"A lovely and insightful compendium for the conscious home cook."

—ALISSA WAGNER, cofounder and chef of Dimes,
Dimes Deli, and Dimes Market

"As a registered dietitian, I am a firm advocate that what you eat affects
your health. I was lucky enough to fulfill a dream of mine and attend the
Chef's Training Program at Natural Gourmet Institute where I honed
my skills in the kitchen, learned how to make creative plant-based meals,
and furthered my understanding of the connection between nourishing
food and well-being. Now the school's philosophy and teachings can
be enjoyed in this gorgeous cookbook that will not only make you happy to
eat the food you are creating, but make you feel fabulous as well."

—MIRANDA HAMMER, MS, RD, CDN, registered dietitian
and natural foods chef, crunchyradish.com

"This book is a testament to the incredible food and
culinary foundation that has shaped so many remarkable true
food-as-medicine pioneers. This is the real deal!"

—STEFANIE SACKS, MS, CNS, CDN, graduate of
Natural Gourmet Center, culinary nutritionist, and author
of What the Fork Are You Eating?

THE
COMPLETE
VEGAN
COOKBOOK

THE
Complete
Vegan

COOKBOOK

OVER 150 WHOLE-FOODS, PLANT-BASED RECIPES *and* TECHNIQUES

By the **NATURAL GOURMET CENTER**

with **JONATHAN CETNARSKI, REBECCA MILLER FFRENCH,**
and **ALEXANDRA SHYTSMAN**

Photographs by **CHRISTINA HOLMES**

CLARKSON POTTER/PUBLISHERS
New York

*To Annemarie Colbin, PhD, for giving the world a
place where likeminded people congregate, collaborate,
study, and enjoy health-supportive foods.*

*To everyone who has ever walked through our doors—
thank you for sharing your energy and passion with us!*

Contents

FOREWORD

I'm Chloe Coscarelli, a vegan chef, cookbook author, restaurateur, and Natural Gourmet Institute alumna. Studying at NGI (currently known as the Natural Gourmet Center at the Institute of Culinary Education [ICE]) was crucial in helping me reach so many of my career and culinary goals. I'm excited that the school has opened its kitchen to cooks and foodies around the globe so they, too, can experience some of the magic that happens there. But, first, I want to tell you a little bit about my journey and why Natural Gourmet is so special to me.

While I was an undergraduate student at Berkeley, I was faced with a dilemma that is familiar to many young people: What was I going to do with my life, and how could I make it meaningful? My friends were off to law school and med school, but all I really wanted to do was cook and bake. I decided that I would try to combine my passion for food with my lifelong love for animals, so after graduation I packed up my knives and whisks and headed to New York City to begin my formal culinary education at Natural Gourmet. My experience learning and growing as a student there built the foundation for me to go forward and make my dreams a reality—like winning Food Network's *Cupcake Wars,* publishing four cookbooks, and cooking the first ethical vegan dinner at the James Beard House—just to name a few highlights!

When I think about what I gained during my time at the school, what comes to mind is so much more than learning traditional culinary techniques. Sure, I learned to julienne, brunoise, and chiffonade with the best of them, but I also learned about the healing properties of natural, whole foods and how to make them incredibly flavorful and exciting to eat. This has since become the centerpiece of my approach to vegan cooking: Vegetables no longer have to be boring! What a concept, right? Natural Gourmet broke the mold of the traditional culinary school because it was one of the first institutions in the country to redefine how a "complete" meal is constructed. A big hunk of meat in the middle of the plate with a few limp string beans on the side? Not anymore! The school was truly a pioneer of the radical notion that a dish consisting entirely of plants could be considered not only a real meal, but an exciting and nourishing one as well. I believe that the school continues to have its finger on the pulse of the future of food, and at a time when mainstream, plant-based cooking is moving further and further away from steamed broccoli and iceberg-lettuce salads, there is hardly a more exciting place to be.

Another wonderful and unique quality about Natural Gourmet is that it fosters a deep sense of community. Some of my very best, lifelong friends—and all the amazing women on my culinary team—are also graduates of the program. These chefs have been alongside me through thick and thin. I definitely would not be the same person or chef without the creativity, support, and passion that my incredible team brings to the table. Female chefs are continuing their meteoric rise to the top of today's food scene, and we Natural Gourmet grads have our trailblazing founder, Dr. Annemarie Colbin, to thank for building a community where women are encouraged to be bold leaders in the food world. Even though Dr. Colbin has since passed, I still hold her story as a pioneer of vegan cooking close to my heart as inspiration to keep breaking down barriers in my own career.

The recipes in this cookbook will allow you to explore the school's distinctive culinary philosophy in your own kitchen. One of the things I love most about Natural Gourmet is that its mission unites people all over the world, due to a shared interest in its philosophy. I met classmates from Brazil, Chile, South Africa, and New Zealand during my time at the school, and through them I learned about so many different ingredients and dishes that still influence my cooking to this day. It's also inspiring to know that a holistic, whole-foods approach to eating is popular around the world, and that Natural Gourmet is truly at the forefront of a global culinary revolution. Now you get to join our community by cooking through this book from your own home, wherever in the world you might be.

Happy cooking!

Chef Chloe

PS. I'll leave you with one of my favorite pieces of kitchen wisdom that one of my instructors, Chef Rich LaMarita, shared with my class years ago, and it still makes me laugh: "Salting your food after it's been cooked is like putting makeup on after the date." Truer words have never been spoken!

When my mother, Annemarie Colbin, was a teenager, she loved bread and butter so much she decided to eat only that. Her experiment lasted a week, and her distressed tummy offered a simple yet profound epiphany: What you eat affects your health.

She started the Natural Gourmet Cookery School, as it was then called, in 1977 in our apartment when I was four. She would put me to bed and then head into the kitchen where her students awaited. As a single parent, teaching people how to create delicious, healthful meals allowed her to earn a living—and make a contribution to the greater good of teaching others how to nurture themselves.

Two years later, my mom wrote *The Book of Whole Meals* (originally printed by Autumn Press and reprinted by Ballantine Books) on our first computer, an Apple IIc. To save a file, she had to remove the program disk from the single floppy drive and insert a blank disk; the maximum file size was eleven pages. The process of writing a 231-page cookbook with over 240 recipes was indicative of her tenacity.

My mother wrote several more books, earned a PhD, and won many awards. She put her heart and soul into the school, nurturing it for decades so it could become the superb institution it is today. Accolades aside, I believe her greatest accomplishment is the positive impact she has had on thousands of people—people who now understand the connection between how you eat and how you feel, and who have the tools to act on that understanding.

This book is one of those tools. May you enjoy it in the best of health.

—Kaila Colbin

My mom raised me to save every morsel of food, so recently, when I accidentally overcooked some asparagus, I instinctively stored the green mush in the refrigerator until I could figure out what to do with it. The next day, I stood staring at it with little enthusiasm. What to do?

"Make a soup," I heard the voice of my mother say in a very pragmatic tone. She was a kind, generous woman whom you could depend on to say exactly what she meant. Although she died several years ago, I can sometimes still hear her voice as if she were standing right next to me.

I like the idea of intuitive cooking, a process that resonated with my mother. So instead of looking for a recipe, I went with my gut. I chopped an onion, a shallot, a Portobello mushroom, and a small potato—and put them all into a soup pot with a bit of olive oil.

"Okay, Ma, now what should I add?"

Then I heard her voice again. "Curry powder." *Curry powder?* I thought. *Really?*

I took the risk, adding a heaping teaspoon of the spice blend to the sautéing vegetables. I added some water and then simmered everything until the ingredients were soft enough to blend. Then I added the asparagus mush. I used an immersion blender, given to me years ago by my mother, to purée the mixture. I also added a few drops of umeboshi vinegar—one of my mother's go-to ingredients. The end result was creamy and delicious.

Ironically, my mother always described herself as a good "home cook," not a chef. Yet the cooking school she started has grown to be the leader in training thousands of people in how to be professional chefs with a knowledge base of health-supportive foods and techniques. My mother's dedication to wellness through whole foods never wavered. Sounds simple enough, especially in this day and age. However, in the 1980s, Oscar Meyer bologna was a delicacy, Wonder Bread was *the* bread, and the only real thing was Hellman's Real Mayonnaise. The food movement hadn't officially begun. So she started an unintentional food revolution in our two-bedroom apartment on the Upper West Side. I assure you, my sister and I were the only children for miles who were eating oatmeal with seaweed and tamari for breakfast.

This cookbook is a testament to the continued success of the school she started. I know if my mother were here, she would beam with pride at the accomplishments of the staff at Natural Gourmet. Her influence and philosophies remain strong in the school today. And her influence is steadfast in my own household as well. My husband, our two children, and I eat oatmeal with seaweed and tamari regularly. Our palates are wide and varied. We know where our food comes from. We all offer continual thanks to my mother, their Oma, Annemarie Colbin.

—Shana Colbin-Dunn

Introduction

*Our bodies are designed by nature
to live on the foods that nature provides.*

—ANNEMARIE COLBIN, PhD

Food. It nourishes, sustains, unites, and defines us. Eating good food can be joyful, emotional, and even spiritual, while talking about food and sharing it with others can be a universal commonality that allows people to connect with one another. The preparation of food, the rituals of serving, and the act of eating are traditions that define communities and bridge generations. In recent times, we find ourselves at a crossroads, where the once simple process of eating has become complicated and potentially hazardous, with many unsure of what to put on their plates or perhaps unaware of the powerful impact their food choices have on their health and well-being.

Annemarie Colbin founded Natural Gourmet Cookery School in 1977 to teach people about the relationship between food and health—long before it was the subject of household conversation. She was fascinated by the effects of food on overall well-being, and spent her life studying theories and systems that reference both Western and Eastern philosophies, such as macrobiotics, Ayurveda, and even quantum physics. When comparing diets, she theoretically proved that one is neither better nor worse, only different. She translated this to the idea that, philosophically, there's no one right way to eat. This is how she came to her own practical guide to mindful eating: the Seven Principles of Food Selection (more on pages 22 to 23), which state that food should be Whole. Seasonal. Local. Traditional. Balanced. Fresh. Delicious.

Natural Gourmet has often been considered "progressive," and in the early days, we were even sometimes called "that hippie school." (Maybe it's because we were touting the benefits of brown rice while everyone else was discovering TV dinners!) In actuality, we were ahead of the curve, and today we are a leading source for health-supportive culinary training.

We have graduated thousands of professional chefs from all over the world with a culinary education focused on food that is healthy for people, communities, and the planet. Through our recreational programs, we have helped countless "everyday cooks" learn how to create health-supportive meals. You could say that Natural Gourmet has been *the* culinary school dedicated to teaching the craft of natural, plant-based, and healthful cooking long before cooking this way was trendy.

We like to think of our school as unique, and it's hard not to feel a certain magic when you're in one of our classrooms. There's a convivial camaraderie that's apparent among our students, who care deeply about food, its future on a global scale, and each other. While we do keep abreast of trends and work constantly to evolve, we stay grounded in our ethos. And while the foundation of our Chef's Training Program is rooted in classic French and Japanese culinary techniques, we ultimately look at the greater picture: how the foods we eat affect us and the world we live in. Our mission is to teach people how to prepare healthful, satisfying meals, and to navigate the often-confusing food conversation with confidence.

Our culinary grads can be found in places like Los Angeles and São Paulo, Paris and Tokyo, and everywhere in between. We find nothing more gratifying than seeing our alumni take what they've learned and use it to feed others in restaurants, work as nutrition coaches, cook for people with illnesses, and advocate for food security and justice in impoverished areas.

The school has been asked for years to create a cookbook and we are excited to finally fulfill that request. This book contains decades of wisdom from the very experts responsible for training some of the culinary industry's most progressive natural foods chefs, and this volume is the first time we have gathered our recipes to share with a public audience. All the dishes featured in the chapters that follow are vegan because we want to encourage you to start thinking about your meals in a way that does not have to revolve around meat in the middle of the plate, or the necessity to include any animal products for that matter. While most of our classes are plant-based, our school does include education about meat in the curriculum because for some people, a moderate amount of animal protein can be part of a healthy diet. In this book, though, we are focusing on plant-based foods and cannot wait to show you how to incorporate a wide variety of vegan ingredients into your meals. We share with you our arsenal of favorite ingredients that give our dishes depth, interest, and harmony. While many of these recipes are part of our professional Chef's Training

Program, this is not a handbook for chefs-to-be, but rather a collection for home cooks—a way for you to bring our school home. We've modified our recipes, distilling them to their basic techniques, making them accessible to beginners, yet preserving complex flavors and textures to make them satisfying for the accomplished cook.

As Annemarie used to say, "Chemistry is limiting. You can't see vitamins or minerals, but you can taste food." With that in mind, we're not going to talk about the nitty-gritty of nutrients in this book. Instead, we're going to do what we do best—show you how to cook whole foods through a collection of exciting and innovative recipes unique to our school, just as we have to thousands over the past forty years.

We are dedicated to making healthy food delicious, and we hope our boundless enthusiasm for creating vibrant meals inspires you to do the same. With each recipe we aim to pass along our acquired knowledge, trusted recipes, techniques, ingredient research, and cooking fundamentals that we've honed, refined, and tested. I sincerely hope this book becomes well-worn and passed down from one generation to the next— starting an entirely new food tradition for you.

In 2019, Natural Gourmet Institute began the next chapter of its journey to provide health-supportive culinary education to the masses. Our programs are now taught at the Institute of Culinary Education (ICE), a world-renowned culinary school with campuses in New York City and Los Angeles, as the Natural Gourmet Center. We are excited for this new phase and look forward to immersing you in our school.

Welcome to the Natural Gourmet.

Yours in good health,

Jonathan Cetnarski
PRESIDENT

CHILLED CUCUMBER-AVOCADO SOUP
page 134

WATERMELON GAZPACHO WITH BASIL-INFUSED OIL
page 147

How to Use This Book

After learning about sourcing food (see page 22), stocking your pantry (see page 27), and the difference between mincing and matchsticks (see page 47), you will be ready to begin cooking. We hope that, as you cook through every recipe in this book, you feel as if you were gaining the same insights and encouraging guidance as you would get from being in our classroom with an instructor by your side. You'll also see Chef's Tips peppered throughout the book. These are hints and advice that will help you streamline the cooking process, offer recommendations for ingredient substitutions, or suggest where you can source an off-the-beaten-path ingredient.

We admit that some of these recipes are projects, like the Butternut Squash and Pepita Blue Cheese Cannelloni in White Bean Broth (page 248), but others are a cinch, such as the Red Lentil Lemon Soup with Spinach (page 137). Just like our school, there's something here for everyone and for any occasion.

More than anything, we want you to fall in love with the recipes you come across, and grow familiar with the vibrant vegetables, nutrient-dense grains and legumes, and colorful herbs and spices that make health-supportive cooking exciting, versatile, and deliciously satisfying. We also hope you'll notice how good you feel after eating certain foods—physically, mentally, and spiritually—and how much better you feel as you incorporate even more plant-based whole foods into your life. Aside from providing us with fuel to live our best lives, food is a vehicle for connecting with others, and the social and cultural ties it forges are a meaningful element of the integrative approach we take. On that note, we hope that the people you share this food with find comfort and inspiration in the recipes as well.

Explanation of Our Icons

Throughout the book you'll see we've included the following icons to designate recipes free of common food allergens.

Ⓖ GLUTEN-FREE

Ⓢ SOY-FREE

Ⓝ NUT-FREE

Getting Started

Building a Foundation the Natural Gourmet Way

In this section, we give you the basics to get you started on the right path, such as how to source the best-quality whole-foods ingredients, as well as fundamental techniques you may use to prepare them. These tools provide a foundation and will be the building blocks for what's to come.

Like mastering any skill, great cooking comes with repetition. We can give you the recipes and guide you through them, but our ultimate goal is for you to acquire the techniques through practice, to be able to improvise, to *feel* a recipe. We want you to know when something's done baking by smell or touch, to cook grains without referring to ratios, and to enjoy being in the kitchen because you're a confident cook!

Sourcing Your Food

Juicy tomatoes, creamy beans, vibrant greens. There is nothing more important to the taste of a dish than the ingredients from which it's made, and we feel strongly that the quality of those ingredients forms the foundation for good cooking. We encourage you as a home cook to seek out the best-quality ingredients you can afford, whether from a farmers' market, a mainstream supermarket, or your own garden. That is how delicious meals begin.

You may be thinking this is easier said than done. With marketing buzzwords plastered on every food package and supermarket sign—ORGANIC, ALL-NATURAL, NON-GMO—how do you begin to decipher which foods you should buy?

To begin, we follow our founder Annemarie Colbin's Seven Principles of Food Selection, which still ring true even forty years after their inception. These criteria do not depend on scientific studies, rigid diets, fat and calorie counters, or individual nutrients, but instead on high-quality ingredients eaten the way nature intended.

1. Whole: Annemarie used to say, "Carrots have vitamin A, fiber, and water, but you can't put those elements in a jar and shake it up and make a carrot." At Natural Gourmet, we believe you should eat foods as nature provides them, with all their edible parts intact, such as whole grains with their bran and germ, and apples with their skins. Whole fruits and vegetables contain fiber and other plant compounds, such as vitamins, minerals, and antioxidants, which is why they are preferable to juices or vitamin pills. We believe whole foods, as opposed to singled-out nutrients, are a key element to optimal health because the whole is greater than the sum of its parts.

2. Seasonal: Choosing foods that are in harmony with our environment's natural growth cycle can have a profound result on almost any dish we cook. Because in-season produce is riper, it is also typically juicier, more fragrant and colorful, and therefore more delicious. Not only are seasonal foods often cheaper when they are purchased in season (think cucumbers!), but they also contain more nutrients than foods that have been transported long distances. Shopping at farmers' markets is a good way to find out what's available locally during any given season. If your area doesn't have an outdoor market in the wintertime or

farmstands in the summer, many grocery stores are now labeling where produce comes from. And if they aren't, you can always ask a produce manager to find out.

3. Local: Local produce often tastes better, usually costs less, and is generally more nutritious because it is allowed to stay on the vine until it is fully ripened. Some of the nutrients in fresh produce begin to decompose from the point of harvesting onward, so the less time food spends traveling, the better. Even large supermarkets, in addition to farmers' markets and smaller locally owned grocery stores, are starting to advertise produce that comes from local farms. Eating locally also does a huge favor to our environment by lessening gas emissions produced in transport. Furthermore, Annemarie was a proponent of seasonal local produce because according to macrobiotic theory (see "Our Macrobiotic Influences," page 27), eat-ing foods that are part of your local ecosystem is better for the health of the individual and the community.

CSA (community-supported agriculture) is a great way to enjoy local produce. Participating in a CSA means you're committing to a "share" of the harvest from a local farm, which you can pick up weekly at a drop-off location in your neighborhood. Bonus: Because you don't usually choose the produce in your share, you get to try cooking new-to-you items and explore new flavors on a regular basis.

OUR SEVEN PRINCIPLES OF FOOD SELECTION

Whole

Seasonal

Local

Traditional

Balanced

Fresh

Delicious

4. Traditional: We should acknowledge what our ancestors ate, as well as the foods that are indigenous to our local region, and incorporate those foods into our diets (see page 25).

5. Balanced: Choose foods that will maintain a balance of protein, carbohydrates, fat, and micronutrients in your diet. It is also important to consider a balance of sweet, salty, sour, and savory flavors, plus a variety of textures to keep our palates satisfied. For example, if you drink sweet smoothies for three meals a day, you may find yourself craving something crunchy or salty.

6. Fresh: The foods you choose should be full of their life energy, which means as minimally processed as possible. Foods should be free of chemical additives, colorings, and preservatives, and not irradiated or genetically modified. Canned and frozen foods are less preferable than fresh, but frozen broccoli is better than no broccoli at all, and canned beans in a fresh tortilla that you assemble yourself are certainly a better option than a fast-food burrito (see page 33 for more on canned foods).

7. Delicious: Healthy food provides nutrition, and when it's delicious, it is also a source of great pleasure. Eating food that tastes good encourages us to eat more of it, and leads us to develop more beneficial eating habits.

When to Buy Organic—
and When It's Okay Not To

When choosing ingredients, we always think about where our food comes from, as it not only impacts the taste of a dish, but our personal health and that of the planet as well. With that in mind, we make a conscious effort to source ingredients responsibly. In fact, at the time of this book's production, nearly 20 percent of all the fresh produce used in our classes came from New York City's famed farmers' market.

Contrary to popular belief, organic isn't always the Holy Grail. Sometimes other considerations surpass growing methods when deciding which product is better for the environment. For example, if you have a choice between two bunches of beets, and one is organic and the other is not, all other things being equal, the organic beets would be the logical choice, since their production can be assumed to be more gentle to the soil and water. But if the organic beets were grown thousands of miles away, while the conventional beets are from a local farm, you have to consider the pollution generated while getting them to you. A lot of organic produce is now shipped to the United States from places as far away as New Zealand. That's a long way, and a lot of fuel, for a fresh vegetable. In this case, conventionally grown beets are the more ecologically sound choice. At the end of the day, this is a personal choice, but it is important to consider the consequences that may result from your purchase.

Furthermore, large-scale conventional farms are more likely to engage in monocropping, the practice of growing the same crop on the same soil for numerous growing seasons in a row. Long-term monocropping depletes soil of its nutrients, among other negative impacts, which poses a danger to our planet's ability to produce food in the not-so-distant future. Small, local farms are more likely to rotate crops (plant a variety of crops on the same land with the change of seasons), which is far healthier for the soil.

With respect to fruit and vegetable sourcing, we follow the recommendations set forth in the Environmental Working Group's Dirty Dozen™ and Clean Fifteen™ lists (page 25). The Dirty Dozen identifies fruits and vegetables grown in conventional systems that may be unsafe to eat because of excessive pesticide residue. The Clean Fifteen identifies produce that, despite being conventionally grown, has minimal amounts of pesticide residue and is, therefore, safer to eat. Foods from the Dirty Dozen side should be purchased organic, whenever possible. In general, when buying fruits and vegetables with skins you will eat (like potatoes, apples, and cucumbers), reach for organic; those that will be peeled/shucked/shelled (such as avocadoes, sweet corn, and grapefruit) can be conventionally grown. Check out the EWG website (ewg.org) for the most recent lists.

The Dirty Dozen™

1. STRAWBERRIES
2. SPINACH
3. NECTARINES
4. APPLES
5. GRAPES
6. PEACHES
7. CHERRIES
8. PEARS
9. TOMATOES
10. CELERY
11. POTATOES
12. BELL PEPPERS

The Clean Fifteen™

1. AVOCADOS
2. SWEET CORN
3. PINEAPPLES
4. CABBAGE
5. ONIONS
6. FROZEN SWEET PEAS
7. PAPAYA
8. ASPARAGUS
9. MANGOES
10. EGGPLANT
11. HONEYDEW MELON
12. KIWI
13. CANTALOUPE
14. CAULIFLOWER
15. BROCCOLI

(Source: EWG's 2018 Shopper's Guide to Pesticides in Produce™)

Eating in Harmony with Tradition

BY CHEF ELLIOTT PRAG

Putting nostalgia and sentimentality aside, why should we eat what our ancestors ate? What do traditional food ways offer us in this time when everything we thought we knew about the connection between food and health is upended by a daily barrage of conflicting information?

On the most fundamental level, our ancestors from four to five generations ago ate a diet that embodied everything we agree to be healthful now—food that was whole, local, seasonal, and organic. Their food choices were simple, uncomplicated by input from the government, fad diets, the latest research, industrial food producers, or the news.

Traditional food choices were ecologically sound. Nothing was wasted. People ate mostly plants, truly "root to frond." Animal protein was more scarce and expensive. When eaten, every part of the animal was used—the skin, flesh, bones, and organs—honoring the sacrifice of the animal.

Before the advent of modern transportation and storage, all food was local, seasonal, and organic.

There were no processing techniques to fracture food's nutritional integrity. People ate what grew near their homes and, as a result, their food was local, seasonal, and natural. And what grew locally helped people best adapt to the challenges of the season: root vegetables to warm their bodies in winter and juicy fruit to cool them in summer.

Today, with increasing technological alacrity, we process and modify food, diminishing its nutritional quality, and rely on vitamin and mineral supplements to fill in the gaps. Our ancestors, by comparison, enjoyed the synergy of the whole. They ate foods with all their edible parts and nutrition intact. We scarcely know what to eat or how to eat anymore because we've outsourced our judgment about food to "experts." We don't need a scientist or a study to tell us that eating in harmony with tradition is a healthier way to live— we know that instinctively. By choosing a seasonal, local, whole-foods diet, we can, as our ancestors did, access well-being in an empowered way, the way nature intended.

WATERCRESS-FENNEL SALAD WITH CITRUS
page 162

Prepping Your Pantry

If you ever take a class at our school, you may notice our refrigerators and pantries are stocked with a variety of jars, vats, and containers housing our favorite sweeteners, vinegars, and other seasoning agents. These are our staples, the ones we use to build layers of flavor. For instance, if something tastes flat or needs contrast, we may add a squeeze of lemon, or head to the pantry for umeboshi vinegar (a briny Japanese staple, see page 31); if a dish lacks depth, we might opt for the savory flavor of shoyu. Don't just rely on recipes to guide your taste buds—trust your palate and taste (and adjust) as you go, working to strike the right balance of sweet, salty, bitter, savory, and astringent. What tastes perfect to one person may need a little something extra to another, so always taste a dish before serving to make sure it's to your liking.

Our Macrobiotic Influences

Macrobiotics is not a diet. It's a way of life—a philosophy, a lifestyle, a way of eating. One of the core principles of macrobiotics is taking responsibility and making choices for one's own life, happiness, health, and well-being. Following thousands of years of tradition, macrobiotics offers a practical, balanced approach to daily life: a flexible way to live, eat, adapt, and heal.

Since the school's founding, macrobiotics's guiding principles have deeply influenced our ideology, specifically our criteria for food selection: food of the highest quality that is whole, local, seasonal, natural, and organic.

A Glossary of Commonly Used Ingredients

We use a variety of health-supportive, minimally processed ingredients to convert conventional recipes to their healthiest versions. Although you've probably heard of quinoa by now, here is a list of ingredients you may be unfamiliar with.

SWEETENERS

BARLEY MALT SYRUP: A liquid sweetener made by sprouting, roasting, curing, mashing, cooking, and concentrating whole-grain barley. This traditional process takes over a month. Barley malt syrup contains trace amounts of B vitamins and potassium. It can be used in cooking and baking in place of molasses for a distinctive, malty taste, but is usually used in combination with other sweeteners because it's not sweet enough to bake with on its own.

BROWN RICE SYRUP: A liquid sweetener made by combining soaked brown rice with barley enzymes to break down its complex carbohydrates into sugars. The grains are then roasted and boiled with water to create the syrup. Less intense than other commonly used natural syrups, it lends a neutral, gentle sweetness that can balance any recipe. Look for certified gluten-free versions if you're following a gluten-free diet.

COCONUT SUGAR: A granulated sweetener made from evaporated coconut sap that can be used in place of regular granulated sugar. Like maple crystals, coconut sugar is dark in color and molasses-y in flavor, so its bold taste is likely to come through in baked goods.

AGAVE SYRUP: When you need a neutral-tasting sweetener, use agave. Its sugar content is quite concentrated, so you can use less: ¾ cup of agave syrup is as sweet as 1 cup of white sugar. Agave works best in smoothies, mousses, fruit compotes, and sauces, rather than in baking.

MAPLE CRYSTALS: A granulated sweetener made from evaporated maple syrup. Maple crystals are minimally processed and contain trace minerals, such as calcium and magnesium. You can use this ingredient as a cup-for-cup substitution for white or brown sugar in baking, but, with its distinct flavor and tan color, it's best used in recipes that include other strong foreground flavors and colors—such as chocolate, peanut butter, or banana—if you want to mask the maple taste, that is.

MAPLE SYRUP: A liquid sweetener derived from maple trees with a sweetness equivalent to cane or beet sugar. We use maple syrup in dressings, sauces, and glazes, and in baking. Maple syrup is a great alternative to honey for those adhering to a strict vegan diet. Prior to 2015, maple syrup was classified by grades A, B, and C. The grades did not signify level of processing, but rather the syrup's color and flavor, with grade A being the lightest in color and the mildest in flavor, B being darker and more robust in flavor, and C being the darkest and the most flavorful (typically not sold in stores, but rather used for commercial food production). Currently, all maple syrup is labeled grade A and classified with four descriptors instead: "Golden Color, Delicate Taste," "Amber Color, Rich Taste," "Dark Color, Robust Taste," and "Very Dark Color, Strong Taste." No grade is inherently better than another; it's simply a matter of preference. We prefer grade A Amber Color, Rich Taste.

Using Alternative Sweeteners

BY CHEF ANN NUNZIATA

Students often come to our baking classes hoping to learn which sweeteners are "good" and which are "bad." Unfortunately, there are no hard-and-fast rules, because all sweeteners are still a form a sugar. While natural sweeteners have minute amounts of minerals or other nutrients, they still have few, if any, health benefits.

That said, white sugar is a highly refined, addictive, and inflammatory ingredient made from evaporated sugarcane juice that is then processed through a centrifuge. This high-temperature, high-powered machine crystallizes the sucrose molecules, which are then cleaned and bleached. Animal bone char is often used as a decolorizing agent, and for this reason many vegans do not use white sugar. The taste of white sugar provides no satiety, so our bodies crave more and more of it. It takes only ten days to wean yourself off white sugar and reset your palate. It doesn't take long for your body to appreciate the more nuanced, complex flavors of whole-food sweeteners, such as maple syrup, which is naturally satiating. Keep in mind, though, that not all sweeteners can be used interchangeably, and it may take some experimentation to get the hang of the varying properties of each.

PROTEINS

TOFU: A good source of plant-based protein, iron, and calcium, tofu is made by coagulating soy milk and pressing it into blocks. It comes in four forms: extra-firm and firm (best for searing and stir-frying), and soft and silken (best for dressings, sauces, puddings, etc.). Tofu has a relatively neutral flavor, so it's a good idea to marinate it and/or let it simmer in a sauce or spice blend before cooking, as in our Tofu Teriyaki (page 212). Tofu should be odorless and not slimy; otherwise it is most likely spoiled.

TEMPEH: Unlike tofu, tempeh is made from whole soybeans that have been soaked, cracked, and fermented into blocks. Some tempeh contains grains, like barley or brown rice, so be sure to read the label carefully if gluten is a concern. Its firm texture makes it perfect for slicing and cubing, searing in a skillet or on the grill, or crumbling up to resemble a ground-meat texture, as in our Tempeh Bolognese (page 228). It's a good idea to marinate, steam, or simmer tempeh in a seasoned bath (see page 231) before cooking to eliminate its naturally bitter flavor.

SEASONINGS

BROWN RICE VINEGAR: Made from fermented rice wine, this vinegar is great for pickling liquids, dressings, and marinades. Commercial manufacturers pasteurize it to prevent bacteria from forming a "mother" while sitting on the retail shelf; pasteurization may weaken the flavor, so choose a raw, probiotic variety, if possible. We prefer brown rice vinegar to the more common white variety because it's made from a whole-food source. Brown rice vinegar is also slightly less acidic than white rice vinegar.

MISO: A savory-salty paste made by fermenting soybeans, barley, rice, or chickpeas in cedar vats for one to three years. It comes in a variety of types and colors—the darker the color, the stronger the flavor. Miso is praised for its umami-enhancing properties and commonly used in soups, sauces, marinades, and vegan cheeses. As with other naturally fermented foods, miso is rich in beneficial microbes that colonize the lower gut and maintain the health of the gastrointestinal tract. If miso makes contact with boiling water, its live digestive enzymes are destroyed, so take extra care to keep liquids it is added to at a gentle simmer. When adding miso to a soup, like Chef Elliot's Famous Miso Soup (page 136), turn the heat off and dissolve the miso in a bit of hot broth before stirring it into the pot.

SEA SALT: Produced by the evaporation of seawater, sea salt is less processed than all-purpose table salt, as well as devoid of additional chemicals such as

SEEDED MIXED-GRAIN CRACKERS
page 109

anti-caking compounds. Sea salt also contains trace minerals. We use fine sea salt for everyday cooking and coarse sea salt (such as Maldon or fleur de sel) as a finishing salt.

SHOYU AND TAMARI: Shoyu is a Japanese style of soy sauce made from fermented roasted soybeans and koji (fermented wheat). It is typically aged from one to two years. We use it to add saltiness and umami to everything from dressings and marinades to stir-fries and soups. Similarly, tamari is made from fermented soybeans, salt, and water, typically without wheat; if you're following a strict gluten-free diet, look for a certified gluten-free version. Tamari is traditionally a by-product of miso production, so its flavor is slightly stronger and saltier than that of shoyu, but the two can still be used interchangeably.

UMEBOSHI PASTE AND VINEGAR: This salty-sour paste is made from unripe ume plums that are pickled in a salt brine with red shiso leaves (also known as perilla). The muted red condiment is a Japanese and macrobiotic kitchen staple. We use it to add umami, and to balance sweetness in dressings, sauces, glazes, and broths; it can also be used in combination with miso to flavor vegan cheeses. Umeboshi vinegar is the brine left over after pickling the plums. Although not a true vinegar, it has enough acidity to act as one, due to the sour flavor of the plums. It is highly concentrated, so use it sparingly to brighten up dressings and marinades.

FUN FACT: According to macrobiotic theory, umeboshi curbs the symptoms of hangovers, morning sickness, and fatigue.

SEEDS

CHIA SEEDS: These small, black, flavorless seeds are native to Mexico and Guatemala. Chia seeds are high in fiber and are a good source of plant-based

Why Soy Is Steeped in Controversy BY CHEF CELINE BEITCHMAN

Soybeans—whole, gently processed, and fermented—have been in the human diet since 3500 BCE. Soybeans are legumes and complex carbohydrates, rich in fiber and calcium. They are also complete proteins (containing all essential amino acids), a rarity in the plant kingdom. As a high-quality protein source with a profile akin to animal foods, it can be a great addition to a whole-foods, plant-based diet.

Yet soy is steeped in controversy. A lot of the concern stems from soy's concentration of phytochemicals, called isoflavones. These bioactive substances, which are naturally present in soybeans, have an estrogen-like chemical structure and are thought to exert hormone-like effects in the body. (Estrogens are hormones governed by the endocrine system, which are responsible for the growth of cells, reproduction, and metabolism in general.) Links between hormone disruption and soy intake seem to occur when extreme and concentrated doses are consumed—think soy powders, soy supplements, and soy junk food, such as processed protein bars—not four ounces of tempeh and one glass of unsweetened soymilk. Multiple studies over the years have disputed these concerns, challenging the notion that soy has any effect on human reproduction, fertility, or sterility. In fact, as it turns out, isoflavones may actually have cardioprotective benefits, including lowering LDL cholesterol and reducing the risk of prostate cancer in men.

In closing, soy should not be a major concern for the average person, and a moderate intake of whole, fermented, or lightly processed soy can be a part of a healthy plant-based diet.

calcium, protein, and omega-3 fatty acids. They are easy to incorporate into smoothies, granolas, and energy bars. When combined with a liquid, chia seeds plump up and take on a gel-like consistency, which makes dishes like chia pudding possible. Chia seeds can also be ground and mixed with water to form a "chia egg."

FLAXSEEDS: High in omega-3 fatty acids, flaxseeds are sold whole or ground, or as an oil. Flax is highly perishable, due to its high fat content, so be sure to store it in the fridge. Whole, lightly roasted seeds can be used as a topping to add crunchy texture and nutty flavor to a variety of foods. Be careful not to overtoast, since high temperatures will destroy the vital fats. Use flaxseed oil raw and unheated to preserve its nutritional properties. Like chia seeds, ground flaxseeds (flaxseed meal) can be combined with water to form a "flax egg" and used as a vegan egg substitute in baking.

HEMP SEEDS: Also known as hemp hearts, these small, beige seeds are seeds of the hemp plant. Although marijuana comes from the same plant (*Cannabis sativa*), hemp seeds contain only trace amounts of THC, so eating them will not result in any psychoactive effects. The seeds have a mild

flavor and are rich is omega-3 and omega-6 fatty acids. They are also high in protein and numerous minerals. They make a delicious milk (see page 61) or a nutritious addition to smoothies, oatmeal, or avocado toast.

SEA VEGETABLES

Coastal cultures in Asia, Northern Europe, Scandinavia, the Caribbean, and even the Americas have eaten edible seaweeds in various forms for centuries. In the United States, the most common sea vegetables are kombu, dulse, nori, hijiki, agar, and arame (see "Why We Eat Sea Vegetables," page 116). Sea vegetables are particularly noteworthy for their nutrient density—they contain minerals, complex carbohydrates, and amino acids. Try the Hiziki Caviar with Tofu Sour Cream (page 118) to check out sea vegetables in action.

THICKENERS

AGAR: Also known as agar-agar or kanten, this sea vegetable is a great vegan alternative to gelatin as it's odorless and flavorless. It consists of 80 percent insoluble fiber, making it great for improving digestion; it also expands in the stomach, acting like an appetite suppressant. It comes in two forms: flakes and powder. The flakes are more commonly found in stores and require 15 minutes of soaking time before cooking, while the concentrated powder does not need soaking. Agar can be used for setting puddings, custards, and Almond Mozzarella (page 62).

ARROWROOT: This starch is made from soaked, mashed arrowroot (a tropical tuber grown in South America), which is washed to separate the starch, then filtered and ground. Flavorless and versatile, think of this product as an alternative to cornstarch. It can be used to thicken sauces, stews, and pie fillings, and for dredging foods before frying.

Vegan Egg Substitute

A chia or flax "egg" can be used to replace the binding power of a dairy egg in most baked goods, like muffins or quick breads, as well as waffles and pancakes. We prefer this homemade egg substitute to packaged store-bought options because it is made from a whole-foods source.

To make 1 vegan egg replacement, combine 1 tablespoon of ground chia or flaxseeds with 3 tablespoons of water, and chill for about 10 minutes. The mixture will thicken and take on a slightly viscous texture.

KUZU: A starch extracted from the kuzu root (sometimes called kudzu), this plant is native to Japan and grows prolifically in the southern United States. Kuzu is used to thicken liquids in the same way as other root starches, like corn, potato, tapioca, and arrowroot. It is prized in traditional Chinese medicine and macrobiotics as a carminative (relieving flatulence) and as a digestive aid. While one is not a replacement for the other, combining kuzu and agar creates a creamy texture in gelatin-type desserts (see Chocolate Pudding, page 294).

COOKING OILS

Fat is one of the three essential macronutrients our bodies need for energy (protein and carbohydrates are the other two). Fat performs various metabolic functions we cannot live without and it also makes food taste satisfying. As with many other ingredients, the science is ever-evolving, but a good rule of thumb is to purchase oils that are organic, non-GMO, and cold-pressed. Try to buy oil that comes in dark-colored bottles or tins, which keep out the light and heat that speed spoiling.

CANOLA OIL: We like to use organic, non-GMO canola oil for its neutral flavor and relative affordability. It has a high smoke point, which makes it a great option for high-heat cooking, such as deep-frying or stir-frying. Refined organic avocado or sunflower oils are other options appropriate for high-heat cooking.

COCONUT OIL: Virgin (unrefined) coconut oil should be used in dishes you want to taste like coconut, such as sweets, granola, or even a stir-fry. Refined coconut oil has been stripped of its coconut-y flavor, and is great for high-heat cooking.

EXTRA-VIRGIN OLIVE OIL: This go-to cooking fat is best for low-temperature cooking, dressings, or used as a finishing oil. Pricier bottles from small-batch producers (sometimes labeled "estate-harvested") indicate a conscientious producer and an oil made with extra oversight and care. This oil is generally more flavorful, brighter, and greener in color, and should be reserved for raw uses if you want the flavor to stand out.

A Word on Heating Oil in a Pan

When heating cooking oil in a pan, we recommend warming up the pan first and then adding the oil. Continue warming up the pan with the oil until the oil flows evenly and easily in the pan when you tilt it. We find that if you hold your hand about 6 inches above the pan and feel the heat, it's ready to go. If you see the oil shimmering gently, you want to get whatever you're cooking in the pan immediately, because the oil is hot. If the oil starts to smoke, discard the oil and start over; heating oil past its smoke point damages the oil and creates harmful free radicals (not to mention an off flavor). You have a rather short time frame before oil starts to smoke in a hot pan, so watch it carefully. Finally, it's important to note that lighter pans (like small nonstick skillets) need less time to preheat; heavier materials (think cast-iron skillets or Dutch ovens) need a bit longer.

A Note on Canned Foods

In line with our Seasonal principle (see page 22), there are times when canned foods may be preferable and other times when they're not. For example, fresh local tomatoes in August are preferred to the canned variety, while in January the canned works better than buying imported fresh ones from far away. We also understand that fresh organic foods are pricey and sometimes canned organic foods are the better option.

When buying canned foods, always read the ingredient label and avoid canned beans that contain disodium EDTA, a synthetic preservative. The ingredients list should reflect what you cook with at home. Always rinse canned beans before using them, and don't store open cans in the refrigerator (acidic ingredients will pick up a metallic taste)—transfer the leftover contents to an airtight container instead.

Cracking the Coconut

In some parts of the world, the coconut tree is known as the "tree of life," and in Indian culture the tree is known to offer "selfless service," represented by its multiple uses, both culinary and otherwise. Virtually every part of the tree can be used for a number of purposes, such as crafting baskets and furniture from coconut palm leaves to making drums and bowls from hollowed-out coconut shells. Then there are all the delicious edible parts that can be turned into a plethora of goodies, from coconut chips to candies, and, of course, our favorites—coconut water, milk, cream, and butter.

So what's the difference?

COCONUT WATER: Also known as coconut juice, this relatively clear liquid is found inside fresh, green coconuts. More akin to water than milk in viscosity, this liquid is sweet and tasty, and is known for its relatively high concentration of potassium. We like to drink it straight and use it in smoothies.

COCONUT MILK: Not to be confused with the water, coconut milk is made by infusing grated coconut meat with boiling water and then straining the mixture. We use rich canned coconut milk as a base for curries, creamy dairy-free tarts and desserts, and also in some beverages to add richness. (The coconut milk found refrigerated in cartons is not the same as canned milk, as it's often thinned with water to make it more palatable for drinking. This type should be used for adding to coffee or enjoying with your morning granola.)

COCONUT CREAM: When coconut meat is soaked in hot water, a cream rises to the top, and this is known as coconut cream. Just as you would assume, it is thicker in consistency than the milk that is left behind. We like to whip coconut cream just as you would traditional dairy cream for a luscious dessert topping (see page 101).

COCONUT BUTTER: Also called coconut manna, coconut butter is not coconut oil (see page 33), which is fat extracted from coconut meat; instead, it's made from coconut flesh that's puréed into a butter that can be used as a spread. Coconut butter and coconut oil cannot be used interchangeably. If your coconut butter is too hard or crumbly, soften it in a water bath (see Chef's Tips, page 314).

PEPPERY BISCUITS WITH MUSHROOM GRAVY
page 278

Equipment You'll Need

While we teach in kitchens that are fully equipped with everything we need (including commercial dishwashers!), at home you will need a few basic tools to cook through our recipes. Here is our list of appliances and key kitchen utensils that we consider valuable for cooking at home. While you don't need every item mentioned, as you page through the book, notice what recipes you're drawn to and what equipment they require—it may just guide your next kitchen purchase.

POTS AND PANS: The ultimate pan construction is a copper core with an aluminum interior and stainless steel exterior, but these materials make pans pricey. Cast-iron is a good and affordable all-purpose option. While heavy, it is excellent for heat retention and, when seasoned properly, develops an effective nonstick surface.

Nonstick cookware is an option, too. These pans are useful for times when you'd like to use less oil, such as searing a starchy food or cooking delicate items like veggie burgers or pancakes. Nonstick surfaces are also useful for searing proteins, such as tofu, that are prone to sticking to pans.

However, these surfaces may become dangerous at high heat, as they emit potentially toxic chemicals from their coating, so avoid high heat when using them. Also, avoid scratching the surface by using appropriate non-scratch tools, and don't scour the pans when washing. If they do become scratched, it's best to replace them.

KNIVES: You can really do all you need in the kitchen with three types of knives: a chef's knife, which is an all-purpose knife with an 8- to 10-inch blade; a paring knife, with a blade about 3 to 4 inches long (good for peeling produce and other small jobs like coring tomatoes); and a serrated knife, which can either be in the 5- to 7-inch category and considered a utility model, or an 8- to 12-inch model, which is called a bread knife. Both work well on bread, hard-to-cut melons, and even delicate tomatoes. If you're going to invest in a professional knife (and we highly recommend that you do), put your funds toward the chef's knife—you'll be using it 90 percent of the time. Higher-quality knives tend to have a balanced weight, which makes them easier to handle, and the grips are usually more comfortable because they're

Throughout this book, we refer to pots, pans, and skillets as small, medium, and large; we recommend at least one or preferably a few of each.

SMALL POT OR SAUCEPAN:
1½ to 2 quarts

MEDIUM POT OR SAUCEPAN:
4 to 6 quarts

LARGE STOCKPOT:
12 to 16 quarts

SMALL FRYING PAN OR SKILLET:
6 to 8 inches in diameter

LARGE FRYING PAN OR SKILLET:
10 to 12 inches in diameter

thoughtfully designed from better materials (which tends to mean higher prices as well). Good-quality blades hold their sharp edges longer, too, so you can anticipate using it for years, or even decades, to come.

CUTTING BOARDS: A large, good, sturdy cutting board made from wood or thick plastic is essential. Steer clear of cutting boards that are too thin or too small, as they may warp or make chopping produce more difficult than it should be.

FOOD PROCESSOR: This kitchen workhorse easily chops, dices, slices, shreds, grinds, purées, and even kneads many foods. It is relatively inexpensive and compact in size, so if you are going to purchase just one countertop appliance, let it be this one.

HIGH-SPEED BLENDER: We use Vitamix, one of the original manufacturers of high-speed, restaurant-grade blenders. You'll find there are several quality high-speed machines on the market today. Although a standard blender works for dressings and some soups, a high-speed model is more versatile and achieves smoother, creamier results when blending ingredients like nuts, seeds, and leafy greens. High-powered blenders are pricey, though, so consider your needs before investing: Will you occasionally use it for smoothies or daily for soups, nut butters, juices, and even vegetable purées and dips?

One of our favorite tips: Lay a damp paper towel under your cutting board to prevent it from moving around or slipping while you're cutting on it. This also works for mixing bowls for jobs like emulsifying vinaigrette.

IMMERSION BLENDER: This compact, handheld blender is tall, narrow, and has a rotary blade at one end. It can be immersed right into a pot of soup or a saucepan to purée or chop the contents.

RASP GRATER: Smaller and handier than a box grater, this specialized grater is typically referred to by its better-known manufacturer's name, Microplane®. This tool comes in a variety of blade and handle sizes, and works wonders with a wide array of ingredients, from nutmeg and ginger to citrus zest.

MANDOLINE: This handheld slicer is convenient when you need to slice vegetables thinly and evenly. Because the blade position is stationary, the slicer maintains uniform cuts, which is great for garnishes and salads, and can create paper-thin slices of virtually any fruit or vegetable. The exposed blades are extremely sharp, though, so always be sure to use a hand guard or a cut-resistant glove. Japanese models are usually made from plastic, and are therefore lighter in weight and less expensive than French ones, which tend to be made of high-quality stainless steel; this makes them more substantial, but also bulkier than their Japanese counterparts. Both versions come with additional blade attachments for making julienne cuts.

PRESSURE COOKER: A cooking pot with a locking, airtight lid and a valve system to regulate internal pressure, this beloved gadget can reduce the cooking time of beans and vegetables like beets and winter squash by as much as two-thirds. This pot is useful for foods that would normally be cooked with moist heat, such as soups, stews, and beans because the steam that builds up inside cooks food at a very high temperature. Beans cooked in a pressure cooker (or a multicooker/electric pressure cooker) tend to be creamier, plumper, and more evenly textured than those boiled in a regular pot. Be cautious not to fill a pressure cooker more than halfway. The pots are outfitted with a safety valve, which automatically vents the steam should there be a malfunction.

COLD-PRESS (SLOW) JUICER: Also known as a masticating juicer, this machine crushes then presses fruits and vegetables to extract fresh juice. Slow juicers are considered superior to the more popular centrifugal models, which extract juice with a spinning metal blade that pulverizes produce into a mesh filter that separates juice from pulp with centrifugal force. Although more affordable, centrifugal juicers' high spinning speed produces some heat, which can kill some of the micronutrients and enzymes in fresh juice. While pricier, cold-press models retain more of the juice's nutrients and a tiny bit more of the fiber, are better at extracting juice from leafy greens, and are quieter, too.

CITRUS REAMER OR JUICER: A reamer is a ridged, teardrop-shaped tool with a handle used for juicing citrus fruits by hand. A citrus juicer has a ridged cone onto which a halved piece of citrus is pressed and holes on the top strain seeds and pulp while the bottom cup collects juice.

FINE-MESH STRAINER OR SIEVE: A good, sturdy model with a long handle is indispensable for straining stocks; rinsing small amounts of vegetables or grains; and draining noodles and small legumes. You'll almost always find a cone-shaped sieve, called a chinois, in professional kitchens as well. While they are not essential to a home kitchen, this fine-mesh workhorse comes in handy when trying to achieve an ultra-smooth texture by straining. If you make homemade stocks or sauces often, a chinois may be a worthwhile investment.

SPROUTED MUNG BEANS
page 56

GINGER JUICE
page 74

CHEESECLOTH: This lightweight, natural cotton cloth has a multitude of culinary uses, including straining liquids and forming a packet for herbs and spices (bouquet garni, page 75). It comes in both fine and coarse weaves and does not fall apart when it comes into contact with food. Cheesecloth is interchangeable with a nut milk bag in most applications, but it cannot be reused. You can also use squares of lightweight unbleached muslin in its place.

NUT MILK BAG: This reusable nylon drawstring bag has a finer weave than cheesecloth and is perfect for straining nut milks or other thin liquids. We prefer using nut milk bags because they are easy to wash, store, and reuse, whereas cheesecloth is one-time-use only and can be harder to manage.

TAWASHI BRUSH: Similar to a loofah, this Japanese scrub brush made from tightly bound palm fibers is both effective and environmentally friendly. We use it to scrub topical pesticide residue off conventionally grown vegetables like potatoes, cucumbers, and summer squash, whose skins we intend to eat or juice.

PARCHMENT PAPER: Lining cake pans and baking sheets with this disposable, nonstick, food-safe paper (not to be confused with wax paper) prevents foods from sticking and can help when lifting food out of pans. It also makes for easy cleanup.

SPIRALIZER: This tool turns vegetables and fruit into long, curly noodles, which are sometimes called zoodles or courgetti. Spiralized vegetables make a great gluten-free, grain-free replacement for traditional pasta.

MORTAR AND PESTLE (*SURIBACHI* AND *SURIKOGI*): A mortar, or *suribachi,* is a bowl-shaped container and a pestle, or *surikogi,* is a rounded, handheld instrument. These two items, usually made from the same material, such as marble, hardwood, porcelain, or stoneware, are used together to grind and pulverize spices, herbs, and other foods.

SPICE GRINDER OR COFFEE GRINDER: This small, powerful, electric machine usually has an exposed, disk-style blade inside a jar-like container that can be used to grind nuts, seeds, and whole spices. Some home cooks dedicate separate units for grinding spices and coffee beans so as not to cross-contaminate flavors. There are also models available with multiple interchangeable bowls.

ICE CREAM MACHINE: For home chefs, the less expensive electric model—which consists of a small basin that is frozen and put into the machine—is most practical. The basin turns and the dasher (the scraping blade) stays still. The more expensive models are self-contained, countertop machines that have a built-in freezing unit. In those, the dasher spins to churn the ice cream.

FRYING SPIDER: Especially useful for deep-frying and blanching, this long-handled, slotted skimmer basket is used to submerge and remove food from a pot. Wide and shallow, the basket is usually made from wire mesh and the handle is often wooden, bamboo, or metal. Lightweight and durable, it's handy for fritters, pasta, and vegetables.

FISH SPATULA: While you won't find any fish recipes in this book, this flexible spatula allows the transfer of delicate foods without breakage and works particularly well for frying tofu or flipping fritters and pancakes. Perforations allow drippings to pass through so foods are transferred cleanly from pan to plate.

RUBBER SPATULA: Constructed of a wooden or plastic handle and a flat, tapered scraper made of flexible, usually heat-resistant rubber, this tool is considered indispensable. It is perfect for folding dry ingredients into wet ones (like pancakes) or scraping thick or sticky foods out of bowls or food processors.

Cooking Fundamentals

One of *the* most important things you can do to incorporate healthier eating into your life is cooking for yourself. If cooking is new to you, there are a few fundamentals that will make you more facile in the kitchen: staying organized; learning indicators; and mastering basic techniques, including knife skills and cooking methods. With these few essentials under your belt, meal prep will become more intuitive, and, hopefully, you'll feel freer, more creative, and less wed to recipes.

Mise en Place

If you've ever watched restaurant chefs cook in open kitchens, you've probably seen an array of chopped vegetables, garnishes, and sauces at their stations—that's the *mise en place* (pronounced MEEZ-ahn-PLAAS), a culinary term that translates roughly from French as "everything in place." This approach is as useful at home as it is in commercial kitchens for staying organized. Readying your *mise en place* before turning on a burner allows you to pay more attention to what's happening on the stove once you're actually cooking (instead of going back and forth between stove and cutting board while the cooking is already in progress). *Mise en place* is especially important for recipes where many different ingredients are gradually added to a pot or pan in quick succession.

Learning Indicators

When students ask how long they should roast the beets, we like to tell them, "Until they're done." Look beyond cooking times and check for doneness when you start to smell the food, see if it turns a certain color, or if it feels a certain texture. Don't be afraid to open the oven door, touch a cake, or gently poke at a bread. We like to say, "If you can smell it, you can check it."

MISE EN PLACE

To prepare your *mise en place*, read through a recipe's ingredient list, prep all the items as needed (toast the nuts, mince the garlic, etc.), organize them in individual dishes (we like the metal nesting bowls available at any restaurant supply store), and have them ready to go.

Basic Knife Skills

Cutting food is integral to meal preparation, and the process deserves significant attention. We can't underscore enough how important good knife skills are to your success in the kitchen. Learning proper knife skills will reduce your prep time and make your food look better, too.

Finding a knife you're comfortable with should be one of every home cook's first priorities. If you don't have a sharp knife, it'll make food preparation difficult, if not dangerous, as you risk the knife slipping off the food you're preparing. Thus, a sharp knife is ultimately safer than a dull one.

Knives are typically made from carbon steel or stainless steel. Most home chefs prefer stainless steel knives because they are much easier to care for than carbon steel models, which may initially take a sharper edge, but don't hold an edge long, stain easily, and are very expensive. In other words, they are high-maintenance. The blades of stainless steel knives are essentially carbon steel with added chromium, which makes the blade resistant to abrasion, corrosion, and stains. If you're looking to invest in a knife, go to a kitchen supply store or a knife specialty store and hold a few knives in your hand to see what feels best. Ask about the materials the knives are made from as well. We equip our students with 8-inch Mercer knives, which are comfortable, durable, and affordable. With any knife, if you keep it sharp and maintain a proper grip, you'll likely be cutting like a pro in no time.

KNIFE CARE

Always cut on a wood, plastic, or hard rubber cutting board, never on metal or a polished stone surface, which will dull your edge. To check if your knife is sharp, try cutting through a piece of paper. If your knife doesn't cut easily through it, you probably need to sharpen it.

Never soak a knife or put it in a dishwasher, as this dulls the blade. Storing knives properly when not in use helps protect the edges and keeps them from getting nicked. Never keep them loose in a drawer. Wooden blocks or sheaths work well for proper storage. And for safety's sake, don't leave knives in a sink of soapy water or any place where they cannot be seen. If you must carry a knife from one end of your kitchen to the other while other people are present, keep your knife pointed down, parallel to your thigh, and warn passersby with an audible "Knife behind."

SHARPENING AND HONING KNIVES

A knife-sharpening stone is a flat, rectangular tool usually about 9 inches long and 1 to 2 inches wide. Also known as a whetstone, this piece of kitchen equipment keeps knives sharp and should be used at home every couple of months or so, and more often by professional chefs who slice and dice all day. A honing steel is a thin tool, usually about 10 inches long, that's attached to a handle. The honing steel does not sharpen knives, but rather realigns the edge, which helps them work more efficiently. A honing steel should be used each time before cooking. To learn to use these tools properly, we highly recommend you take a knife skills class at a culinary school (we know just the place!), ask for a demo at a local kitchen supply store, or look for knife sharpening tutorials online.

HOW TO GRIP A KNIFE

When you grip a knife, it should feel natural. To begin, take the knife in your palm and grip the handle or heel, with your thumb on one side and the index finger, curled up, on the other. The finger should never point outward along the top edge of the knife. When you grip the handle toward the top, near to where it meets the blade, you gain more control and strength when cutting. It is a strong, confident, and safe grip.

HOW TO CUT LIKE A CHEF

Once you've mastered your grip, you're ready to cut. Stand with your back straight, your arms bent at the elbows near your sides, and your forearms straight out in front of you.

Secure the item you are cutting with one hand using a "bear claw" grip, which means you tuck the tips of your fingers under in a claw shape while still holding the food item. Your fingertips should never be exposed. Curling them under your first knuckles protects them from the blade. This grip does not mean you're using your knuckles to hold the food or vegetable you're cutting. Instead, your knuckles slightly overhang your fingertips, which ultimately hold the food in place. This may feel awkward at first, but with practice, it will start to feel more natural.

To cut, use a down and forward cutting motion. To slice, bring the knife down, the tip a bit lower than the heel, and hit the vegetable with the blade about 1 to 2 inches from the tip of the knife, then slice forward and down, and bring the knife back up, so your hand makes a circular motion. The tip stays on the cutting board and the heel slides across the cutting board. You can build great speed with this motion, and it's also safer than raising your knife repeatedly up and down off the board. The motion stays close to the board while your other hand holds on to the food you're cutting with a bear claw grip. Slicing backwards (pulling the knife toward you), which many novices naturally tend to do, is neither efficient nor fast. This forward rocking motion is one worth practicing on a few zucchini or cucumbers at your leisure.

When choosing the best cut for your food item, think about the cooking time. The larger the cut, the longer the cooking time. For example, if you are making a quick-cooking soup and add chunks of quartered beets, they will increase your cooking time, possibly by as much as 45 minutes. Conversely, if you use a quarter-inch dice, your cooking time will be greatly reduced.

We teach our students both traditional French and Japanese cuts. The main difference is that Japanese cuts don't have measurements attached to them and French cuts do.

JAPANESE VEGETABLE CUTS

DICING: Cut the vegetable crosswise into rounds. Slice each round into strips then slice each strip into matchsticks. Finally slice the matchsticks crosswise into cubes.

MINCING: A very small dice.

CHOPPING: A more casual, coarse dice that doesn't necessarily have to be uniform in size.

ROUNDS: Slice vegetables, such as carrots or zucchini, crosswise into thin or thick rounds.

DIAGONAL CUT: Slice vegetables on the diagonal by holding the vegetable at an angle. The angle of the vegetable and the knife determine the length of the pieces.

HALF-MOONS: Cut the vegetable lengthwise through the middle into two halves. Then cut each half crosswise into slices.

QUARTER-MOONS: Slice the vegetable lengthwise as you do with half-moons then cut each half down the center again. Lastly cut each section crosswise into slices.

MATCHSTICKS: The vegetable is cut on the diagonal and then each diagonal piece is sliced into thin matchsticks.

IRREGULAR OR ROLLING STYLE: Cut the vegetable on a diagonal, rotating the vegetable toward you 90 degrees after each cut. The pieces should be the same size but irregularly shaped.

FRENCH VEGETABLE CUTS

Follow the same procedure as for Japanese cuts, using the following specific measurements.

MINCE: ⅛ inch or less.

SMALL DICE: ¼ inch × ¼ inch × ¼ inch.

MEDIUM DICE: ½ inch × ½ inch × ½ inch.

LARGE DICE: ¾ inch × ¾ inch × ¾ inch.

JULIENNE: Similar to a matchstick cut, food items are cut into long thin strips that are ⅛ inch × ⅛ inch × 2½ inches.

BRUNOISE: Similar to a small dice but even smaller, ⅛ inch × ⅛ inch × ⅛ inch.

CHIFFONADE: A thin or thick ribbon cut, often used for leafy greens or herbs. Stack leaves so they go in the same direction, roll them like a cigar, and slice perpendicular to the roll to the desired width.

CHEF'S TIP: Using the chiffonade technique to cut leaves not only looks pretty, but it also helps prevent the browning of certain herbs, like basil, mint, and sage, that can occur when you roughly chop them, which can bruise the delicate leaves.

BRUNOISE

SMALL DICÉ

MINCE

MEDIUM DICE

CHIFFONADE

LARGE DICÉ

JULIENNE

DICE

MINCE

MATCHSTICK

ROUND

CHOP

DIAGONAL

HALF-MOON

QUARTER-MOON

ROLLING/IRREGULAR

About Grains

Rice is a staple food crop for more than half the world's population, yet the ability to cook it well still seems elusive to many. The hardest thing to do is nothing at all when cooking grains. Resist the temptation to stir, toss, or lift the lid to peek while your grains are cooking. Following are tips and techniques for grains frequently used in this book.

SELECTING, STORING, AND WASHING GRAINS

To ensure fresh grains, buy them from a store that has a quick turnover or from mail-order companies that specialize in grains. Always smell grains before using them. Fresh grains smell faintly sweet, or have no smell at all. If they smell off, discard them. Unprocessed whole grains, with the germ intact, have a higher oil content than processed grains, and thus are more perishable and prone to rancidity and pests. To prolong the shelf life of grains, keep them tightly covered in a cool, dry place, and refrigerate or freeze grains you use infrequently to keep them from becoming rancid.

WASHING GRAINS

While most grains sold today are free of debris, it's always a good idea to wash them to clean away dust or chaff. However, if you are short on time, it's good to know that grains like white rice and polenta have been washed during processing, while whole grains like brown rice and wheat berries should be washed.

Contrary to what may seem intuitive, rinsing grains in a colander under running water does not thoroughly clean them. To wash grains, place the measured amount in a bowl or pot. Add cold water to cover them by at least 2 or 3 inches. Swirl the water and grains with your fingers to loosen the dust, chaff, and dirt. Gently pour off most of the water. Repeat until the water is clear; usually three times will do the trick. On the last rinse, pour the grains into a fine-mesh strainer. If you are soaking your grains, discard the soaking water and rinse before using.

COOKING GRAINS

Freshness, grain size, and the presence or absence of a seed coat (whole grains versus processed) will determine the cooking technique and timing best suited to the specific grain at hand. For tender, more succulent grains, cook slowly, covered in just enough water to allow for proper expansion.

The standard method for cooking grains is to bring the measured amount of water, salt, and grain to a boil (in general, ¼ teaspoon or a generous pinch of fine sea salt per 1 cup of grain is sufficient to make the grain taste lightly seasoned; more salt can be added, to taste, after cooking), cover, and reduce the heat to the lowest setting, then begin timing according to the Grains-at-a-Glance Cooking Guide (page 52). Do not lift the cover. At the end of the cooking time, check to see that the grain is the desired texture and all the water or liquid is absorbed. Remove the pot from the heat and set it aside to steam, covered, for a minimum of 5 minutes. Fluff with a fork before serving.

> **CHEF'S TIPS:** We often like to dry-roast grains to bring out their nutty aroma and speed up cooking. To do this, put grains in a pan or pot over moderately low heat, stirring constantly, and toast until fragrant and slightly colored, about 3 to 5 minutes. Remove the toasted grains from the pan immediately, so they don't continue to cook, and use as desired.
>
> For fluffy, more separate grains (like rice), add the grain to boiling liquid at the beginning of cooking. For chewier, stickier grains (like oatmeal), start cooking the grains in a cold liquid.

GRAINS-AT-A-GLANCE COOKING GUIDE

GRAIN AMOUNT	LIQUID AMOUNT	PROCEDURE
1 cup Arborio rice (for risotto)	4 to 5 cups warmed stock	Wash the rice and drain. In a medium saucepan, sauté the rice in 1 tablespoon oil. Add stock in ½-cup increments, stirring constantly between each addition until the grain has absorbed the liquid. The grain should be creamy and a bit al dente when done, 20 to 30 minutes (you may not use all the stock).
1 cup short-grain brown rice (oven)	1¾ cups boiling water	Preheat the oven to 375°F. In a small lidded baking dish, dry-roast the rice (see Chef's Tips, page 51). Add the boiling water, ¼ teaspoon salt, and cover (you can use foil if your dish doesn't have a lid). Bake until all the water is absorbed and the grain is chewy, about 60 minutes. (This method works best for larger batches.)
1 cup long-grain brown rice (stovetop)	1¾ cups boiling water	In a small pot, dry-roast the grain (see Chef's Tips, page 51). Add the boiling water and ¼ teaspoon salt, cover, and return to a boil. Lower the heat and simmer for 45 minutes. Remove from the heat and let stand, covered, 15 minutes more to steam. Fluff with a fork before serving.
1 cup wild rice	4 cups water	In a small pot, combine the rice, water, and ¼ teaspoon salt. Bring to a boil, cover, reduce the heat, and simmer until the rice is tender, 45 to 50 minutes (the rice should butterfly slightly). Transfer the rice to a colander and drain any excess water.
1 cup medium or coarsely ground cornmeal	3 cups water	In a small saucepan over high heat, combine the cornmeal, 2 cups of the water, and ¼ teaspoon salt, whisking until smooth. Bring the mixture to a boil, stirring constantly, until it has thickened. Add the remaining 1 cup water, a little at a time, stirring well to mix thoroughly. Simmer, stirring constantly, until the mixture pulls away slightly from the sides of the pan, 20 to 30 minutes.
1 cup millet	1¾ cups water	In a small pot, sauté the millet in 1 tablespoon of oil. Add the water and ¼ teaspoon salt, bring to a boil, and cover. Reduce the heat and simmer until all the liquid is absorbed, 25 to 30 minutes.
1 cup quinoa	1¾ cups boiling water	In a small pot, combine the quinoa, boiling water, and ¼ teaspoon salt. Bring to a boil, reduce the heat, and simmer until all the liquid is absorbed, about 20 minutes. Remove from the heat and let stand, covered, for 10 minutes more to steam. Fluff with a fork before serving.
1 cup couscous	1 cup boiling water	In a small pot, sauté the couscous with 1 tablespoon of oil and ¼ teaspoon salt. Remove the pot from the heat, add the boiling water, and cover. Steam until all the water is absorbed, 5 to 10 minutes. Fluff with a fork before serving.
1 cup bulgur wheat	1¾ cups boiling water	In a small pot, dry-roast the bulgur (see Chef's Tips, page 51). Add the boiling water and ¼ teaspoon salt. Cover and cook for 1 minute. Remove from the heat and let stand, covered, for 45 minutes more to steam. Fluff with a fork before serving.

COCONUT BASMATI RICE
WITH LIME ZEST AND PISTACHIOS
page 187

About Beans

We use beans in many recipes, from soups and stews to dips and burgers. Beans consist of about 20 to 25 percent protein, as well as calcium, iron, B vitamins (niacin, B6, and folic acid), and fiber. In many traditional cuisines, grains and beans are served in tandem. When the two are served together, the amino acids complement each other to form complete proteins, a very important factor for anyone following a vegetarian or vegan diet.

Protein and a Plant-Based Diet

We often get asked the question, "Can I get enough protein from a plant-based diet?" And the answer is a resounding, "Yes!" When you eat a variety of whole foods, including vegetables, whole grains, legumes, nuts, and seeds, protein needs are easily met for a healthy adult since, essentially, all the aforementioned foods contain some protein. The difference between animal- and plant-based proteins is usually the amount of amino acids they contain. So while animal products provide complete proteins (containing all the essential amino acids in one food), most plant-based sources have some amino acids but are usually low in certain others and thus need other plant-based foods to complement them. For example, grains are low in lysine. Legumes, on the other hand, are high in lysine but low in methionine. Many cultures pair grains and legumes in traditional dishes, like rice or corn and beans in Central and South America, and soybeans and rice in Asia to make a complete protein. The good news: Complementary amino acids do not need to be consumed at the same time, but may be eaten over the course of a day.

While the USDA makes recommendations for the amount of protein we should get daily, there are other signals your body sends that usually tell you when you have adequate protein intake, including being satisfied after meals, no excessive cravings for sweets and fats, enough energy for daily activities, and appropriate mental focus and clarity.

BEAN COOKING TIMES

Note that cooking times vary depending on the age of the beans, soaking method, and cooking method.

VARIETY OF BEAN	COOKING TIME (for boiling method—bring to boil, reduce to simmer, and cook until tender)
BEANS REQUIRING NO SOAKING	
Red lentils	20 minutes
Green lentils	45 minutes
BEANS THAT REQUIRE SOAKING OVERNIGHT	
Black-eyed peas	20 to 25 minutes
Great Northern beans	45 to 60 minutes
Navy beans	45 to 60 minutes
Kidney beans	45 to 60 minutes
Black beans	45 to 60 minutes
Pinto beans	45 to 60 minutes
Adzuki beans	60 minutes
Mung beans	60 minutes
Lima beans (large and small)	60 to 90 minutes
Yellow or green split peas	60 to 90 minutes
Garbanzo beans (chickpeas)	1 to 3 hours

Purchase beans from a store where there is quick turnover. Beans toughen as they age, and the older they are, the longer they take to cook.

Spread the beans you're going to use on a plate or tray and sort through them, discarding any clumps of dirt, grains, cracked beans, stones, etc. This is especially important for lentils.

Transfer the beans to a bowl or pot and cover with at least 2 to 3 inches of cold water. Swirl the water and beans with your fingers. Gently pour off most of the water and any floating matter or debris into the sink. Repeat until the water is clear. After the last rinse, drain the beans completely.

CHEF'S TIP: A good rule of thumb: Every cup of most dried beans, once soaked and cooked, triples in volume.
1 cup dried beans = about 3 cups cooked

SOAKING BEANS

Most beans should be soaked for maximum digestion; however, lentils are soft enough that they don't require soaking. Soaking also shortens the cooking time and helps beans cook evenly. Soak beans for 8 to 10 hours (start them when you head out the door for the day). If you must soak them for more than 10 hours, drain and replace the soaking water. If you soak beans for longer than 24 hours, they may start to germinate.

How To Soak Beans

COLD-SOAK METHOD
Place sorted, washed beans in a bowl or container and cover with 3 to 4 inches of water. Put the soaking beans in the refrigerator for 8 to 10 hours. Discard the soaking water and rinse the beans; use as desired.

HOT-SOAK METHOD
Place sorted, washed beans in a pot and cover with 3 to 4 inches of water. Bring the water to a boil and cook for 5 minutes. Remove the pot from the heat, cover, and let the beans soak in hot water for 2 hours. Discard the soaking water and rinse the beans; use as desired.

COOKING BEANS

The two most common ways to cook beans are on the stovetop or in the oven in liquid, which takes a very long time. For stovetop cooking, put soaked and washed beans in a pot and add enough water to cover the beans by 2 to 4 inches. We believe you should never cook beans in water alone. Adding aromatics, such as fresh or dried herbs, or vegetables, like celery and carrots, flavors the beans from the inside out. Adding sea vegetables, like kombu (see page 116), to the cooking water enhances their digestibility and adds minerals, too. Don't add all the salt at the start because it can toughen the skins—begin with ¼ teaspoon per 1 cup of beans. Bring the beans to a boil, lower the heat, and continue to cook at a little more than a simmer. Keep the beans uncovered and taste 10 minutes before they're done. Add the last of the salt at that time because it'll give the beans time to absorb it. Test a few beans for doneness, not just one, because individual beans can cook at different rates. A perfectly cooked bean should be cooked through with no hardness; it should be tender but never mushy.

If you are not going to use the cooked beans right away, transfer them to a shallow pan to cool quickly before refrigerating. If time is not an issue, let the beans cool in the pot with their cooking liquid. The bean skins may split if you cool beans out of their liquid (which is fine if you're going to purée them). Cooked beans keep in the refrigerator for about 5 days.

A NOTE ON PRESSURE COOKERS

A pressure cooker is a tightly sealed pot that holds steam under pressure. The trapped steam's temperature rises above the standard boiling point (212°F to 250°F). Beans cooked under pressure are typically done 15 to 30 minutes faster than those cooked on the stovetop or in the oven. The disadvantage is that you can't test beans along the way for doneness. If you release the steam from a pressure cooker and the beans aren't done, you can always continue to cook them in a regular pot on the stovetop (or just bring them back up to pressure). To cook beans in a pressure cooker, follow the manufacturer's instructions but, in general, cover the beans with water by an inch (don't fill the pressure cooker more than halfway full), place the lid on top, seal the pressure cooker, and start timing them after the water reaches pressure.

Toasting

Some techniques enhance depth of flavor for certain ingredients, and toasting—making something hot, crisp, and brown by dry heat—is one of them. The difference may be subtle, but oftentimes subtlety is what differentiates novice cooks from experienced ones.

Use a small skillet to toast small round nuts and seeds, such as pine nuts, sliced almonds, and sesame and sunflower seeds on the stovetop. Because the heat needs to penetrate the nut or seed, refrain from stirring until you hear them crackle, which should start within a few minutes, then shake the pan. Turn off the heat and transfer to a plate or bowl immediately.

Toast larger nuts, such as walnuts, peanuts, pecans, pistachios, and Brazil nuts, in the oven so they cook more evenly. Preheat the oven to 350°F. Spread the nuts on a baking sheet in a single layer. Bake until they are fragrant and lightly golden, 5 to 10 minutes, tossing halfway through cooking to ensure even toasting.

CHEF'S TIP: Always cool nuts before grinding them. When you heat nuts, their oils become fluid, so if you put them in a food processor or blender before cooling, you'll end up with nut butter instead of chopped nuts.

Sprouting

We like to add sprouted beans and seeds to dishes like fried rice and salad for extra texture and nutrition. You can sprout many types of legumes and seeds, including adzuki beans, peas, lentils, and pumpkin seeds. Sprouts can take anywhere from 2 to 5 days to grow. To sprout beans, put ½ cup of dried beans or seeds in a large bowl and cover them with several inches of cold water. Cover the bowl with a plate or towel and leave the beans to sit overnight. In the morning, drain and rinse the beans; they are now activated. Keep the beans in a strainer over a bowl covered with a light cloth, rinsing them two to four times a day. You may also do this same process in a jar covered with cheesecloth secured with a rubber band (see photo, page 40); fill the jar with water and turn it upside down to drain out the water through the cheesecloth (or buy a sprouting jar specifically for this purpose). Over the next few days, $\frac{1}{8}$- to 2-inch-long sprouts will appear. Refrigerate the sprouts for up to 2 days. (The sprouted beans or seeds will be two to five times their original size.)

Sweating, Sautéing, and Searing

SWEATING

Traditionally, in a culinary context, sweating means cooking something over low heat with a small amount of fat to release flavors and moisture (akin to its name). You are not browning food, but softening and tenderizing it. Covering the pan while sweating speeds up the process. It is a technique often referred to when cooking onions, carrots, or other aromatics.

SAUTÉING

Sautéing refers to cooking something quickly in a small amount of fat over moderately high heat and allowing the food to brown without absorbing much of the fat. When sautéing, avoid crowding the pan, which can create steam and stew the food in its own juices instead of caramelizing it. You also want to preheat your pan and any fat or oil you're using (see "A Word on Heating Oil in a Pan," page 33). Cooking vegetables this way can wonderfully enhance their natural flavors, and we often use this method to make simple vegetable side dishes. Sautéing also lends itself well to incorporating fresh herbs and seasonings. (Spices are often added at the beginning of cooking, while herbs are usually added at the end to preserve their bright and fresh flavor.)

SEARING

Searing refers to browning food on all sides over high or very high heat. Unlike sautéing, seared foods are left in the pan undisturbed to brown. For instance, we like to sear tofu to give it a nice, crispy exterior (see Tofu Teriyaki, page 212).

Baking Versus Roasting

Both baking and roasting involve cooking food with hot, dry air; however, baking is often done at lower temperatures (think cakes, sweets, and breads), while roasting implies higher oven temperatures to brown foods. As with sautéing, you don't want to crowd your pan when roasting so the heat is evenly distributed among the food. Applying this basic technique to vegetables will give you a base for many other, more complicated dishes, such as Chili Beet Tacos with Creamy Cabbage-Pineapple Slaw (page 227).

Blanching and Shocking

These techniques are widely used in restaurants and deserve to be used more in home kitchens! Blanching refers to partially and very briefly cooking an item in boiling (usually salted) water to either improve or preserve color (as with the Basil-Infused Oil, page 78), loosen peels, improve flavor, or parcook vegetables in advance and then finish them right before serving. Most often, blanching is followed by shocking: plunging the precooked items into ice water to halt cooking. This further helps preserve color and texture, as with the green beans in the Springtime French Lentil Salad (page 171). Blanching and shocking are also useful for crudités that are not as desirable eaten raw, such as broccoli and cauliflower.

Herbs and Spices

We often prefer fresh herbs to dried, especially when it comes to delicate herbs like cilantro, parsley, and basil, which lose much of their flavor when dried. Dried hardy herbs like rosemary and thyme pair well with longer-cooking stews and soups.

There's no question that spices purchased already ground are more convenient, but the flavors are inferior to those of freshly ground spices. You can grind spices by hand using a mortar and pestle, or an electric or manual coffee or spice grinder (you can purchase one for around $20). If you decide to invest in the process, though, consider purchasing a grinder dedicated solely to spices, so you don't end up with cumin-flavored coffee. You can make spices even bolder and more fragrant by toasting them: If you have a few extra minutes to spare, place whole spices in a dry skillet over medium-low heat and toast just until they smell fragrant, 1 to 2 minutes; cool before grinding. In general, whole spices last up to a year and ground spices about six months.

Creating Flavor Profiles

When a chef "flavor profiles," he or she starts by layering distinct sets of aromatic base ingredients before adding main flavoring ingredients, then finishing with ingredients that amplify the qualities they wish to express. A single recipe—vegetable soup, for instance—will project a Mediterranean, Thai, North African, or South American personality when seasoned with the precise spice profile of the region. Take, for example, *mirepoix* (pronounced meer-pwah), a well-known European aromatic made of diced celery, carrots, and onion. If you hone that sweet vegetable base with herbs like basil, oregano, rosemary, or thyme, you get a French, Spanish, Greek, or Italian essence. Thai aromatics start with the "Thai holy trinity" of galangal (a ginger-like rhizome), makrut lime leaves, and lemongrass. Thai profiles then evolve by using curry pastes of chili peppers, shallots, coriander, anise, and fermented condiments. A balanced use of herbs and spices can infuse ordinary ingredients with vibrant, signature flavors evocative of faraway places.

Salt is highly suspect today. However, we do need a small amount of it for survival—for nerve transmission, electrolyte balance, and muscle contraction. Salt and freshly ground pepper, also referred to as "seasonings," are a chef's best friends. When a dish is bland, often a sprinkle of each of these may bring out the flavors. Home cooks tend to underseason for fear of oversalting. Unless you need to eliminate salt for health reasons, a few grains to a modest dose of sea salt, free of additives and iodine, can be beneficial. The salt in highly processed foods, however, is often used by manufacturers with abandon as a preservative and as a way to mask the flavor of artificial ingredients. The sodium in these products should be a bigger cause for concern than the table salt used in from-scratch home cooking.

There's a point at which the right amount of salt makes flavors pop. It's the element of flavor that brings out all the other flavors. Always start with less, and season as you go, tasting as needed. After adding salt, you may notice the sweet flavors of a dish more, or its acidity. When you slowly add salt, there's always a moment when you suddenly taste the cumin, the coriander, or other spices present. A pinch of salt in sweets can even heighten their flavors.

If you make the mistake of adding too much salt to a dish, you can add some liquid such as water or stock, or a fat like oil or butter, to mellow it out. If something is too bitter, never add more salt, as that will intensify the flavor. Instead, add something sweet. The addition of salt can also help repair the flavor of a dish that is too sweet.

**BENGALI DAHL WITH CUMIN,
FENNEL, AND MUSTARD SEEDS**
page 155

CHAPTER 1

Plant-Based Essentials

Basic Nut Milk

MAKES 4 CUPS

NOT ONLY DOES HOMEMADE nut milk taste better than store-bought "alt-milks," it doesn't contain the stabilizers, emulsifiers, and preservatives. Almond and hazelnut milks taste very nutty, while cashew milk is more neutral-tasting. You may also want to flavor your milk with a bit of maple syrup and vanilla if you plan to use it for sweet applications. A nut milk bag makes it easy to strain out the gritty pulp; you can pick one up for under $15 at most kitchen supply stores or online. Save the pulp from almond or hazelnut milk to make Almond Pulp Crisps (page 103) or Cookies (page 104). Don't expect much pulp from cashews—they mostly disintegrate into the liquid.

1 cup raw almonds, hazelnuts, or cashews, soaked for at least 8 hours or overnight, drained, and rinsed

Pinch of fine sea salt

1 to 2 teaspoons maple syrup (optional)

1 teaspoon pure vanilla extract (optional)

SPECIAL EQUIPMENT

Nut milk bag or a fine-mesh sieve lined with cheesecloth

1. In a blender, combine 4 cups of water with the nuts, salt, maple syrup, and vanilla, if using. Blend for 1 to 2 minutes, until the nuts are completely pulverized and the mixture begins to resemble milk.

2. Strain through a nut milk bag or a fine-mesh sieve lined with cheesecloth, squeezing out as much liquid as possible. Transfer the milk to an airtight container and refrigerate for up to 4 days.

CHEF'S TIP: Nut milk stays fresh in the fridge for 2 to 4 days, so make half a batch if you don't plan on using it within this time frame.

Hemp Seed Milk

MAKES 5 CUPS

HEMP MILK IS ONE of our favorites because it does not need to be strained. This means there is no nut milk bag to wash, and you get to reap the benefits of whole hemp seeds, which contain healthy fats, iron, and antioxidants, plus 10 grams of protein per 3 tablespoons of seeds. We love to serve this warm atop Amaranth Porridge with Ginger Peaches and Pistachios (page 257).

2 cups shelled hemp seeds

2 pitted Medjool dates, soaked in hot water for 10 minutes

1 teaspoon pure vanilla extract

¼ teaspoon fine sea salt

In a blender, combine 5 cups of water with the hemp seeds, dates, vanilla, and salt. Blend for 1 to 2 minutes, until the seeds are completely pulverized and the mixture begins to resemble milk. Transfer the milk to an airtight container and refrigerate for up to 4 days.

Almond Mozzarella

MAKES SIX 3-INCH ROUNDS OF MOZZARELLA Ⓖ Ⓢ

1½ cups blanched almonds (Chef's Tip, page 173), soaked overnight

¼ cup plus 3 tablespoons agar flakes

¼ cup plus 3 tablespoons arrowroot starch

¼ cup nutritional yeast flakes

¼ cup canola oil

1 tablespoon brown rice vinegar

1½ teaspoons fine sea salt

½ teaspoon garlic powder

SPECIAL EQUIPMENT:

Nut milk bag or fine-mesh sieve lined with cheesecloth, 6-cavity semispherical silicone mold with 3-inch cavities (available online and at kitchen supply stores)

CHEF'S TIP: Don't forget to taste this in step 4 to make sure the cheese mixture doesn't taste starchy. If it does, continue cooking

IF YOU'RE NEWLY VEGAN and miss eating cheese, then you are in for a treat. This recipe is made with fresh almond milk, thickened with arrowroot, and set with agar, a sea vegetable with gelatin-like qualities (see page 32). This recipe is on the slightly more complicated side, but once it's ready, you won't believe your mouth (the nutritional yeast adds that distinct cheesy flavor!). The mozzarella can be sliced, or frozen and grated atop pizza, such as Pear and Leek Spelt Pizza with Pesto (see page 243) or Grilled Spelt Flatbreads with Caramelized Onions and Oyster Mushrooms (page 244)—just note that it won't be as gooey or have the "pull" of dairy mozzarella.

1. In a high-speed blender, combine the almonds and 4 cups of water, and purée until smooth, 1 to 2 minutes. Strain the almond milk through a nut milk bag or a fine-mesh sieve lined with wet cheesecloth, squeezing out as much liquid as possible (reserve the nut pulp for another use). Measure out 3 cups of almond milk, and reserve the rest for another use (refrigerate in an airtight container for up to 5 days).

2. In a medium pot, combine 2 cups of almond milk with the agar, and whisk to combine. Set the pot over a low flame, bring to a bare simmer, and cook for about 5 minutes, stirring almost constantly, until the mixture thickens slightly and the agar is dissolved. (To check if it has dissolved, tilt the pan forward—if you still see flecks of agar on the bottom, continue cooking.) Remove from the heat and set aside.

3. In a medium bowl, combine the remaining 1 cup of almond milk with the arrowroot, nutritional yeast, oil, vinegar, salt, and garlic powder, and whisk to dissolve.

4. Pour the milk-arrowroot mixture into the milk-agar mixture, and return the pot to the heat, cooking over medium-low until the mixture is very thick and viscous, and no longer tastes starchy, 3 to 5 minutes, stirring constantly.

5. Using a ladle, divide the mixture among the silicone molds, making the tops as smooth as you can. Refrigerate until firm, 30 to 60 minutes. Unmold and use as desired. Refrigerate leftovers in an airtight container for up to 4 days.

Cashew Sour Cream

MAKES 1 CUP

THIS VEGAN SOUR CREAM substitute is simple to make. The only time-consuming element is waiting for the cashews to soak. Don't be tempted to skimp on time here; let them sit. Soaking is what gives the sour cream its smooth, silky texture. We like to use this as a base for dips and as a topping for soups or stews. Of course, it goes without saying (but we'll say it anyway), a nice big dollop completes a taco.

1 cup cashews, soaked for at least 4 hours or overnight, drained, and rinsed

¼ cup lime juice (from 3 or 4 limes)

¼ cup neutral oil, such as avocado or canola

2 scallions (white parts only), coarsely chopped

2 teaspoons brown rice vinegar

½ teaspoon fine sea salt, or more to taste

1. In a food processor or blender, combine the cashews, lime juice, oil, scallions, vinegar, and salt, and purée until completely smooth and creamy.

2. Taste and adjust seasonings, if needed. Refrigerate in an airtight container for up to 4 days.

CHEF'S TIP: To make flavored sour cream, try adding some finely chopped fresh or pickled jalapeños, chopped dill, or a chopped canned chipotle.

Vegan Mayonnaise

MAKES 1 CUP

THIS MUST-HAVE CONDIMENT RELIES on soft tofu for its creaminess, and comes together in a breeze with the help of a blender. Add a canned chipotle, a combo of fresh cilantro and lime, or a few reconstituted sun-dried tomatoes for a flavored option.

7 ounces soft tofu (half a standard package)

1 tablespoon fresh lemon juice (from about ½ lemon), or more to taste

1 teaspoon Dijon mustard

1 small garlic clove, grated or crushed

½ teaspoon fine sea salt, or more to taste

2 tablespoons canola oil or another neutral oil

1. In a blender, combine the tofu, lemon juice, mustard, garlic, and salt, and purée until creamy.

2. With the motor running, slowly stream in the oil. Taste and season with more lemon juice or salt, if needed. If a thinner consistency is desired, add up to 2 tablespoons of water, 1 tablespoon at a time. Store in an airtight container in the refrigerator for up to 4 days.

Vegan Ricotta

MAKES ABOUT 1 CUP

THIS CREAMY SPREAD GRANTS you all the indulgence of ricotta without any of the dairy. We love to serve it on cucumber rounds or in endive spears as an elegant hors d'oeuvre. It's also great on crostini drizzled with maple syrup or Basil-Infused Oil (page 78), or layered into a veggie lasagna.

1 head of garlic

2 tablespoons plus 1 teaspoon extra-virgin olive oil

1 cup raw pine nuts or cashews, soaked overnight and drained

1 tablespoon chickpea miso or white miso

1 tablespoon fresh lemon juice (from about ½ lemon)

1½ teaspoons umeboshi paste (see page 338 for resources)

Pinch of fine sea salt and freshly ground black pepper to taste

1. Preheat the oven to 350°F.

2. Slice off the top ¼ inch from the head of garlic and discard. Rub the exposed garlic cloves with 1 teaspoon of oil and wrap the garlic in foil with the exposed cloves facing up. Bake until it is soft and golden-brown, about 35 minutes. Unwrap and cool to room temperature. Once cool enough to handle, peel away the papery parts and squeeze out the mushy cloves.

3. In a food processor, combine the garlic paste, pine nuts, miso, lemon juice, umeboshi paste, and the remaining 2 tablespoons of oil. Purée until the mixture resembles ricotta cheese, 1 to 2 minutes. Season with salt and pepper to taste. Refrigerate in an airtight container for up to 3 days.

Pickled Onions

MAKES ABOUT 1 CUP

WHEN YOU'RE IN NEED of extra brightness, a little tang, or some subtle crunch in a dish, think pickled red onions. They are simple to make, keep well in the fridge, and are versatile enough to be used on everything from our Massaged Kale Salad (page 166) to our Butternut Squash and Pepita Blue Cheese Cannelloni (page 248). If you don't have apple cider vinegar on hand, use white or brown rice vinegar instead. Feel free to experiment with other crunchy vegetables, too, like carrots or fennel.

¾ cup apple cider vinegar

1 tablespoon maple syrup

¼ teaspoon fine sea salt

Pinch of red pepper flakes

1 medium red onion, sliced

In a small pot, combine the vinegar, maple syrup, salt, pepper flakes, and ¼ cup water, and bring to a simmer. Turn the heat off and add the onions. Let stand until cooled to room temperature. Refrigerate in an airtight container for up to 1 week.

Pepita Blue Cheese Spread

MAKES 4 CUPS

7 ounces firm tofu (half a standard package), drained

1½ cups toasted pepitas (page 56)

1 medium garlic clove, coarsely chopped

2 tablespoons apple cider vinegar

2 tablespoons extra-virgin olive oil

1 tablespoon Dijon mustard

1 tablespoon white miso

4 teaspoons umeboshi paste (see page 338 for resources)

½ teaspoon fine sea salt

Pinch of freshly grated nutmeg

SPECIAL EQUIPMENT

Cheesecloth

CHEF INSTRUCTOR OLIVIA ROSZKOWSKI is the creative mind behind many of our vegan cheese recipes, transforming health-supportive ingredients into umami-packed deliciousness. A combination of miso, umeboshi paste, and mustard here contributes to the savory flavor that tastes like blue cheese. We like to use little dollops of it as a flatbread topping (page 244) and because it's quite creamy, it works as a dip with fresh veggies—you can always stir in a tablespoon or two of soy milk to make it creamier—or even just eat it straight from the spoon! You'll notice we blanch the tofu here. We do this to improve the flavor of the tofu and remove any chalky aftertaste.

1. Bring a medium pot of water to a boil. Lay the tofu on a few layers of cheesecloth, gather the ends, and tie them up. Using a slotted spoon or a frying spider, lower the tofu into the water and simmer for about 4 minutes. Lift the cheesecloth-covered tofu out of the pot and set it aside until cool enough to handle, about 30 minutes. Gently press out any excess water before unwrapping it.

2. In a food processor, combine the tofu, pepitas, garlic, apple cider vinegar, oil, mustard, miso, umeboshi paste, salt, and nutmeg, and purée until smooth. Taste and adjust seasonings, if needed. Refrigerate in an airtight container for up to 4 days.

Shiitake Bacon

MAKES ABOUT 1 CUP

THIS BACON MADE FROM shiitake mushrooms is one of the best loved recipes by anyone who walks through our doors. It uses only three ingredients—and two of them are oil and salt! As the mushrooms dehydrate in the oven, their umami flavor concentrates and their texture morphs from chewy to crisp. Serve these crunchy slices alongside the Tomato Tofu Scramble (page 267), atop Baked Mac and Cheese (page 233), or crumbled on the Sweet Potato Waffles (page 283) and drizzled with maple syrup, for a sweet-savory brunch treat.

¾ pound shiitake mushrooms, stemmed and thinly sliced

3 tablespoons extra-virgin olive oil

½ teaspoon fine sea salt

Preheat the oven to 375°F. In a large bowl, toss the mushrooms with the oil and salt. Transfer to a baking sheet and spread into an even layer. Bake for 20 to 25 minutes, until the mushrooms are browned and crisp, stirring once halfway through cooking. The mushrooms will crisp up even more as they cool. These are best served immediately; though they may be stored in the refrigerator in an airtight container for several days, they will lose their crispness.

Shiitake Crumble

(Vegan Bacon Bits)

MAKES ABOUT 1 CUP

½ pound shiitake mushrooms, stemmed

¾ cup refined coconut oil or another oil with a high smoke point

Fine sea salt to taste

CHEF'S TIP: Save the cooking oil to sauté or roast potatoes or other root vegetables.

WHEREAS THE SHIITAKE BACON on page 71 simply gets sliced and baked, this crumble gets its crunchy texture by finely chopping and then deep-frying the mushrooms. Think of it as a meatless alternative to bacon bits, great on salads, sprinkled over avocado toast, or to finish a soup like Cream of Corn (page 144).

1. Put the mushrooms in a food processor and pulse until they are broken down into small bits.

2. Set a fine-mesh strainer in a heat-safe bowl; set aside.

3. Heat the oil in a large nonstick skillet over medium heat. (To check that the oil is hot enough to fry, place a mushroom bit in the oil— if it sizzles right away, you're ready to fry.) Add the mushrooms and fry until they are crisp and browned—they should be gently sizzling— 5 to 10 minutes.

4. Carefully strain the mushrooms in the prepared strainer setup; reserve the oil for other uses. Season the mushrooms with salt to taste and cool. The crumble is best served immediately but may be stored in an airtight container at room temperature for several days.

Quick Shiitake Stock

(Vegetarian Dashi)

MAKES 2 QUARTS

TRUE TO ITS NAME, this simple stock (also called vegetarian dashi when used in Japanese culinary applications) makes a quick base for soups, stews, and even risotto. This is a great recipe to add to your plant-based stock arsenal, since both dried shiitakes and kombu are shelf-stable, and you can store them in your pantry for stock-making anytime. The strained mushrooms and kombu can be sliced and used in soup or to garnish other dishes.

2 ounces (about 2 cups) dried shiitake mushrooms

One 8-inch piece of kombu

1. In a small stockpot, combine the mushrooms with 2 quarts (8 cups) of water. Let stand for 30 minutes.

2. Add the kombu and bring the mixture to a boil. Reduce the heat and simmer gently for 5 minutes.

3. Strain the stock through a fine-mesh strainer or chinois, pressing firmly on the solids to extract as much liquid as possible. Refrigerate for up to 5 days, or freeze up to several months.

Homemade Teriyaki Sauce

MAKES ABOUT 2 CUPS *

SALTY AND SWEET, SYRUPY and thick, this crowd-pleasing condiment enhances many savory foods, including vegetables, tofu, and even grains. As with most sauces, we prefer homemade to store-bought because we can make it to our exact taste preferences, including the types of sweeteners we choose, replacing commonly used corn syrup or white sugar with unrefined coconut sugar and brown rice syrup.

1 cup shoyu or tamari

½ cup coconut sugar

¼ cup brown rice vinegar

¼ cup brown rice syrup

3 medium garlic cloves, minced

2 tablespoons fresh ginger juice from about a 6-inch piece (see page 74)

½ teaspoon toasted sesame oil

1. In a medium pot, combine the shoyu, sugar, vinegar, rice syrup, garlic, ginger juice, and oil with 1 cup of water, and bring to a gentle simmer.

2. Reduce the heat to medium-low and simmer until the mixture thickens and can coat the back of a wooden spoon, 10 to 15 minutes. Store in the refrigerator for up 2 weeks.

*if made with tamari

How to Make Ginger Juice

To make ginger juice, line a small bowl with cheesecloth and grate a peeled piece of ginger onto the cheesecloth with a microplane grater. Gather up the cheesecloth ends and squeeze the grated ginger into the bowl that has already collected some of the juice. Depending on how fresh your ginger is, you may need upwards of ¼ cup grated ginger for 1 tablespoon of juice.

Carrot-Onion Stock

MAKES ABOUT 3 QUARTS (G)

1 tablespoon extra-virgin olive oil

3 medium yellow onions, halved and coarsely chopped

3 medium carrots, peeled and coarsely chopped

2 shallots, halved and coarsely chopped

3 or 4 celery stalks, coarsely chopped

6 garlic cloves, peeled and smashed

Bouquet garni, made with 1 fresh thyme sprig, 1 fresh bay leaf, and 4 parsley stems, tied together with cotton cooking twine

CHEF'S TIP: We recommend storing stock in plastic quart or pint containers (the kind takeout usually arrives in), so that it's always premeasured. These containers are especially handy if you're freezing the stock because you can pull out and thaw the exact amount you need.

THIS VERSION OF STOCK is lighter than our Brown Vegetable Stock (page 76), in both color and flavor. It makes a great base for mild sauces and soups. Stock is kind of a silent stalwart—part of the whole but in a supportive way. You never want your stock to overpower other ingredients in a recipe, but rather enhance the overall flavor. Here we use a bouquet garni for aromatics, which simply means we tie fresh herb sprigs together. This makes the stems easy to remove after cooking. When straining stock, we like to use a chinois, a metal fine-mesh strainer that has a conical shape. While a rounded strainer works just fine, the cone shape has more stability when straining large amounts of liquid.

1. Heat the oil in a large stockpot over medium-high heat. Add the onions, carrots, shallots, celery, and garlic, and stir to coat. Sauté until the vegetables are soft and the onions and shallots become translucent, about 15 minutes.

2. Add 3½ quarts (14 cups) of water and the bouquet garni. Bring the stock to a boil, skimming off the foam that rises to the surface. Simmer, partially covered, for 1 to 1½ hours (the longer you cook it, the more concentrated the flavor will be). Taste and make sure the liquid has a well-rounded flavor before straining.

3. Strain through a fine-mesh strainer or chinois into another pot, and discard the solids. Refrigerate in an airtight container for up to 5 days, or freeze for up to several months.

Brown Vegetable Stock

MAKES 5 QUARTS

½ cup dried white beans, soaked overnight, drained, and rinsed (or use the Hot-Soak Method, page 55)

¾ cup brown lentils, rinsed and drained

4 medium carrots, cut into ¼-inch diagonal pieces

3 celery stalks, cut into ¼-inch pieces

2 large yellow onions, halved and thinly sliced

2 medium shallots, thinly sliced

1 parsnip, peeled and cut into ¼-inch pieces

¼ cup extra-virgin olive oil

4 plum tomatoes, halved, seeded, and chopped

2 garlic cloves, peeled

¼ cup dry red wine

1 cup roasted walnuts

Sachet d'épices, made with 3 parsley stems, 1 sprig fresh thyme, 5 peppercorns, and 2 bay leaves

1 tablespoon shoyu or tamari

*if made with tamari

*if made without shoyu/tamari

THE LONGER YOU COOK vegetable stock, the more flavorful it becomes. We roast the vegetables first for this stock and then deglaze the pan with red wine to make the stock darker and give it a more complex flavor. This stock is quite rich, comparable in flavor to beef stock. We use a *sachet d'épices* (see Making an Herb Sachet, below) here instead of a bouquet garni as we do in the Carrot-Onion Stock (page 75) because this method of bundling aromatics in a cheesecloth keeps ingredients like peppercorns contained.

1. Preheat the oven to 400°F.

2. Combine the white beans, lentils, and 6 quarts of water in a large stockpot set over high heat. Cover, and bring to a boil, skimming off any foam that rises to the top. Lower the heat, partially cover, and continue to simmer, about 45 minutes, while you roast the vegetables.

3. Place the carrots, celery, onions, shallots, and parsnips on a baking sheet and toss with the oil to coat. Roast, stirring occasionally, until lightly browned, about 25 minutes. Add the tomatoes and garlic to the vegetables in the oven and continue to roast until everything is aromatic and browned, 10 to 20 minutes more. Add the roasted vegetables to the beans in the stockpot.

4. Set the baking sheet on a flat surface and deglaze it by pouring the red wine on the hot pan and carefully stirring, scraping any bits that are stuck to the pan. Pour the liquid from the baking sheet, along with any browned bits, into the stockpot. Add the walnuts, sachet d'epices, and shoyu and simmer, partially covered, 60 to 90 minutes (the longer you cook it, the more concentrated the flavor will be). Strain using a fine-mesh sieve or chinois, discard the solids, and use the stock as desired. Refrigerate for up to 5 days, or freeze up to several months.

MAKING AN HERB SACHET: The French term *sachet d'epices* translates to "little bag of spices." To make one, place the aromatics (herbs and spices) in a square of cheesecloth, gather the corners to form a pouch, or bag, and use cotton cooking twine to tie it closed. The ingredients in the sachet fully flavor the stock with the advantage that the pouch is easy to remove.

Basil-Infused Oil

MAKES ¾ CUP   Ⓝ

HOMEMADE INFUSED OILS MAKE a beautiful garnish for soups—like our Watermelon Gazpacho (page 147)—or an unexpected and flavorful replacement for olive oil in a dressing. They're also great for drizzling over basically anything and everything, from lunchtime grain bowls to Vegan Ricotta (page 67) on crostini. Here, the basil is blanched and shocked (see page 57) in order to keep its bright-green color; soft, blanched basil also blends more smoothly than raw. Feel free to experiment with other tender herbs as well, such as cilantro, dill, or parsley.

3 cups packed fresh basil leaves (about 3 ounces)

¾ cup canola oil

Pinch of fine sea salt

1. Bring a medium pot of water to a boil and prepare an ice bath.

2. Put the basil in the boiling water and simmer just until it wilts and turns bright-green, 10 to 15 seconds. Using a frying spider or slotted spoon, immediately transfer the basil to the ice bath to cool completely. Remove the cooled leaves and squeeze out all the water.

3. In a blender, combine the basil, oil, and salt, and blend until completely smooth. Chill for at least 30 minutes, or overnight.

4. Strain the basil oil in a nut milk bag or a fine-mesh sieve lined with wet cheesecloth. Use immediately or refrigerate for up to 7 days.

Homemade Tofu

MAKES ONE 10-OUNCE BLOCK OF TOFU (G) (N)

2 cups dried soybeans, soaked overnight and drained

2 teaspoons nigari

**SPECIAL EQUIPMENT
(SEE PAGE 338 FOR RESOURCES)**
Tofu mold, very large stockpot, high-speed blender

CHEF'S TIP: Plastic or wooden tofu molds (which are different from a tofu press) are available online or at specialty Asian food markets for as little as $10 apiece. You can also make your own by repurposing a plastic fruit container, such as a quart strawberry container, which usually already has holes in the bottom for draining, or a container from store-bought tofu with holes poked into the bottom to allow for drainage.

MAKING TOFU IS SIMILAR to making cheese, in that you add a coagulant to a "milk" to create curds and whey and then separate them from one another. We use nigari to do this, a coagulant made up of minerals such as sodium chloride, magnesium chloride, and calcium sulfate, among others. It is the by-product of removing sea salt from sea water. You can find nigari at specialty Asian food markets or online. All the steps may seem onerous—making and straining the milk, separating the curds, etc.—but the end result, creamy tofu with an earthy flavor, is well worth the effort.

1. Line a wooden tofu mold with 2 layers of wet cheesecloth. Set aside.

2. Heat 7½ cups of water in a very large stockpot over medium-high heat until it just comes to a simmer.

3. In a high-speed blender, purée the soybeans in 2 batches with 3 cups of cold water for each batch, about 2 minutes per batch. Add the puréed soybean-water mixture to the pot with the simmering water. Stir constantly, bringing the soybean mixture to a gentle boil. Be careful not to heat it too rapidly, as the liquid has a tendency to boil over suddenly.

4. Strain the soybean-water mixture through a nut milk bag or a fine-mesh sieve lined with a double layer of wet cheesecloth and into a second large pot (or another large container), pressing out all excess liquid. Discard the soy pulp (called *okara*) or reserve it for later use. You should have about 3 quarts of soy milk.

5. Return the strained soy milk to the pot and bring it to a boil, stirring constantly, again being careful because it can boil over quickly. Reduce the heat and gently simmer, uncovered, for about 10 minutes. Remove the pot from the heat.

6. Dissolve the nigari in 1 cup of cold water. Slowly stir one-third of the nigari mixture into the hot soy milk. Cover the pot and allow it to stand for about 3 minutes, or until the milk has separated into soft white curds.

7. Add half the remaining nigari mixture, stirring, and cover for about 3 minutes, then repeat with the remaining nigari. The soy milk should now be completely separated into curds and whey.

8. Pour the mixture through a clean nut milk bag or cheesecloth, squeezing out as much liquid as possible (discard the liquid). Transfer the curds to the cheesecloth-lined tofu mold, folding over the extra cheesecloth on top of the curds. Press the curds down with a 2- to 3-pound weight (such as cans of beans) until the curds are firm and solid, 25 to 30 minutes. Use immediately or store in fresh water for up to 5 days (drain and add fresh water daily).

Homemade Ketchup

MAKES ABOUT 1¼ CUPS

¼ cup golden raisins

1½ cups tomato purée

2 garlic cloves

1 teaspoon sweet paprika

1 teaspoon fine sea salt

Pinch of cayenne pepper

Pinch of cinnamon

1 tablespoon canola oil

1 teaspoon vegan Worcestershire sauce

1 teaspoon fresh lemon juice (from about ¼ lemon)

KETCHUP COULD WELL BE considered America's national condiment. Our version is so full of tangy flavor that you'll be looking for reasons to use it. We purée golden raisins as a sweetener (many store-bought brands use corn syrup), which enhances overall flavor. Feel free to add more sweetener, spices, or acid to reach the perfect balance for your own palate.

1. Soak the raisins in ¼ cup warm water until plump, 10 to 15 minutes.

2. In a blender, combine the raisins with their soaking liquid, the tomato purée, garlic, paprika, salt, cayenne, and cinnamon. Purée until completely smooth.

3. Heat the oil in a medium saucepan over high heat. Slowly add the tomato mixture. Lower the heat to low and simmer, stirring occasionally, until the mixture is thickened, about 20 minutes. Stir in the Worcestershire sauce and lemon juice, and simmer for 5 more minutes. Taste and adjust seasonings, if needed. Refrigerate in an airtight container for up to 2 weeks, or freeze up to several months.

CHEF'S TIP: Vegan Worcestershire sauce can be found in health food stores or online.

Homemade Barbecue Sauce

MAKES ABOUT 2 CUPS

¼ cup golden raisins, soaked in hot water for 10 minutes and drained

1¾ cups tomato purée

2 garlic cloves

3 tablespoons apple cider vinegar

2 tablespoons vegan Worcestershire sauce

2 tablespoons molasses

1 teaspoon fine sea salt

1 teaspoon sweet paprika

1 teaspoon onion powder

¼ teaspoon dried red pepper flakes

STORE-BOUGHT BARBECUE SAUCE CAN be cloyingly sweet, and the ingredients inside the bottle are often unrecognizable and even unpronounceable. Like our ketchup (page 82), this simple homemade version is sweetened with raisins (you'll be surprised how well they work here!), and the red pepper flakes give it a nice kick at the end. It's the perfect finishing touch to our Pulled Barbecue Mushroom Sandwiches (page 240).

l. In a high-speed blender, combine the raisins, tomato purée, garlic, vinegar, Worcestershire sauce, molasses, salt, paprika, onion powder, and pepper flakes, and blend until smooth.

2. Transfer to a saucepan, bring to a simmer over medium-low heat, and cook for about 15 minutes, stirring occasionally, until slightly thickened. Let cool to room temperature before serving or storing. Refrigerate in an airtight container for up to 2 weeks, or freeze for several months.

CHEF'S TIP: Vegan Worcestershire sauce can be found in health food stores or online.

Sherry Vinaigrette

MAKES ABOUT ½ CUP

WE ALL NEED A delicious, reliable back-pocket salad dressing in our arsenal. This vinaigrette is emulsified, meaning the oil and vinegar, which would usually separate after a few minutes, come together and remain smooth and stable, thanks to the creaminess of mustard, the emulsifying agent. The thicker consistency also makes it cling better to salad leaves. Feel free to substitute different types of vinegars, sweeteners, and oils (like our Basil-Infused Oil on page 78), as you like.

3 tablespoons sherry vinegar

4 teaspoons maple syrup

1½ teaspoons Dijon mustard

1 small garlic clove, minced

¾ teaspoon fine sea salt

¼ cup extra-virgin olive oil

In a small bowl, whisk together the vinegar, maple syrup, mustard, garlic, and salt. Gradually whisk in the olive oil until the vinaigrette is creamy and emulsified. Alternatively, add the ingredients to a jar with a tightly fitted lid and shake vigorously to combine. Refrigerate for up to 1 week.

Avocado Green Goddess Dressing

MAKES 1 CUP

A BEAUTIFUL SHADE OF green, as the name implies, this dressing gets its color not only from fresh herbs but from an avocado base, which replaces the mayonnaise traditionally found in Green Goddess dressing. This creamy blend is great tossed with vegetables and lettuces like romaine and kale (more delicate greens may wilt under its weight). It also works well as a dip for fresh vegetables—just use a little less liquid for an even thicker consistency.

½ medium shallot, peeled and coarsely chopped

1 ripe avocado, halved, pitted, and peeled

½ packed cup fresh cilantro leaves

1 to 2 tablespoons fresh basil leaves

4 tablespoons fresh lime juice (from 3 to 4 limes)

2 tablespoons extra-virgin olive oil

½ to ¾ teaspoon fine sea salt

Freshly ground black pepper to taste

Put the shallot in a food processor (use the mini bowl insert if you have one) and pulse until finely minced. Add the avocado, cilantro, basil, lime juice, oil, ½ teaspoon of salt, pepper, and ½ cup of water and process until smooth and creamy. Add more water, if needed, until the desired consistency is reached. Taste and add more salt if desired. Refrigerate in an airtight container for up to 1 day.

CHEF'S TIP: Try adding a seeded jalapeño for a little kick, or sub out the basil and cilantro for other favorites, like tarragon, parsley, dill, and/or chives.

To prevent the dressing from oxidizing quickly, hold on to the avocado pit and store it in the container with the dressing.

SHERRY VINAIGRETTE
page 85

AVOCADO GREEN GODDESS DRESSING
page 85

Creamy Horseradish Dressing

MAKES ABOUT 1 CUP

THE SHARP FLAVOR OF horseradish, a root prized for its medicinal qualities, gives a nice kick to this creamy dressing. To prepare horseradish, treat it as you would a carrot or parsnip—remove the skin using a vegetable peeler and finely grate with a Microplane or another fine grater. We blanch the tofu here because blanching makes it last longer—the hot water is meant to kill any lingering bacteria, since tofu is such a fresh, perishable item. Blanching it also improves the flavor by removing any raw, chalky aftertaste.

4 ounces silken tofu

¼ cup unsweetened soy milk

2 tablespoons extra-virgin olive oil

2 tablespoons miso

2 tablespoons fresh lemon juice (from about 1 lemon)

1 tablespoon brown rice vinegar

1 tablespoon peeled, freshly grated horseradish

½ teaspoon Dijon mustard

1 garlic clove

Freshly ground black pepper to taste

Hot sauce to taste

1. Bring a medium pot of water to a boil.

2. Wrap the tofu in cheesecloth and tie it closed with cotton cooking twine. Lower the tofu into the boiling water and blanch it for 2 to 3 minutes. Drain well. Let the tofu stand until cool enough to handle.

3. In a blender, combine the blanched tofu, soy milk, oil, miso, lemon juice, vinegar, horseradish, mustard, and garlic. Process until smooth and creamy. Season with black pepper and hot sauce to taste. Refrigerate in an airtight container for up to 4 days.

CREAMY HORSERADISH DRESSING

Basic Basil Pesto

MAKES ABOUT ¾ CUP

3 cups packed basil leaves
(about 3 ounces)

¼ cup toasted pine nuts
(see page 56)

1 tablespoon miso

1 small garlic clove, chopped

Pinch of fine sea salt

½ cup extra-virgin olive oil

CHEF'S TIP: If the price of pine nuts is a deterrent to making this recipe, replace them with walnuts or sunflower seeds. You may substitute arugula, spinach, or kale for the basil as well (we won't tell *nonna*).

THIS FRAGRANT, NUTTY STAPLE sauce should be seemingly straightforward—put all the ingredients in a food processor and you're good to go. But, oh, how easy it is to upset the trinity of basil, garlic, and oil! We find the most common way to throw off the balance is with a too-large clove of garlic. If your clove is large, consider cutting it in half and starting out small. While you may like a strong garlic flavor, you don't want your pesto to become bitter or have an overpowering garlicky taste. And while traditional pesto alla Genovese is made using Parmesan cheese, we opt for a tablespoon of miso in its place so our vegan version maintains a similar sweet and subtle umami.

In a food processor, combine the basil, pine nuts, miso, garlic, and salt. Pulse until everything is coarsely chopped. With the motor running, stream in the oil through the feeder tube. Taste and adjust the seasonings if needed. Use as desired or refrigerate in an airtight container for up to 4 days.

Salsa Roja

MAKES ABOUT 1½ CUPS

2 dried chipotle chilies

1 (14½-ounce) can diced fire-roasted, tomatoes

2 tablespoons extra-virgin olive oil

½ medium white onion, minced

6 medium garlic cloves, minced

1½ teaspoons ground cumin

¼ teaspoon fine sea salt, plus more to taste

HERE IS A FIERY, smoky salsa you can rely on to spice up a meal. Use it on a tofu scramble (page 267), as an accompaniment to beans, or with our Avocado Fritters (page 129). Pan-roasting the chilies makes them pliable so it's easier to remove the seeds.

1. Heat a small cast-iron pan over medium-high heat and cook the dried chilies until soft and pliable, 30 to 40 seconds. Slice the chilies open and scrape out the seeds.

2. Transfer the chilies to a small pot, cover them with water, and bring to a simmer over medium heat. Simmer until the chilies soften, about 5 minutes.

3. Drain the chilies and put them in a food processor. Add the tomatoes and purée until smooth.

4. Heat a skillet over medium heat, add the oil, and heat until it just starts to shimmer. Add the onion and cook until translucent, 5 to 7 minutes. Stir in the garlic, cumin, and salt, and cook until fragrant, about 1 minute more. Add the tomato-chili mixture and simmer for about 10 minutes. Season to taste. Cool to room temperature before serving. Refrigerate in an airtight container for up to 4 days.

Rich Béchamel Sauce

MAKES 3 CUPS

2 teaspoons refined coconut oil

1 small shallot minced

¼ cup oat flour

6 cups homemade almond milk (see Basic Nut Milk, page 61)

Pinch of freshly grated nutmeg

1 sprig fresh thyme

1 dried bay leaf

2 to 3 tablespoons fresh lemon juice (from about 1 large lemon)

½ teaspoon fine sea salt, plus more to taste

¼ teaspoon freshly ground black pepper, plus more to taste

CHEF'S TIP: Add a few spoonfuls of nutritional yeast for a "cheesy" version of this sauce.

CREAMY AND SMOOTH, BÉCHAMEL is one of the five French mother sauces and is an essential component to classic French cuisine—it's also key to dishes like mac and cheese, a creamy gratin, and potpie. We use the traditional method of making the sauce by starting with a roux (pronounced ROO), a thickening agent made up of equal parts flour and fat, but we've replaced the butter fat with coconut oil, the dairy milk with almond milk, and the wheat flour with oat flour (if you have a gluten intolerance, check the oat flour label to make sure it wasn't processed in a facility that also processes wheat flour). This gluten-free vegan version is as rich and versatile as the original.

1. Heat a medium saucepan over medium-high heat, add the oil, and heat until it just starts to shimmer. Add the shallot and stir to coat with the oil. Cook until the shallot is translucent, 5 to 8 minutes.

2. Add the flour, reduce the heat to low, and cook, stirring constantly, for 3 to 5 minutes.

3. Slowly whisk in the almond milk and add the nutmeg, thyme, and bay leaf. Increase the heat to medium and bring the sauce to a simmer. Continue cooking, stirring often, until the sauce thickens, 20 to 25 minutes.

4. Strain the sauce through a fine-mesh sieve into a bowl. Stir in the lemon juice and season with salt and pepper. Use as desired or refrigerate for up to 3 days.

Sweet Potato–Cassava Tortillas

MAKES ABOUT 10 TORTILLAS

1 medium sweet potato

1⅓ cups cassava flour

1 teaspoon fine sea salt

3 tablespoons refined coconut oil or extra-virgin olive oil, plus more for brushing the tortillas

CHEF'S TIP: If you prefer, you can make the dough in a food processor using a dough blade instead of mixing the dough by hand.

THESE GRAIN-FREE TORTILLAS ARE a combination of sweet potato and cassava flour, which is made from the root of the cassava plant (also known as yuca). We love this gluten-free, gut-friendly flour—now sold in many markets and online—for its mild flavor and binding qualities. Slightly less pliable than traditional corn tortillas, these flatbread-like rounds have an almost chewy yet tender texture and a faintly sweet taste. Top them with raw or roasted vegetables, or serve them as a side to a hearty stew or soup.

1. Preheat the oven to 375°F. Pierce the sweet potato all over with a fork, wrap it in foil, and bake until fork-tender, 60 to 90 minutes. Remove from the oven, unwrap, and cool completely.

2. Make a slit down the center of the potato, scoop out the inside, and discard (or eat!) the skins. You should get about 1¼ cups of cooked sweet potato.

3. Put the sweet potato in a large bowl and add the flour and salt. Place a ½-cup measure of water near the bowl. Work the mixture together with your hands (it gets messy, then comes together), squeezing the potato and flour together until it won't combine any further, then sprinkle with 2 tablespoons of water over the mixture and continue to form it with your hands. After a few squeezes, add another 2 tablespoons of water, continuing the process until you've used all the water. Once the dough comes together in a ball, knead it until smooth, about 5 minutes.

4. Divide the dough into 10 equal pieces (about the size of a ¼-cup measure) and form each piece into a ball. (Keep the dough pieces covered with a damp towel to prevent them from drying out.)

5. Line each side of the inside of a tortilla press with plastic wrap and press each dough ball to about a ⅛-inch thickness, about 5 inches in diameter (or see Chef's Tip, page 95). Keep the tortillas covered.

6. Heat a cast-iron skillet, griddle, or nonstick pan over medium-high heat and coat lightly with oil. Place a tortilla on the skillet. Brush the top of the dough with oil. If the dough sticks to the skillet, work a small amount of oil underneath the tortilla. Cook each tortilla until lightly browned and golden, 2 to 3 minutes per side. Remove from the pan, and cover the tortillas with a kitchen towel to keep them warm.

7. Serve warm. Refrigerate for up to 2 days, or layer the tortillas with parchment paper, wrap in plastic, place in a sealed container or in a resealable plastic bag, and freeze for up to a month.

Homemade Corn Tortillas

MAKES 12 TORTILLAS

2 cups masa harina

½ teaspoon fine sea salt

1½ cups hot water

CHEF'S TIP: You can buy a tortilla press for under $20 at most chef's supply stores, or you can simply put a dough round between 2 pieces of parchment or plastic wrap and press it flat with a flat-bottomed pot or pie plate.

CHEF INSTRUCTOR SUE BALDASSANO has led numerous tours to Mexico throughout her career and has developed a curriculum, which includes this recipe, to teach our students about the country's regional dishes and techniques (underscoring the "traditional" principle of our Seven Principles, pages 22–23). While in parts of Mexico fresh tortillas are made to order from dried corn ground with a *metate*, or a simple grindstone, in the United States most cooks buy the corn already ground in flour form, called masa harina. The corn used to make this flour is soaked and cooked in an alkaline solution before it is hulled and ground. This process, known as *nixtalimazation*, tenderizes the grains, making them easier to grind, while also improving their flavor and nutritional profile. Once you taste fresh tortillas, there is no going back to store-bought!

1. In a large bowl combine the masa harina and salt. Add the hot water and stir to combine.

2. Using your hands, knead the dough until it becomes smooth and forms a ball, about 5 minutes. It should start to feel springy and resist slightly when you press against it. If the dough feels dry, incorporate more water, and if it feels too wet and sticks to your hands, add a bit more flour. Cover the dough with a damp towel and allow it to rest for at least 20 minutes.

3. Remove the dough from the bowl and press it into a ½-inch-thick rectangle. Cut the dough in half then divide each half into 6 equal pieces. Form each piece into a ball. (Keep the dough balls covered with a damp kitchen towel to prevent them from drying out while you shape each one into a ball.)

4. Line each side of the inside of a tortilla press with plastic wrap and press each dough ball to about a ⅛- to ¼-inch thickness, about 6 inches in diameter. Alternatively, you may press each ball with a heavy-bottomed pan.

5. Heat a cast-iron skillet, griddle, or nonstick pan over medium-high heat. Place a tortilla on the griddle and cook for about 45 seconds on each side, or until some brown spots start to appear and the edges look slightly dry. Keep the tortillas warm and pliable by wrapping them in a kitchen towel until ready to serve. Fresh tortillas are best eaten immediately.

Basic Pastry Crust

MAKES ONE 8-INCH CRUST

(S) (N)

⅔ cup whole-wheat pastry flour

⅔ cup unbleached all-purpose flour, plus more for dusting

1 tablespoon maple crystals, coconut sugar, or organic raw sugar

¼ teaspoon baking powder

Pinch of fine sea salt

¼ cup refined coconut oil, partially solid (refrigerate, if necessary, to get the texture of soft butter)

2 tablespoons maple syrup

1 tablespoon pure vanilla extract

About ¼ cup ice water

CHEF'S TIP: For added convenience, you can freeze unbaked pie crusts right in pie pans. Roll them out as directed above, place them in pie pans, wrap tightly with plastic wrap, and freeze. No need to thaw before cooking. Simply fill and bake (you may need to adjust the cooking time, making it slightly longer).

WE USE COCONUT OIL and whole-wheat pastry flour to make this dough, which creates a slightly nutty crust that's more toothsome than a traditional butter-based one. Whole-wheat pastry flour is made from soft white wheat and has a lower protein content, making it more tender for baking compared to traditional whole-wheat flour, which is made from hard wheat. This crust works great for galettes and pies, and can even be rolled out, sprinkled with cinnamon sugar, and cut into cookies.

1. In a medium bowl, whisk together the flours, maple crystals, baking powder, and salt. Add the oil and, using a pastry cutter or a large fork, work the oil into the flour. The dough should have a coarse, sand-like consistency.

2. Using a wooden spoon, stir in the maple syrup and vanilla until combined. Gradually add water, 1 tablespoon at a time, while continuing to stir. The dough should just hold together and be hydrated but not wet.

3. Place the dough on a piece of plastic wrap, gather the sides, and shape the dough into a ball. Press the ball down to form a disk shape about 1 inch thick and refrigerate for 10 to 15 minutes.

4. Remove the dough from the refrigerator and let it rest at room temperature for 5 to 10 minutes, or until it's malleable and can be rolled out without cracking. Use as directed. The dough can be made up to 3 days in advance; wrap and store the disk in the refrigerator until ready to roll out, or store in the freezer for up to 3 months.

Whipped Coconut Cream

MAKES ABOUT 1 CUP ⒼⓈⓃ

SLIGHTLY THICKER AND RICHER than traditional dairy whipped cream, a dollop of this dairy-free topping adds creamy decadence to anything it garnishes. Depending on your preference, you may add sweetener or not. When you chill coconut milk, as the recipe calls for, the cream separates and hardens at the top of the can, which is what you scoop out to whip. Save the remaining coconut water for smoothies.

1 (13.5-ounce) can full-fat coconut milk, or 1 (5-ounce) can coconut cream, very cold from the fridge

1 tablespoon powdered maple crystals (page 28), or another powdered sugar

1 teaspoon pure vanilla extract

SPECIAL EQUIPMENT

Stand mixer or hand mixer

Scrape the coconut cream into the chilled bowl of a stand mixer (or a large bowl if you're using a hand mixer). Beat the cream until light and fluffy. Add the maple crystals and vanilla, and beat to combine. Refrigerate until ready to serve. The cream will firm up when chilled. Soften at room temperature before serving and rewhip, if necessary. Store refrigerated in an airtight container for up to 1 week.

CHEF'S TIP: Keep a few cans of coconut milk or coconut cream in the refrigerator at all times so you can whip up a batch at a moment's notice. Also, if your sugar is not ultra-fine, or powdered, put it in a high-speed blender and run it until the sugar becomes ultra-fine (we prefer to steer clear of store-bought powdered sugar because it typically contains highly processed cornstarch).

Whipped Cashew Cream

MAKES 2 TO 3 CUPS, DEPENDING ON THE THICKNESS OF THE CREAM Ⓖ Ⓢ

COMPARABLE TO A VEGAN crème fraîche, this velvety, creamy dessert topping keeps its structure more than the Whipped Coconut Cream (previous recipe). To make a chocolate version, whisk in a tablespoon or two of sifted cocoa powder.

2 cups raw cashews, soaked for at least 4 hours or overnight, drained and rinsed

2 tablespoons agave syrup

2 teaspoons pure vanilla extract

Pinch of fine sea salt

In a blender, combine the cashews, agave, vanilla, and salt. Purée, gradually adding water in ¼-cup increments and blending for 1 to 2 minutes between additions, scraping down the sides as needed, until the cream is smooth and airy. Refrigerate in an airtight container for up to 4 days.

CHEF'S TIP: The thick cream may be diluted with water to create to a pourable sauce.

CHAPTER 2

Snacks & Starters

Almond Pulp Crisps

MAKES ABOUT 10 CRACKERS

HOMEMADE ALMOND MILK HAS only one downside: leftover almond pulp. Although some of the fat gets extracted into the almond milk, much of the protein and fiber of almonds remains in the pulp. Here, we show you how to turn it into light, free-form crackers. Almond pulp can be frozen for several months, and this recipe easily doubles or triples to make sure no pulp goes to waste.

1 cup almond pulp, reserved from making almond milk (see Basic Nut Milk, page 61)

2 tablespoons maple syrup or agave syrup

½ teaspoon lemon extract, or 1 teaspoon lemon zest

Pinch of fine sea salt

1. Preheat the oven to 350°F. In a medium bowl, stir together the almond pulp, maple syrup, lemon extract, and salt until combined.

2. Turn the mixture out onto a sheet of parchment paper, cover with another sheet of parchment paper, and roll out to a ¼-inch thickness. Remove the top sheet of parchment and transfer the bottom sheet (with the dough) to a baking sheet. Bake until crisp and lightly golden, rotating the baking sheet after about 8 minutes, 15 to 20 minutes total.

3. Cool completely, then break into 10 crackers. Store in an airtight container at room temperature for up to 1 week.

Spiced Roasted Chickpeas

MAKES ABOUT 1½ CUPS

ROASTED CHICKPEAS ARE A great high-protein snack to keep at your desk for midday munching, or to sprinkle on soups or salads. You can flavor these any way you like, with curry powder, Cajun seasoning, or za'atar. Be sure to really use your elbow grease when drying the chickpeas—if they're not fully dried, they'll never get crispy.

1½ cups cooked chickpeas (page 54), or 1 (15-ounce) can chickpeas, drained and rinsed

2 tablespoons extra-virgin olive oil

½ teaspoon ground fennel

½ teaspoon ground cumin

¼ teaspoon smoked paprika

¼ teaspoon fine sea salt

Pinch of dried red pepper flakes

1. Preheat the oven to 375°F. Pat the chickpeas very dry between paper towels and transfer them to a baking sheet.

2. Add the oil, fennel, cumin, paprika, salt, and pepper flakes, and toss to coat. Roast until golden and crispy, about 25 minutes.

3. Cool completely before serving. Store at room temperature for up to 1 week. (A paper bag is preferable. If you store them in a plastic bag they will lose their crispiness.)

Almond Pulp Cookies

MAKES ABOUT 2 DOZEN COOKIES Ⓖ Ⓢ

1 cup dehydrated almond pulp (see step 1)

¼ cup arrowroot starch

Pinch of fine sea salt

2 tablespoons melted coconut oil

2 tablespoons maple syrup

2 tablespoons tahini or banana purée

CHEF'S TIP: To make the cookies chocolate-flavored, use only ¾ cup of almond flour and add ¼ cup cocoa powder to the dry ingredients.

JUST LIKE THE ALMOND Pulp Crisps on page 103, these light and crumbly, marzipan-like cookies are an excellent way to use up the fiber-rich pulp left over from making almond milk. Feel free to use additional flavorings, if you like, such as vanilla, cinnamon, orange zest, and/or ground cardamom.

1. To dehydrate the almond pulp left over from making milk, preheat the oven to 250°F. Spread the pulp on a parchment paper–lined baking sheet and bake until dehydrated, about 1 hour. Cool completely, then transfer to a food processor and grind until it is light and fluffy. Reserve the baking sheet with parchment. Measure out 1 cup of the resulting almond flour for the cookies.

2. Increase the oven temperature to 350°F. In a medium bowl, combine the almond flour, arrowroot, and salt.

3. In a small bowl, stir together the oil, maple syrup, and tahini. Add the wet ingredients to the dry and stir, using a rubber spatula, until the dough comes together; it should be thick but hydrated.

4. Using a tablespoon measure, scoop the dough onto the reserved baking sheet, spacing the cookies 1 to 2 inches apart (you should get about 12). Lightly flatten the cookies with the palm of your hand. Bake until lightly golden around the edges, about 10 minutes. Cool completely before serving. Store in an airtight container for up to 5 days.

Sunflower Pâté

A **COMBINATION OF NUTS** and seeds makes this plant-based pâté rich and satisfying. The spread literally comes together in seconds. The only extra time needed is for soaking the walnuts and sunflower seeds, which is important because it helps the nuts and seeds blend to a creamy, smooth consistency. Serve it as an appetizer, or try it for lunch as a spread on bread in place of nut butter.

1½ cups raw walnuts, soaked overnight and drained

1½ cups raw sunflower seeds, soaked for 4 to 6 hours and drained

½ cup packed fresh dill, coarsely chopped

2 tablespoons fresh lemon juice (from about 1 lemon)

1 tablespoon shoyu or tamari

1 tablespoon finely diced red onion

1 medium garlic clove

Fine sea salt to taste

Cucumber rounds and/or crackers, such as Seeded Mixed-Grain Crackers (page 109), for serving

1 cup sunflower sprouts, for serving

*if made with tamari

1. In a food processor, combine the walnuts, sunflower seeds, dill, lemon juice, shoyu, onion, and garlic. Purée until completely smooth, scraping down the sides as needed. Taste and season with salt, if desired. Transfer to an airtight container and refrigerate for up to 3 days.

2. Serve chilled, spread on cucumber rounds or crackers, and sprinkle with the sunflower sprouts. Alternatively, scrape the pâté into a shallow bowl and serve as a dip.

SEEDED MIXED-GRAIN CRACKERS
page 109

EDAMAME-SCALLION SPREAD
page 108

VEGAN RICOTTA
page 67

POPPY SEED CRACKERS
page 111

BEET TARTARE
page 110

Edamame-Scallion Spread

SERVES 8

¼ cup canola or another neutral oil

1 large clove garlic, minced

1 (16-ounce) bag frozen shelled edamame, thawed

1 tablespoon fresh lemon juice (from about ½ lemon)

1 tablespoon fresh ginger juice (from about a 3-inch piece; see page 74)

¼ teaspoon fine sea salt, plus more to taste

2 tablespoons thinly sliced scallions (white and green parts), for sprinkling

Crackers, crudités, or bread, for serving

EDAMAME, WHICH ARE IMMATURE soybeans, are an easily digestible form of whole soy, containing fiber, protein, thiamin, iron, magnesium, and other minerals. If you're looking for an alternative to your typical hummus, this creamy, garlicky, eye-catchingly green spread is sure to become a staple in your repertoire. It's terrific with the Seeded Mixed-Grain Crackers on the following page.

1. Heat a small skillet over low heat, add the oil, and heat for about 1 minute. Add the garlic and cook just until it begins to sizzle, about 1 minute. Remove the pan from the heat immediately and transfer the garlic and oil to a bowl so the garlic doesn't burn.

2. In a food processor, combine the edamame, lemon and ginger juices, salt, and garlic-oil mixture. Purée until smooth, adding a teaspoon of water if needed to achieve a smooth consistency. Taste and season with salt, if needed.

3. Transfer to a bowl and sprinkle with the scallions. Serve with crackers, crudités, or bread.

Seeded Mixed-Grain Crackers

MAKES ABOUT 40 CRACKERS

¼ cup rolled oats

¼ cup sliced almonds

¼ cup spelt flour

2 tablespoons fine cornmeal

¼ teaspoon ground cumin

1 tablespoon plus 1 teaspoon extra-virgin olive oil

1 tablespoon plus 1 teaspoon maple syrup

½ teaspoon fine sea salt

1 teaspoon black or white sesame seeds

1 teaspoon flaxseeds

1 teaspoon caraway seeds

1 teaspoon poppy seeds

THESE CRACKERS ARE SERIOUSLY addictive. They are crunchy, a bit thicker than most crackers, and slightly sweet from the cornmeal and maple syrup. We love the variety of textures the sesame, flax-, caraway, and poppy seeds provide, but if you can't locate all four at your grocery store, feel free to use more of whichever seeds you have on hand.

1. Preheat the oven to 375°F. In a food processor, grind the oats, almonds, flour, cornmeal, and cumin to a fine meal. In a small bowl, whisk together the oil, maple syrup, and salt. With the food processor motor running, stream in the oil mixture through the chute and then pulse until thoroughly combined. The mixture should form a ball. If the dough is too dry or crumbly, add 1 to 2 teaspoons of water, as needed.

2. Roll out the dough between 2 sheets of parchment paper to a thickness of ⅛ inch. Remove the top sheet and sprinkle the sesame, flax-, caraway, and poppy seeds over the dough. Replace the top sheet of parchment and roll the seeds into the dough. Remove the top sheet of parchment.

3. Score the dough into 2-inch crackers of your desired shape, like squares or diamonds (you should get about 40 crackers). Transfer the dough, along with the parchment paper, to a baking sheet and bake until golden and crisp, about 15 minutes. Let cool completely, then separate the crackers. Store them in an airtight container at room temperature for up to 1 week.

Beet Tartare

SERVES 6 TO 8

2 pounds small red beets (about 10 beets), scrubbed

4 fresh thyme sprigs

½ teaspoon freshly ground black pepper

4 teaspoons fine sea salt

3 tablespoons white balsamic or champagne vinegar, or to taste

2 tablespoons extra-virgin olive oil

4 teaspoons vegan Worcestershire sauce

1 garlic clove, minced

1 batch Vegan Ricotta (page 67), for serving (optional)

Poppy Seed Crackers (see following page), for serving (optional)

WITH ITS RUBY-RED COLOR and light-catching glisten, this sophisticated appetizer resembles a pile of jewels on a plate. Serve it with the Poppy Seed Crackers at your next cocktail party.

1. In a medium pot, combine the beets, thyme, black pepper, and 3 teaspoons of salt with enough water to cover the beets. Cover, bring to a boil over high heat, reduce the heat to low, and simmer until the beets can be pierced with a fork with no resistance, about 45 minutes. Drain and cool the beets until they can be easily handled.

2. Rub the cooled beets with gloved hands or paper towels to remove the skins. Coarsely chop the beets and, working in batches, pulse them in a food processor into small chunks, making sure not to purée them completely. Transfer the ground beets to a mixing bowl and stir in the vinegar, oil, Worcestershire sauce, garlic, and the remaining teaspoon of salt. Toss to combine and chill for up to 4 hours before serving. Serve alongside the Vegan Ricotta and Poppy Seed Crackers.

Poppy Seed Crackers

MAKES ABOUT 24 CRACKERS

1 cup old-fashioned rolled oats

1 cup sunflower seeds

1 cup whole-wheat flour

2 teaspoons garlic powder

2 teaspoons fine sea salt

⅓ cup extra-virgin olive oil

⅓ cup maple syrup

3 tablespoons poppy seeds

CHEF'S TIP: Bake a single cracker to test the crunch factor. If you'd like them a little crispier, roll out the dough a little thinner.

WHILE MAKING HOMEMADE CRACKERS may seem intimidating, they are actually a great starting place for beginning bakers because they are almost foolproof. The dough comes together easily in a food processor, then you roll it out. Even if you have a hard time getting the dough thin enough to achieve a crispy cracker, you'll still get a cracker, just a little chewier. It's also much more economical to make your own, since artisanal crackers can get pricey. We like to serve these with Beet Tartare (see previous page) and Vegan Ricotta (page 67), but you can pair them with any dip you like, or just eat them plain.

1. Preheat the oven to 325°F. In a food processor, combine the oats and sunflower seeds and pulse until pulverized. Add the flour, garlic powder, and salt, and pulse to combine. With the motor running, stream in the oil and maple syrup, and purée until the dough forms a ball, adding 1 to 2 tablespoons of water if the mixture appears too dry.

2. Roll out the dough between 2 sheets of parchment paper to a thickness of ⅛ inch. Remove the top sheet and sprinkle with the poppy seeds. Replace the top sheet of parchment and roll the seeds into the dough. Remove the top sheet of parchment.

3. Transfer the dough with the parchment paper to a baking sheet and score it into about 2 dozen 1½-inch diamond-shaped pieces. Bake until firm, about 20 minutes. When cool enough to handle, break the sheet into crackers along the scored indentations. Store them in an airtight container at room temperature for up to 1 week.

Rosemary–White Bean Purée, Tomato, and Arugula Toast

SERVES 6 TO 8

FOR THE TOAST

1 cup white beans, soaked overnight, drained, and rinsed

4 cups store-bought vegetable stock or Carrot-Onion Stock (page 75)

3 sprigs fresh rosemary, stemmed and minced, plus 1 whole sprig

1 dried bay leaf

¾ teaspoon fine sea salt

1 garlic clove, minced, plus 1 clove, halved lengthwise

¼ teaspoon freshly ground black pepper

1 whole-wheat Tuscan or peasant bread loaf, cut into ½-inch-thick slices and toasted

2 plum tomatoes, halved, seeded, and finely diced

1 cup arugula, coarsely chopped (about 1 ounce)

FOR THE ROSEMARY OIL

5 sprigs fresh rosemary (about 1 ounce), finely chopped (with stems)

1 cup extra-virgin olive oil

*if served on gluten-free bread

THIS BEAN PURÉE IS light, creamy, and flavored throughout with everyone's favorite Italian power duo—garlic and rosemary. The recipe makes more rosemary oil than you'll need, so reserve the rest for sautéing or roasting vegetables, or incorporating into a salad dressing. You may also serve this purée as a dip—just spoon it into a shallow bowl and garnish with extra rosemary oil and black pepper.

1. Cook the beans: In a large pot, combine the beans, stock, 1 sprig of rosemary, bay leaf, and ¼ teaspoon salt. Cover and bring to a boil over high heat. Reduce the heat to low and simmer with the lid ajar until the beans are tender, about 30 to 40 minutes. Discard the rosemary sprig and bay leaf, and drain the beans, reserving all the cooking liquid.

2. Meanwhile, make the rosemary oil: Combine the rosemary and oil in a small saucepan over high heat until the mixture begins to sizzle, about 5 minutes. Continue to cook for about 10 more seconds, then remove from the heat, and swirl the pot a few times. Strain the oil through a cheesecloth-lined fine-mesh strainer and into a medium bowl, pressing down on the rosemary to extract all the flavor. Discard the rosemary.

3. Heat a large skillet over medium heat, add 2 tablespoons of the rosemary oil, and heat until it just starts to shimmer. Add the minced rosemary, minced garlic, cooked beans, pepper, and the remaining ½ teaspoon salt, and cook, stirring, for about 5 minutes, adding some reserved bean cooking liquid if the beans begin to dry out. Turn off the heat and mash the beans with a fork to make a chunky paste. Taste and adjust seasonings, if needed.

4. To serve, rub the halved garlic cloves on the bread and brush with a bit of rosemary oil. Spread the bean paste on the toast and top with tomatoes and arugula.

Why We Eat Sea Vegetables

BY CHEF JILL BURNS

Seaweed—also known as sea vegetables, edible plants from the sea, or simply algae—is a wonderful addition to a natural foods kitchen. These unique plants are among the very first organisms to thrive on planet Earth and have been part of traditional diets for thousands of years, particularly among people living along coastlines who gather food from the sea.

Sea vegetables have endured time and climate change, and are considered nutrient-dense foods. They bring a variety of colors, flavors, and textures to meals that are unlike any offered by vegetables grown on land. They may be dark-brown, black, burgundy, or deep-green in color, and their flavor can range from mildly sweet–salty to deep ocean–briny. Seaweed can be added to soups, stews, salads, side dishes, casseroles, pickles, and even desserts.

Seaweed is known for its rich mineral content—often higher than that of land vegetables—including iodine, potassium, sodium, calcium, magnesium, iron, sulfur, nitrogen, zinc, boron, copper, and manganese, which are great for bones, teeth, hair, and nails. Seaweeds are also rich in fiber and contain alginic acid, which can bind with harmful heavy metals in the body and assist in their removal.

Most natural food markets carry dried seaweed, as do many online retailers. The most common varieties are agar, arame, hijiki, kombu, kelp, dulse, nori, and wakame. You can store them almost indefinitely in the pantry, although sometimes they absorb moisture from the air and the pieces may soften. But not much else will happen (and even softened pieces are okay to use).

Seaweed can be harvested by hand or mechanically by large boats. Keep in mind that quality control is greater when plants are cut by hand in pristine water while ensuring a sustainable harvest for the following season.

Some sea vegetables should be rinsed and rehydrated before cooking, though small pieces of wakame or kombu can be dropped directly into a soup, stew, or pot of beans. The easiest way to introduce sea vegetables into meals is to keep them in the background of a dish. Then as the flavor and texture become more familiar, they can take on a starring role as a side dish. Check out Hiziki Caviar with Tofu Sour Cream (page 118) and Adzuki Bean Stew (page 150) for ways to incorporate sea vegetables into your diet.

Traditional Muhammara

SERVES 6 TO 8

2 large red bell peppers

2 tablespoons plus 2 teaspoons
extra-virgin olive oil

3 small garlic cloves, coarsely
chopped

1 cup toasted walnuts
(see page 56)

1 tablespoon pomegranate
molasses

1 tablespoon fresh lemon juice
(from about ½ lemon)

¼ cup plain dried bread crumbs

2 tablespoons vegetable stock
or water

1½ teaspoons sherry vinegar

¼ teaspoon fine sea salt

¼ teaspoon freshly ground black
pepper

Chopped fresh flat-leaf parsley
or cilantro, for serving (optional)

Crudités and/or pita chips,
for serving

IF HUMMUS IS YOUR go-to dip, try switching things up with this classic Levantine red pepper–and–walnut spread, a colorful addition to any mezze-style meal. The steps of freshly roasting peppers and toasting the nuts, as minor as they may seem, contribute greatly to a more intense, sophisticated flavor than if you used jarred peppers and raw nuts. If you don't have pomegranate molasses on hand, you may use aged or reduced balsamic vinegar instead.

1. Preheat the oven to 450°F. Line a baking sheet with parchment paper. Rub the bell peppers with 1 teaspoon of oil each. Put on the prepared baking sheet and roast until the skins are blistered and charred, 25 to 30 minutes.

2. Transfer the peppers to a bowl and cover with plastic wrap to steam. When cool enough to handle, peel off the skins, pull off the tops, and discard the ribs and seeds.

3. In a food processor, combine the peppers, garlic, walnuts, pomegranate molasses, and lemon juice, and purée until broken down, about 30 seconds. Add the bread crumbs, stock, vinegar, salt, black pepper, and the remaining 2 tablespoons of oil, and purée until smooth. Taste and adjust seasonings, if needed. Transfer to a serving bowl, sprinkle with herbs, if using, and serve with crudités and/or pita chips.

Hiziki Caviar

with Tofu Sour Cream

SERVES 6 *

FOR THE SOUR CREAM

7 ounces soft tofu (half a standard package)

2 tablespoons fresh lemon juice (from about 1 lemon)

2 tablespoons extra-virgin olive oil

½ teaspoon fine sea salt

1 tablespoon minced fresh dill

FOR THE CAVIAR

3 tablespoons sesame oil or another neutral oil

½ cup loosely packed hiziki (about ½ ounce), soaked for 10 minutes, drained, rinsed, and minced

2 tablespoons shoyu or tamari

3 large garlic cloves, minced

1 small shallot, minced

1 tablespoon fresh lemon juice (from about ½ lemon)

2 tablespoons fresh ginger juice from about a 6-inch piece (see page 74)

Fine sea salt to taste

Cucumber rounds, crostini, or crackers, for serving

*if made with tamari

CHEF INSTRUCTOR JILL BURNS is our sea vegetable guru. Over fifteen years ago she wrote *Vegetables from the Sea* with the intention of bringing these "gifts from the sea" to the mainstream, because seaweed is among the most nutrient- and mineral-rich foods on the planet. There are many different varieties of sea vegetables (see page 116), and we incorporate them often into our meals. Hiziki (known in Japan as *hijiki*), with its dark color and briny quality, lends a sea flavor reminiscent of caviar to this appetizer.

1. Make the sour cream: In a food processor, combine the tofu, lemon juice, oil, salt, and 1 tablespoon of water, and purée until smooth. Add the dill and purée to combine. Transfer to a medium bowl and chill for 20 minutes or overnight.

2. Meanwhile, make the caviar: Heat a medium skillet over medium-high heat, add 2 tablespoons of oil, and heat until it just starts to shimmer. Add the minced hiziki and cook until it's well coated with the oil, about 3 minutes. Add enough water to cover and bring to a boil over high heat. Add the shoyu, reduce the heat to low, and simmer until all the liquid is evaporated, about 15 minutes. Transfer the hiziki to a small bowl and wipe out the skillet.

3. Return the skillet to medium-high heat and heat the remaining 1 tablespoon of oil until it just starts to shimmer. Add the garlic and shallot and sauté, stirring occasionally, until the shallots are browned, 2 to 3 minutes.

4. Add the shallot-garlic mixture to the hiziki and stir to combine. Season to taste with the lemon and ginger juices. Season with sea salt, if needed.

5. To serve, place the caviar on cucumber rounds, crostini, or crackers, and top with a small dollop of the tofu sour cream.

CHEF'S TIP: If you find the folding technique too finicky, fill and roll the phyllo into a roulade shape instead, score it with slits, and bake. Slice through completely after baking.

Phyllo Triangles

with Tofu and Spinach

MAKES 35 TO 40 TRIANGLES

14 ounces firm tofu (1 standard package)

1½ bunches spinach (about 1 pound), stemmed

3 tablespoons extra-virgin olive oil, plus more for brushing the dough

6 small shallots, minced

½ teaspoon ground fennel

½ teaspoon ground cumin

½ teaspoon smoked paprika

½ teaspoon fine sea salt, or to taste

3 tablespoons chickpea miso or white miso

2 tablespoons umeboshi paste (see page 338 for resources)

½ pound phyllo dough (8 sheets), preferably whole-wheat phyllo

FOR OUR VEGAN VERSION of spanakopita—a Greek spinach-feta pie—we use firm tofu instead of feta cheese for body, and a mixture of miso and umeboshi paste to give the pie a briny, salty bite. We like whole-wheat phyllo dough, but since it can be difficult to work with and hard to find, feel free to use regular phyllo instead.

1. Put the tofu on a paper towel–lined plate, cover with another few paper towels, and top with a weighted plate. Let stand for 30 minutes to drain the excess water. Discard the paper towels and crumble the tofu into a medium bowl; set aside.

2. Rinse the spinach and shake off the excess water, but don't dry the spinach completely. In a medium pot over medium-low heat, add the spinach and warm until wilted, 2 to 3 minutes, stirring occasionally. Transfer the spinach to a bowl and, once it is cool enough to handle, squeeze out the excess moisture and finely chop.

3. Preheat the oven to 375°F. Line 2 baking sheets with parchment paper and set aside.

4. Heat a large skillet over medium heat, add the oil, and heat until it just starts to shimmer. Add the shallots, fennel, cumin, paprika, and salt and cook, stirring frequently, until the shallots are translucent, about 5 minutes. Transfer the mixture to the bowl with the tofu, and stir in the spinach, miso, and umeboshi. Taste and adjust the salt, if needed.

5. Lay 1 sheet of phyllo on a sheet of parchment paper with the short end facing you, keeping the remaining dough covered with a damp kitchen towel. Lightly brush the phyllo with oil. Spoon seven 1-tablespoon dollops of the tofu filling across the bottom edge of the phyllo at equal distances. Cut the phyllo into long strips between each dollop, and fold the dough up "flag-style" to make triangular shapes. Transfer the phyllo triangles to the prepared baking sheet and brush the tops with more oil. Repeat with the remaining phyllo and filling. Right before baking, brush all the triangles again with oil. Bake until golden-brown, about 20 minutes. Serve warm.

Potato Pakoras

with Mint-Cilantro Raita

SERVES 4 TO 6   (N)

CRISP AND GOLDEN, THESE Indian-style fritters are so light they're almost fluffy. They are loaded with soft chunks of potato that give them a satisfying bite. They also get a spicy kick from the chili and cayenne, which is a nice contrast to the cooling mint and cilantro in the yogurt-based raita. Along with chutney, raita is one of many condiments served with most Indian meals.

FOR THE RAITA

2 cups fresh mint leaves

2 cups fresh cilantro leaves

1 Thai green chili, seeded and finely diced

2 teaspoons fresh ginger juice, from about a 3-inch piece (see page 74)

1 cup dairy-free plain yogurt

1 tablespoon fresh lime juice (from about 1 lime), or more to taste

1 teaspoon agave syrup

½ teaspoon fine sea salt

¼ teaspoon chaat masala, or more to taste (see Chef's Tip)

FOR THE PAKORAS

1 cup chickpea flour

¼ teaspoon baking powder

½ teaspoon ground cumin

½ teaspoon ground turmeric

⅛ teaspoon cayenne

1 teaspoon fine sea salt

¾ pound russet potatoes (1 or 2 medium potatoes), peeled and cut into ⅛-inch cubes

1 Thai green chili, seeded and finely diced

1 medium yellow onion, minced

2 tablespoons finely chopped fresh cilantro leaves

4 cups refined coconut oil, for frying

1. Make the raita: In a food processor, combine the mint, cilantro, chili, and ginger juice, and purée until smooth, scraping down the sides as needed. (Add water, if necessary, to blend easily, but only enough to assist in blending.) Transfer to a small bowl and stir in the yogurt, lime juice, agave, salt, and chaat masala. Refrigerate until ready to serve (it can be made up to one day in advance).

2. Make the pakoras: In a medium bowl, combine the chickpea flour, baking powder, and 6 to 7 tablespoons of cold water. Whisk until smooth. Add the cumin, turmeric, cayenne, and salt, and stir to combine. Next, fold in the potato, chili pepper, onion, and cilantro. The batter consistency should be similar to thick pancake batter.

3. Heat the oil in a wok or a large skillet to 350°F (see Chef's Tips). Using a teaspoon, gently slide a heaping scoop of the batter into the hot oil, using another teaspoon to ease it off the spoon and into the oil without splashing; the batter should sizzle immediately. Fry several pakoras at a time without overcrowding the wok, until the pakoras are golden-brown and cooked through, about 3 minutes total, turning them halfway through cooking. Use a frying spider or a slotted spoon to transfer them to a wire rack or a paper towel. Serve with the raita.

CHEF'S TIPS: Use a candy thermometer to regulate the temperature of the oil; if you don't have one, carefully add a small cube of bread to the oil—if it sizzles immediately and is surrounded by bubbles, the oil is ready.

If you don't have chaat masala (an Indian spice blend), you may omit it or replace it with another blend, such as garam masala.

Endive Boats

with Vegan Ricotta

SERVES 8

2 heads of Belgian endive

1 batch Vegan Ricotta (page 67)

2 tablespoons finely chopped chives

2 tablespoons finely diced red bell pepper

2 tablespoons finely diced yellow bell pepper

3 tablespoons toasted pine nuts (see page 56)

WE LOVE BELGIAN ENDIVE for its slightly bitter flavor and crisp, juicy texture; it is a sophisticated addition to any crudités platter. The tapered, bite-size shape makes it the perfect vessel for a filling like our Vegan Ricotta. You can prepare the ricotta and the toppings a day in advance, making for breezy assembly right before serving.

1. Slice off the bottom of the endive and separate the heads into individual leaves. Arrange the leaves on a platter.

2. Dollop a tablespoon of the ricotta into the wide corner of each endive leaf, top with the chives, bell peppers, and pine nuts, and serve.

Edamame, Leek, and Herb Dumplings

with Ginger-Scallion Sauce

MAKES ABOUT 32 DUMPLINGS

FOR THE DIPPING SAUCE

¼ cup shoyu or tamari

¼ cup brown rice vinegar

2-inch piece ginger, peeled and minced (about 1½ tablespoons)

1 scallion (white and green parts), thinly sliced on a diagonal

FOR THE DUMPLINGS

2 tablespoons canola oil, plus ¼ cup for frying

3 medium leeks, thinly sliced into half-moons and thoroughly cleaned

2 large garlic cloves, minced

1½-inch piece of ginger, peeled and minced (about 1 tablespoon)

¼ teaspoon fine sea salt

10 ounces frozen shelled edamame, thawed

2 tablespoons fresh lemon juice (from about 1 lemon)

1 teaspoon toasted sesame oil

1 teaspoon mirin

2 scallions, thinly sliced

1 tablespoon chopped fresh cilantro

1 tablespoon chives

1 tablespoon chopped fresh mint

Freshly ground black pepper

1 tablespoon arrowroot starch

32 square wonton wrappers

LEEKS BELONG TO THE onion family and, similar to their round cousins, they get sweeter as they cook, lending this dumpling filling a sweet note that pairs well with edamame. If you do not have arrowroot starch, you may use tapioca flour or organic cornstarch to seal the dumplings. The formed dumplings may be refrigerated for several days or frozen in an airtight container for up to several months. The dipping sauce is also a good complement for eggrolls, rice paper rolls, and Sweet Potato Sushi Rolls (page 235).

1. Make the dipping sauce: In a medium bowl, stir together the shoyu, rice vinegar, ginger, and scallion with 2 tablespoons water. Chill until ready to serve.

2. Make the dumplings: Heat a medium skillet over medium heat, add 2 tablespoons of the oil, and heat until it just starts to shimmer. Add the leeks and sauté, stirring frequently, until softened, about 5 minutes. Add the garlic, minced ginger, and salt, and cook for 1 minute more.

3. Transfer the leek mixture to a food processor, and add the edamame, lemon juice, sesame oil, and mirin, and purée until a creamy paste forms. Add the scallions, cilantro, chives, and mint, and pulse just to combine. Season to taste with salt and pepper, if needed.

4. In a small bowl, combine the arrowroot with 3 tablespoons of water and stir to dissolve. To form the dumplings, place a scant tablespoon of the filling in the middle of a wonton wrapper, lightly brush all the edges with the arrowroot slurry, fold the wrapper closed to make a triangle shape, then pull the 2 long corners in toward each other, and pinch them together to form traditional wonton shapes. Put the formed dumplings on a baking sheet and repeat with the remaining wrappers.

5. Heat about ¼ cup of oil in a large skillet over medium-high heat. Cook 6 or 7 wontons at a time, being careful not to overcrowd the skillet, and fry until golden-brown, 3 to 4 minutes per side. Transfer to a paper towel–lined baking sheet and continue cooking the remaining dumplings. Serve with the ginger-scallion dipping sauce.

CHEF'S TIPS: To clean leeks, fill a large bowl with water and add the sliced leeks. Swirl the water with your hands and lift the leeks out of the water, letting the dirt fall to the bottom of the bowl. Replace the water and wash the leeks again until no more dirt remains.

You can find wonton wrappers at Asian markets and most major supermarkets.

Sweet Potato Latkes

with Pear Sauce and Cashew Sour Cream

SERVES 6 TO 8 (MAKES ABOUT 2 DOZEN BITE-SIZE LATKES AND 2 CUPS PEAR SAUCE) (S)

FOR THE PEAR SAUCE

3 Bartlett pears (about 1½ pounds), peeled, halved, cored, and cut into 1-inch chunks

2 tablespoons fresh lemon juice (from about 1 lemon)

Pinch of freshly grated nutmeg

FOR THE LATKES

1 pound sweet potatoes (about 1 large or 2 medium sweet potatoes), peeled and grated

2 scallions (white and green parts), thinly sliced

⅓ cup whole-wheat pastry flour

¼ cup arrowroot starch

¾ teaspoon fine sea salt

½ teaspoon freshly ground black pepper

½ teaspoon garlic powder

About ½ cup canola oil

½ cup prepared Cashew Sour Cream (page 66), for serving

2 tablespoons chopped chives, for serving

THESE FRITTERS TAKE A nod from traditional latkes, served with applesauce and sour cream, but use slightly more unexpected ingredients and are presented in an elegant, bite-size format. Sweet potatoes are a great addition to a health-supportive diet, since they are a concentrated source of beta-carotene, a powerful antioxidant; they also contain fiber and potassium. If you do not have arrowroot starch, you can use tapioca flour or organic cornstarch in the latkes, which helps bind the mixture. Due to their sugar content, these sweet potato latkes can go from golden-brown to burned pretty quickly, so be sure to keep an eye on them while frying. Leftover pear sauce is great on Sweet Potato Waffles (page 283), Amaranth Porridge (page 257), or Spelt Bread (page 286) with nut butter.

1. Make the pear sauce: In a medium pot, combine the pears, lemon juice, and nutmeg with ½ cup of water and bring to a boil over high heat. Reduce the heat to low and simmer, stirring occasionally, until the pears are softened, 10 to 15 minutes. Transfer the pear mixture to a food processor and pulse until smooth. Chill until ready to serve.

2. Make the latkes: In a bowl, stir together the sweet potatoes, scallions, flour, arrowroot, salt, pepper, and garlic powder.

3. Line a baking sheet with paper towels and set aside. Heat enough oil in a large, nonstick skillet over medium-high heat to cover the bottom. Using a tablespoon measure, portion out the latkes, cooking them in batches and making sure not to overcrowd the skillet. Fry the latkes until golden-brown on both sides, about 4 minutes total. Transfer to the prepared baking sheet to drain excess oil and repeat with the remaining potato mixture.

4. To serve, top the latkes with the pear sauce and the Cashew Sour Cream, and sprinkle with chives.

CHEF'S TIPS:
When using avocados, we always recommend getting more than what you think you need, since you might be surprised when you cut one open only to find a dark-brown interior, which may be caused by mishandling/ bruising or exposure to low temperatures before ripening.

Don't be tempted to skip the freezing step; if the balls are not firm, they will fall apart when you fry them.

Avocado Fritters

MAKES 20 FRITTERS

3 gluten-free corn tortillas

2 ripe avocados, peeled, pitted, and coarsely chopped

½ cup minced yellow onion

3 tablespoons fresh lime juice (from 2 or 3 limes)

2 tablespoons finely chopped fresh flat-leaf parsley

2½ teaspoons fine sea salt

1 cup white rice flour

2 cups fine cornmeal

1 teaspoon ground cumin

About 2 cups seltzer water

1 quart (4 cups) canola oil or other high-temperature oil, for frying

Salsa Roja (page 91), for serving

SPECIAL EQUIPMENT

Candy thermometer, frying spider

WE'RE IN LOVE WITH these delicious pillows of creamy avocado ensconced in a crispy, golden coating. Although this recipe is part of our Mexican cuisine curriculum, these fritters are not traditional to Mexico, but rather inspired by the avocados that grow there. Keep your oil nice and hot, so the fritters are as crispy as possible. Pair them with Salsa Roja for a bright, fresh contrast to the mild filling.

1. Preheat the oven to 400°F. Place the tortillas in a single layer on a baking sheet and bake until golden and very crisp (like tortilla chips), about 15 minutes. Set aside to cool, crumble into a food processor, and pulse to make a coarse meal.

2. Transfer the tortilla meal to a medium bowl. Add the avocados, onion, lime juice, parsley, and ½ teaspoon of the salt. Mash with a fork or potato masher until combined but still slightly chunky. Lay plastic wrap directly on the entire surface of the filling (to prevent discoloration) and refrigerate for 20 minutes.

3. Using a tablespoon measure, shape the filling into balls and place on a parchment paper–lined baking sheet. Freeze the balls until firm, about 25 minutes.

4. Make the batter: Whisk the rice flour, cornmeal, the remaining 2 teaspoons of salt, and cumin together in a medium bowl. Slowly whisk in enough seltzer to form a batter similar in consistency to pancake batter. Let the batter rest at room temperature for at least 20 minutes or up to half an hour.

5. Preheat the oven to 350°F. Line a baking sheet with paper towels and set aside. Heat the oil in a Dutch oven or wok over medium-high heat until it reaches 350°F on a candy thermometer. Using a slotted spoon, dip a frozen ball into the batter, place on a spider, and gently lower into the oil. Repeat with a few more balls—be sure not to overcrowd the pan. (If the oil cools below 340°F, increase the heat or wait 1 to 2 minutes before adding the next batch of fritters; if the oil gets too hot, remove it from the heat for a few minutes then return it to the heat.) Fry until golden and then transfer the fritters to the prepared baking sheet to drain the excess oil. Repeat with the remaining frozen avocado balls.

6. Before serving, remove the paper towels from the baking sheet and warm the fritters in the oven for about 5 minutes. Serve with Salsa Roja on the side.

Baked Panelle

with Eggplant Caponata

MAKES 32 PIECES

PANELLE, A POPULAR SICILIAN street food, are deep-fried chickpea fritters that are thin and flat and typically served in a sandwich. We've lightened the recipe by baking the chickpea cakes instead. The appetizer gets a bright summery taste from *caponata*, a summer vegetable–based condiment or side dish (and another Sicilian classic). Other great panelle toppings include Basic Basil Pesto (page 88) or even simply roasted grape tomatoes with a sprinkling of nutritional yeast. We love this as an hors d'oeuvre because it is so flexible—it can be served warm or at room temperature and can be left out for the duration of a dinner or party.

FOR THE CAPONATA

1 medium eggplant (about 1 pound), peeled and cut into medium dice

1 tablespoon plus ½ teaspoon fine sea salt, plus more to taste

5 tablespoons extra-virgin olive oil

1 medium yellow onion, cut into small dice

3 celery stalks, cut into small dice

3 tablespoons tomato paste

3 tablespoons white wine vinegar

2 to 3 tablespoons agave syrup to taste

2 tablespoons drained capers, rinsed and chopped

4 pitted green olives, chopped

Freshly ground black pepper to taste

½ cup Vegan Ricotta (page 67), for serving (optional)

2 tablespoons chopped fresh parsley, for serving

FOR THE PANELLE

2 teaspoons extra-virgin olive oil

2 cups chickpea flour

2 teaspoons fine sea salt

1. Salt the eggplant for the caponata: Put the eggplant in a colander fitted within a bowl and sprinkle with 1 tablespoon of the salt. Weigh down the eggplant with something like a heavy pot, and set aside for 30 minutes to drain.

2. Meanwhile, make the panelle: Grease an 8 × 8-inch baking dish with 1 teaspoon of the oil and set aside. In a medium pot, whisk together the chickpea flour and salt. Place the pot over low heat. Gradually whisk in 5½ cups water, whisking constantly to prevent lumps from forming. Bring to a simmer and cook, partially covered, over low heat for 20 to 25 minutes, until the mixture is very thick but still pourable, whisking every couple of minutes and making sure to scrape the bottom and sides.

3. Using a rubber spatula, transfer the mixture to the prepared baking dish and spread into an even layer. Drizzle with the remaining 1 teaspoon of oil and smooth the top. Once the mixture has stopped steaming, transfer the dish to the fridge and chill for at least 30 minutes or up to 1 day.

4. Rinse the eggplant and press it between 2 kitchen towels to squeeze out the excess moisture.

5. Heat a large skillet over medium-high heat, add 3 tablespoons of the oil, and heat until it just starts to shimmer. Add the eggplant and sauté, stirring occasionally, for 2 to 3 minutes, just until tender and slightly golden on all sides. Transfer the eggplant to a paper towel–lined baking sheet or platter and set aside.

6. To the same pan, add the remaining 2 tablespoons of oil. Reduce the heat to medium and add the onion and celery and cook until the vegetables are tender, 5 to 7 minutes. Stir in the tomato paste, vinegar, agave, the remaining ½ teaspoon salt, and ¾ cup water, and simmer over low heat until the sauce thickens a bit, about 10 minutes. Return the eggplant to the pan and cook until it softens a little, about 5 minutes. Stir in the capers and olives. Taste and season with salt and pepper, if needed. Let the caponata come to room temperature.

7. Preheat the oven to 375°F. Line a baking sheet with parchment paper and set aside.

8. Cut the chilled panelle into 16 squares, then halve each square diagonally to make 2 triangles. Transfer the panelle to the prepared baking sheet, spacing them about 1 inch apart. If the panelle feel dry, brush them with a bit more oil. Bake until lightly golden, 30 to 35 minutes. Let the panelle come to room temperature before serving with a dollop of the caponata, ricotta (if using), and parsley. Caponata can be made a day in advance, and in fact it's even better when made ahead because the flavors meld. Store refrigerated in an airtight container for up to 1 week.

CHAPTER 3

Soups & Stews

Curried Yellow Split Pea Soup

with Coconut Milk

SERVES 6

2 tablespoons coconut oil

1 medium yellow onion,
finely diced

1 medium carrot, peeled and cut
into ½-inch-thick quarter-moons

3 large garlic cloves, minced

1 tablespoon curry powder

½ teaspoon fine sea salt, plus
more to taste

5 cups store-bought vegetable
stock or homemade Carrot-Onion
Stock (page 75)

1 cup yellow split peas

1 dried or fresh bay leaf

½ head of cauliflower, cut into
bite-size florets

1 cup canned full-fat coconut milk

3 tablespoons fresh ginger
juice from about a 6-inch piece
(see page 74)

2 tablespoons fresh lime juice
(from about 2 limes)

Freshly ground black pepper
to taste

2 tablespoons chopped fresh
cilantro, for serving

FLAVORED WITH GINGER, LIME, curry powder, and cilantro, this creamy and satisfying coconut soup combines Thai and Indian flavors into one hearty bowl. Note that the cooking time for the split peas depends on their age, so be sure to taste the soup as it simmers. You can also use red lentils, which typically have a shorter cooking time than split peas.

1. Heat the oil in a medium pot over medium-low heat. Add the onion, carrot, garlic, curry powder, and salt. Cover and cook the vegetables, stirring occasionally, until they begin to soften, about 10 minutes.

2. Add the stock, split peas, and bay leaf, and bring to a boil over high heat. Reduce the heat to low and simmer with the lid ajar until the peas are completely soft, about 45 minutes.

3. Discard the bay leaf. Add the cauliflower and simmer until tender, about 5 minutes.

4. Transfer 2 cups of the soup to a blender, purée until smooth, and return to the pot with the rest of the soup. Add the coconut milk, ginger juice, and lime juice. Season to taste with salt and pepper, and sprinkle with the cilantro.

Creamy Mushroom Soup

SERVES 4

HERE IS AN EXAMPLE of a luscious, creamy cream-less soup. The secret to the smooth texture may be unexpected— we use good old-fashioned rolled oats! When combined with liquid, the oats release their starch and thicken the soup. The result is a puréed soup that is deliciously savory—perfect for sipping on a chilly winter night.

2 tablespoons extra-virgin olive oil

1 pound cremini mushrooms, stemmed and sliced

4 small shallots, finely diced

1 teaspoon fine sea salt, plus more to taste

¼ cup dry sherry

4 cups store-bought vegetable stock or homemade Brown Vegetable Stock (page 76)

¼ cup old-fashioned rolled oats

Freshly ground black pepper to taste

2 tablespoons chopped fresh flat-leaf parsley, for serving

1. Heat the oil in a medium pot over medium heat. Add the mushrooms, shallots, and salt, and sweat until the mushrooms are softened, stirring occasionally, about 10 minutes. Stir in the sherry and cook until most of the liquid is evaporated, about 2 minutes.

2. Add the stock and oats. Increase the heat to high, cover the pot, and bring to a boil. Reduce the heat to low and simmer with the lid ajar for about 30 minutes.

3. Using a blender or immersion blender, purée the soup (in batches, if necessary) until completely smooth. Return the soup to the pot and season with salt and pepper. Sprinkle with parsley before serving.

Chilled Cucumber-Avocado Soup

with Fresh Dill

SERVES 4 TO 6

WE LIKEN THIS REFRESHING soup to a green gazpacho. Umeboshi paste, made from pickled green plums (see page 31), enlivens the summery dish with its salty-sour umami flavor. Serve this soup as a light main course with grilled bread for dipping or in shot glasses as a light and pretty appetizer.

1½ English cucumbers, peeled and diced (about 3 cups)

2 avocados, halved and pitted

6 tablespoons fresh lime juice (from 4 to 6 limes)

4 large garlic cloves, coarsely chopped

2 tablespoons extra-virgin olive oil

1½ teaspoons umeboshi paste (see page 338 for resources)

4 tablespoons coarsely chopped fresh dill, plus more for serving

1½ cups store-bought vegetable stock or homemade Carrot-Onion Stock (page 75)

½ teaspoon fine sea salt, plus more to taste

2 teaspoons minced red onion

½ rib of celery, finely diced

Additional minced red onion, for serving (optional)

1. In a blender, combine 2 cups of the cucumber, the avocado, lime juice, garlic, oil, umeboshi paste, dill, vegetable stock, and salt, and purée until smooth.

2. Pour the mixture into a large bowl. Stir in the remaining 1 cup of cucumber, red onion, and celery. Cover and refrigerate for 1 hour (or up to 24 hours).

3. Pour the chilled soup into serving bowls and finish with fresh dill and minced onion, if desired.

Chef Elliott's Famous Miso Soup

SERVES 8

2 tablespoons sesame oil

1 medium onion, halved and thinly sliced

1 carrot, cut into matchsticks (see page 47)

2 celery stalks, thinly sliced on a diagonal

10 shiitake mushrooms, stemmed and sliced

6 medium garlic cloves, thinly sliced

1 teaspoon fine sea salt

¼ cup wakame, soaked in water for 10 minutes and drained

7 ounces firm tofu (half a standard package), cut into ½-inch dice

1 tablespoon fresh ginger juice from about a 3-inch piece (see page 74)

1 tablespoon fresh lemon juice (from about ½ lemon) or brown rice vinegar

1 cup white mellow miso

2 scallions (white and green parts), thinly sliced, for serving

A few sheets of dried nori, sliced, for serving

THIS MISO SOUP MAKES a regular appearance in our flagship cookie-baking class, where students work in pairs to convert conventional baking recipes using white sugar, refined flour, and other processed ingredients to more whole, vegan alternatives. Soup in a baking class? Let us explain. Bowls of the salty elixir—full of vegetables, live with digestive enzymes, and rich in minerals from seaweed—are the perfect balance for the sugar high the students experience from sampling the large number of baked goods (over 700 portions) made throughout the day.

1. Heat the oil in a large pot over low heat. Add the onion, carrot, celery, shiitakes, garlic, and salt. Cover and sweat until the vegetables soften, stirring occasionally, about 10 minutes. Add the wakame and tofu, and continue to cook, covered, for about 10 minutes more.

2. Add 8 cups of water and bring to a boil over high heat. Reduce the heat to low and simmer, uncovered, 10 to 15 minutes more.

3. Turn the heat off and let the soup stand to cool slightly, 5 to 10 minutes. Stir in the ginger and lemon juices.

4. Ladle 2 cups of the broth into a bowl and stir in the miso until completely dissolved (see note on page 29 regarding tempering miso). Add the mixture back to the soup pot. Sprinkle with scallions and nori before serving.

Red Lentil Lemon Soup

with Spinach

SERVES 4 TO 6

2 tablespoons extra-virgin olive oil

2 medium onions, finely chopped

1 large carrot, peeled and cut into ½-inch dice

2 large garlic cloves, minced

1 teaspoon ground cumin

1 teaspoon ground turmeric

½ teaspoon fine sea salt, plus more to taste

¼ teaspoon freshly ground black pepper, plus more to taste

6 cups store-bought vegetable stock or homemade Carrot-Onion Stock (page 75)

1 cup dried red lentils, picked through for stones and rinsed

1 dried bay leaf

Pinch of cayenne pepper

1 slice of lemon, seeded

3 cups packed spinach leaves (about 3 ounces)

2 tablespoons fresh lemon zest (from about 2 lemons)

Whole cilantro leaves, for serving

A VERSION OF THIS nourishing soup can be found in Annemarie Colbin's cookbook *The Natural Gourmet*, which dates back to 1989. The recipe remains a classic for good reason—it's extremely easy and it cooks in about 30 minutes. We love red lentils because they are highly nutritious and they cook through very quickly—they practically dissolve, creating a thick, comforting soup.

1. Heat a large pot over medium heat. Add the oil and heat until it just starts to shimmer. Add the onions and carrot, and sweat for about 5 minutes, stirring occasionally, until softened. Add the garlic and sauté until fragrant, about 1 minute. Stir in the cumin, turmeric, and salt and pepper.

2. Add the stock, lentils, bay leaf, cayenne pepper, and the lemon slice, and bring to a boil, skimming off any foam as needed. Lower the heat and simmer, covered, until the soup thickens and the lentils are cooked through, about 25 minutes.

3. Stir in the spinach and cook just until wilted, about 1 minute. Turn the heat off. Discard the bay leaf and lemon slice, and stir in the lemon zest. Taste and adjust seasonings, if needed. Sprinkle with cilantro and serve.

Shiitake Broth

with Udon, Tofu, and Baby Bok Choy

SERVES 4

1 tablespoon canola oil or another neutral oil

1 small onion, cut into ½-inch dice

1 small carrot, cut into ¼-inch-thick half-moons

1 garlic clove, thinly sliced

¼ teaspoon fine sea salt, plus more to taste

1 teaspoon Szechuan peppercorns, coarsely ground (optional)

6 cups store-bought vegetable stock or homemade Brown Vegetable Stock (page 76)

1 piece star anise

1 small dried Thai chili

1 lemongrass stalk, tough outer husk removed, stalk bruised and cut into thirds (see Chef's Tips)

3 dried shiitake mushrooms

2 tablespoons shoyu or tamari

1 (14-ounce) block of firm tofu, drained and cut into ¾-inch cubes

2 baby bok choy, ends trimmed and thinly sliced

2 tablespoons fresh ginger juice from about a 6-inch piece (see page 74)

2 to 3 tablespoons fresh lime juice (from about 2 limes)

4 ounces udon noodles, cooked according to package directions, rinsed in cold water, and drained

2 scallions, thinly sliced on a diagonal, for serving

THIS WARMING NOODLE SOUP is a good example of layering flavors, and Szechuan peppercorns (actually not a pepper at all, but the husk of the prickly-ash shrub) make this dish even more interesting. Szechuan peppercorns are unique in that they produce a slight tingly, buzzing sensation in the mouth, which is traditionally used to tame the heat of chili peppers—an essential ingredient of Szechuan cooking. Add ginger and lime juices, and a sprinkle of fresh scallions, and you have a cozy pot of Asian goodness.

1. Heat the oil in a large pot over medium-low heat. Add the onion, carrot, garlic, salt, and peppercorns (if using), and sweat, stirring occasionally, until the onions are translucent, about 4 minutes.

2. Add the stock, star anise, chili, lemongrass, shiitakes, and shoyu. Cover the pot and bring to a boil over high heat. Then reduce the heat to low and simmer for 25 minutes.

3. Remove and discard the star anise, chili, and lemongrass. Remove the shiitakes and slice thinly. Return the shiitakes to the soup and add the tofu, bok choy, and ginger juice. Cook just until the bok choy wilts, about 2 minutes.

4. Turn the heat off, and stir in the lime juice. Taste and season with salt, if needed.

5. To serve, divide the udon noodles among 4 bowls, pour the soup on top, and sprinkle with scallions.

CHEF'S TIPS: To bruise lemongrass, flip your knife and whack the stalk with the back (spine) of the knife throughout the entire length.

If you are unable to find dried shiitakes, substitute by sautéing fresh sliced mushrooms, along with the onion mixture, in step 1.

Autumn Minestrone

MAKES 6 TO 8 SERVINGS

2 tablespoons extra-virgin olive oil

1 large onion, cut into medium dice

1 teaspoon fine sea salt, or more to taste

Pinch of dried red pepper flakes

2 leeks (white and light-green parts), cleaned, halved lengthwise, and thinly sliced into half-moons

2 celery stalks, finely diced

1 large carrot, cut into ¼-inch-thick half-moons

2 large garlic cloves, minced

1 cup white beans, soaked overnight, drained, and rinsed, or 2 (15-ounce) cans of white beans, drained and rinsed

7 cups store-bought vegetable stock or homemade Carrot-Onion Stock (page 75)

1 sprig of fresh rosemary

1 sprig of fresh sage

1 pound butternut squash (about half a medium squash), peeled and cut into medium dice (see Chef's Tip)

1 teaspoon red wine vinegar or apple cider

Freshly ground black pepper to taste

2 tablespoons chopped fresh flat-leaf parsley, for serving

IF YOU NEED A hearty one-pot meal to prep on Sunday and enjoy throughout the week, you've found it. This soup is full of vegetables, fiber- and protein-rich beans, and hardy herbs that will make your house smell like an autumn wonderland. If you prefer, use sweet potatoes instead of the butternut squash. And while we're huge proponents of cooking dried beans from scratch—the tenderness and flavor they impart to soups and stews is unmatched by canned beans—we know time is precious, and sometimes you want a hearty bowl of soup now (and don't want to wait for beans to soak!). In that case, use canned beans.

1. Heat the oil in a large pot over medium heat. Add the onion, 1 teaspoon of salt, and the red pepper flakes, and sweat until the onions are translucent, 5 to 7 minutes. Add the leeks, celery, carrot, and garlic, and continue to sweat until the vegetables soften, another 5 to 7 minutes.

2. Add the beans, stock, rosemary, and sage. Cover, bring to a boil over high heat, then reduce to medium-low and simmer with the lid ajar until the beans are just tender, about 40 minutes. (If you're using canned beans, reduce the cooking time to 15 minutes, then move to the next step.)

3. Add the butternut squash and continue to simmer until the squash begins to break down and the soup thickens, 10 to 15 minutes.

4. Stir in the vinegar and season with salt and pepper. Sprinkle with parsley before serving.

CHEF'S TIP: To prep the butternut squash, use a sharp knife to trim off the top and bottom of the squash, then halve it widthwise, separating the thinner top from the bigger bottom. Stand each half on a flat side and slice off the skin, running your knife from top to bottom around the squash (a good vegetable peeler works, too). Halve the bottom portion lengthwise and using a tablespoon, scrape out the seeds (reserve, if desired). Proceed to prep the squash as instructed.

Beet Borscht

SERVES 8 (G)

2 tablespoons extra-virgin olive oil

1 large yellow onion, diced

1 teaspoon fine sea salt, plus more to taste

3 large garlic cloves, minced

1 small carrot, peeled and cut into ½-inch quarter-moons

1 celery stalk, diced

¼ small head of red cabbage, finely shredded (about 2 cups)

2 tablespoons apple cider vinegar

3 medium beets, peeled and cut into ¼-inch dice

8 cups store-bought vegetable stock or homemade Carrot-Onion Stock (page 75)

¼ cup unsweetened apple juice

2 tablespoons fresh lemon juice (from about 1 lemon)

Freshly ground black pepper to taste

2 tablespoons chopped fresh dill, for serving

Dairy-free sour cream or Cashew Sour Cream (page 66), for serving (optional)

A BEAUTIFUL REDDISH-PINK COLOR, this beetroot soup is popular in many Eastern European countries and can be made with either meat or vegetables. It's thin and brothy, infused with garlic and tinged with apple and lemon juices for a bit of tang. The acid also helps preserve the bright-fuschia color of the beets. As a complement to the delightfully savory, almost tart, elixir-like broth, we like to serve this with a dollop of Cashew Sour Cream, which makes the texture feel even more a luxurious.

1. Heat a medium pot over medium heat, add the oil, and heat until it just starts to shimmer. Add the onion and salt, and sweat until translucent, stirring occasionally, about 5 minutes. Stir in the garlic, carrot, celery, cabbage, and vinegar, and continue cooking until the cabbage softens, 5 to 7 minutes.

2. Add the beets and stock. Cover, bring to a boil over high heat, reduce the heat to low, and simmer with the lid ajar until all the vegetables are tender, about 30 minutes.

3. Add the apple and lemon juices. Season to taste with salt and pepper, and serve with dill and sour cream, if using.

Creamy Carrot Ginger Soup

with Shiitake Crumble

SERVES 4 TO 6 Ⓖ Ⓢ Ⓝ

2 tablespoons extra-virgin olive oil

1 large yellow onion, finely diced

½ teaspoon fine sea salt

4 large carrots (about 2 pounds), coarsely chopped

About 5 cups store-bought vegetable stock or homemade Carrot-Onion Stock (page 75)

½ medium russet potato, peeled and cut into medium dice

1 teaspoon fresh lemon juice

1 to 2 teaspoons fresh ginger juice from about a 2-inch piece (see page 74)

½ cup Shiitake Crumble (page 72) or fresh dill, for serving (optional)

CREAM SOUPS ARE TRADITIONALLY thickened with a butter-flour roux and further enhanced with heavy cream. This recipe utilizes the humble potato instead to turn a handful of simple ingredients into a creamy purée. If you choose to forgo the Shiitake Crumble, sprinkle the soup with chopped dill instead.

1. Heat the oil in a large pot over medium heat. Add the onion and salt, and sweat until the onion is softened, stirring frequently to prevent browning, 5 to 7 minutes. Add the carrots, cover the pot, and cook over low heat until softened, stirring frequently, about 5 minutes.

2. Add the stock and potato to the pot, and bring to a boil. Reduce the heat to low and simmer with the lid ajar until the carrots and potato are very tender, about 25 minutes.

3. Purée the soup in a blender in batches until creamy, adding additional stock, if needed, to achieve the consistency you prefer.

4. Return the soup to the pot. Reheat and season to taste with the lemon and ginger juices. Serve topped with the Shiitake Crumble, if desired.

Cream of Corn Soup

with Red Pepper Coulis

SERVES 4   Ⓝ

FOR THE SOUP

2 tablespoons extra-virgin olive oil

1 medium onion, diced

1 teaspoon fine sea salt

2 tablespoons oat flour

5 cups store-bought vegetable stock or homemade Carrot-Onion Stock (page 75)

8 ears of corn, shucked, kernels sliced off the cob (4 to 6 cups)

FOR THE RED PEPPER COULIS

1 medium red bell pepper

2 tablespoons extra-virgin olive oil

1 to 2 teaspoons hot sauce to taste

½ teaspoon fine sea salt

THE VELVETY TEXTURE OF this soup is achieved by puréeing corn cooked in vegetable stock, which keeps it wonderfully smooth and not cloying or heavy. The sweet taste of the corn is the star, so make this soup at the height of the summer when the golden cobs are at their sweet-best. We like to add a swirl of red pepper coulis (pronounced koo-LEE)—a thick sauce made by puréeing vegetables—for contrasting color and a pop of flavor.

1. Make the soup: In a soup pot, heat the oil over medium heat until it just starts to shimmer. Add the onion and salt and sweat until the onion is softened, stirring often to prevent browning, about 10 minutes. Stir in the oat flour.

2. Add the stock and corn and bring to a boil over high heat. Reduce the heat to low and simmer with the lid ajar for about 25 minutes.

3. Meanwhile, make the coulis: Roast the red pepper on the stovetop directly over a gas burner until uniformly charred on all sides, about 5 minutes. Place the pepper in a bowl, cover with plastic, and set aside to steam for 10 to 15 minutes (if you don't have a gas stove, see Chef's Tips). When cool enough to handle, remove the pepper from the bowl and peel away the charred skin by rubbing it with your fingertips or scraping it with a knife. Seed and coarsely chop the pepper.

4. In a blender, purée the roasted pepper with the oil, hot sauce, and salt. If necessary, add some water to thin the texture so it's pourable; set aside.

5. Transfer the soup to a blender and purée until creamy and smooth. (You can strain the mixture through a fine-mesh sieve for an extra-smooth texture.)

6. Return the soup to the pot. Reheat and adjust the seasonings, as needed. Serve with a small swirl of the coulis.

CHEF'S TIPS: We char the red pepper to impart a smoky flavor and remove the skin. If you don't have a gas stove, you may roast it under a broiler. To do this, cover a baking sheet with foil, rub the pepper with a little olive oil, put it on the baking sheet, and place it under the broiler. After 5 minutes or so, areas of the skin should start to char. When this happens, flip the pepper using tongs. Continue to broil on the other side until the skin blisters. After about 8 minutes of cooking, remove the pepper from the broiler, put it in a bowl, cover with plastic wrap, and continue as directed in step 3.

If you want to create decorative swirls, dots, or stripes atop each bowl of soup, pour the coulis into a squeeze bottle (available online, at a restaurant supply store, or even at your local grocery store or supermarket).

Watermelon Gazpacho

with Basil-Infused Oil

SERVES 6

2 red bell peppers, halved, seeded, and chopped

2 medium cucumbers, peeled and coarsely chopped, plus 1 cucumber, peeled, seeded, and finely diced

2 garlic cloves, chopped

3 tablespoons extra-virgin olive oil

3 tablespoons red wine vinegar, or more as needed

1 tablespoon green Tabasco, or to taste

1 teaspoon fine sea salt, or more as needed

4 cups coarsely diced seedless watermelon

¼ cup fresh mint leaves, chopped

About 2 tablespoons Basil-Infused Oil (page 78), for serving

THIS FRUITY TOMATO-LESS GAZPACHO is the epitome of summer in a bowl (or even a tumbler or shot glass!) and a great example of how to use watermelon in a savory recipe. Be sure to use the best-quality produce you can find here (preferably from your local farmers' market), since the ingredients will not be cooked. Bring this along to your next summer potluck or cookout.

1. In a large bowl, combine the bell peppers, coarsely chopped cucumbers, garlic, oil, vinegar, Tabasco, and salt. Cover with plastic wrap and let sit at room temperature for at least 10 minutes (or up to several hours in the refrigerator).

2. Transfer the mixture to a blender and purée until smooth. Add the watermelon and pulse until it is broken down but the mixture remains a bit chunky. Taste and season with more salt or vinegar, if needed. Chill for at least 30 minutes.

3. To serve, divide the gazpacho among bowls and finish with the remaining diced cucumber, mint, and basil oil.

Chilled Mediterranean Grilled Vegetable Soup

SERVES 6 TO 8

With its assertive mixture of fire-grilled summer vegetables in a light tomato broth, this soup may just transport you to a sun-drenched Mediterranean village. This hearty soup can hold its own as a main dish, especially if served with grilled bread. Seaside view optional.

2 medium fennel bulbs, trimmed, cored, and cut lengthwise into ½-inch slabs

1 small eggplant, cut crosswise into ½-inch-thick rounds

1 medium red bell pepper, halved and seeded

1 small red onion, cut into ½-inch-thick rings

¼ cup extra-virgin olive oil

½ teaspoon fine sea salt

¼ teaspoon freshly ground black pepper

4 cups tomato juice

2 to 3 cups store-bought vegetable stock or homemade Carrot-Onion Stock (page 75)

1 large garlic clove, minced

¼ cup fresh lemon juice (from about 2 lemons)

½ cup red wine vinegar

2 tablespoons ground cumin

2 tablespoons ground coriander

¼ cup chopped fresh flat-leaf parsley

¼ cup chopped fresh basil leaves

1. In a large bowl, combine the fennel, eggplant, bell pepper, onion, oil, salt, and pepper. Set the vegetables aside to marinate at room temperature for 30 minutes.

2. Heat a grill to medium-high heat. Grill the vegetables in batches until they are tender and develop dark grill marks, about 8 minutes total. Remove from the grill and cool.

3. When cool enough to handle, finely dice the vegetables and transfer to a large serving bowl. Add the tomato juice, stock, garlic, lemon juice, vinegar, cumin, coriander, parsley, and basil. Stir to combine and chill for 30 minutes before serving.

Adzuki Bean Stew

SERVES 4 TO 6

ADZUKI BEANS ARE QUITE small, reddish-brown in color, and have an almost sweet, nutty flavor. The beans are widely used in Japan and China, where they are often mashed into a paste for desserts, such as mooncakes or red bean ice cream. For some, these beans are easier to digest than other bean varieties due to their lower phytic acid content. Simmered together with the sweet squash and a few aromatics, the beans create a savory stew that leaves you feeling full and nourished.

2 tablespoons extra-virgin olive oil

1 medium yellow onion, diced

2 large garlic cloves, minced

½ teaspoon fine sea salt, plus more to taste

1 cup adzuki beans, soaked overnight, drained, and rinsed (see page 55)

2-inch piece of kombu (see page 55)

5 cups store-bought vegetable stock or homemade Brown Vegetable Stock (page 76)

1 pound butternut squash, halved, peeled, seeded, and cut into large dice (about 2 cups)

2 tablespoons fresh ginger juice from about a 6-inch piece (see page 74)

2 tablespoons shoyu or tamari, or more to taste

½ bunch scallions (white and green parts), thinly sliced, for serving

*if made with tamari

1. Heat a medium pot over medium-low heat, add the oil, and heat until it just starts to shimmer. Add the onion, garlic, and salt, and sweat until the onion becomes translucent, about 8 minutes. Add the adzuki beans, kombu, and stock. Cover, bring to a boil over high heat, reduce the heat to low, and simmer, partially covered, until the beans are almost tender, about 30 minutes.

2. Add the butternut squash, cover, and continue simmering until the beans and squash are tender, about 20 minutes.

3. Remove and discard the kombu. Add the ginger juice and shoyu, and season to taste with salt, if needed. Sprinkle with scallions and serve.

Smoky Black Bean Soup

SERVES 6 Ⓖ Ⓢ Ⓝ

2 cups boiling water

1 tablespoon Lapsang souchong loose-leaf tea

1 cup dried black turtle beans, soaked overnight, drained, and rinsed, or 2 (15-ounce) cans black beans, drained and rinsed (see Chef's Tip)

5 cups store-bought vegetable stock or homemade Brown Vegetable Stock (page 76)

2 dried bay leaves

1 teaspoon fine sea salt

2 tablespoons extra-virgin olive oil

2 celery stalks, cut into medium dice

1 small yellow onion, cut into medium dice

1 small carrot, peeled and cut into medium dice

2 large garlic cloves, minced

¾ cup canned crushed tomatoes

1 teaspoon chili powder seasoning

½ teaspoon ground cumin

½ teaspoon dried oregano

½ teaspoon ground fennel

Freshly ground black pepper to taste

1 teaspoon fresh lime juice, plus lime wedges for serving

½ small bunch scallions (white and green parts), thinly sliced

1 tablespoon chopped fresh cilantro leaves

¼ cup dairy-free sour cream or Cashew Sour Cream (page 66)

WE ADD BREWED LAPSANG souchong tea to this soup to impart a distinctive smoky flavor. You can find the loose tea in Asian markets or online, but if you don't have the tea, use a guajillo chili instead to infuse a similar flavor; it can be added with the stock, and then removed after 15 to 20 minutes so it doesn't disintegrate. Rich and satisfying, served with side of cornbread or garlic bread, this soup is hearty enough to call dinner.

1. In a small bowl, combine the boiling water and tea. Steep for 5 minutes, then strain out the leaves and set the brewed tea aside.

2. (If you're using canned beans, move on to step 3.) In a medium pot, combine the beans, stock, bay leaves, and ½ teaspoon of the salt. Cover and bring to a boil over high heat. Reduce the heat to low and simmer until the beans are just tender, about 45 minutes.

3. Meanwhile, heat a large pot over medium heat, add the oil, and heat until it just starts to shimmer. Add the celery, onion, carrot, and the remaining ½ teaspoon sea salt. Sweat the vegetables over medium-low heat until slightly tender, 7 to 10 minutes. Stir in the garlic, tomatoes, chili powder, cumin, oregano, and fennel, and continue to cook the mixture until fragrant, about 5 minutes more. Add the beans and their cooking liquid to the pot with the cooked vegetables.

4. Simmer the soup until the vegetables are very tender, about 15 minutes more. Remove the bay leaves and discard. Add 1½ cups of the brewed tea.

5. Ladle half of the soup mixture into a blender and purée until smooth (or purée with an immersion blender). Return the purée back to the soup and stir to combine. If a thinner consistency is desired, add more of the brewed tea. Season to taste with salt, if needed, pepper, and lime juice. Serve with lime wedges, scallions, cilantro, and a spoonful of sour cream.

CHEF'S TIP: If you're using canned beans, skip the bay leaves and simply add the cooked beans and vegetable stock to the pot in step 3.

Oden

(Japanese Root Vegetable Stew)

SERVES 8 (G)* (N)

CHOCK-FULL OF HEARTY VEGETABLES in a simple shiitake broth (also called vegetarian dashi), this comforting stew has several layers of flavor that build as you cook it—and the complexity continues to develop with time, making this a great make-ahead dish. Burdock, a wild root related to the daisy, has been used throughout history in an attempt to cure a plethora of illnesses, from arthritis to cancer; we like the slightly earthy flavor it contributes to this stew. The shapes and colors of the vegetables make a beautiful presentation, even if they do take some time to prep.

FOR THE STEW

7 ounces firm tofu (half a standard package), drained and cut into bite-size triangles

2 tablespoons plus 2 teaspoons canola oil

2 teaspoons arrowroot starch

1 medium yellow onion, diced

1 large burdock root, peeled, halved lengthwise, and cut into thin half-moons

¼ teaspoon fine sea salt

1 small carrot, peeled, halved lengthwise, and cut into half-moons

4 garlic cloves, thinly sliced

½ large daikon radish, cut into large rounds

1 medium kabocha squash (about 2 pounds), peeled, halved, seeded, and cut into large dice

3 tablespoons fresh ginger juice from about 2 (4-inch) pieces (see page 74)

2 tablespoons fresh lemon juice (from about 1 lemon)

½ bunch thinly sliced scallions (white and green parts), for serving

1½ cups cooked long-grain brown rice, for serving (optional)

FOR THE DASHI

2 ounces dried shiitake mushrooms (about 18 mushrooms)

2-inch piece of kombu (see page 55)

¼ cup shoyu or tamari

*if made with tamari

1. Press the tofu: Line a plate or cutting board with paper towels and arrange the triangles on top in a single layer. Lay another paper towel on top of the tofu and then another plate or cutting board and weigh it down with heavy cans. Let stand for 30 minutes.

2. Meanwhile, make the dashi: In a large pot, combine the mushrooms, kombu, shoyu, and 12 cups of water. Bring to a boil over high heat, then lower the heat and simmer, uncovered, for 30 minutes. Strain the stock into another large pot and set aside. Thinly slice the kombu and shiitake caps (discard the stems or save for another use), and set aside.

3. Make the stew: Preheat the oven to 400°F and line a baking sheet with parchment paper. In a large bowl, gently toss the pressed tofu with 2 teaspoons of the oil, sprinkle it with the arrowroot, and gently toss to coat. Arrange the tofu in a single layer on the prepared baking sheet and bake until it's crispy and golden, about 25 minutes, flipping the tofu halfway through cooking. Set aside.

4. Heat a separate large pot over medium heat, add the remaining 2 tablespoons oil, and heat until it just starts to shimmer. Add the onion, burdock, and salt. Cook, stirring occasionally, until the burdock begins to soften, 7 to 10 minutes.

5. Add the carrot and garlic, and continue cooking until all the vegetables are slightly tender, about 5 minutes. Add the daikon radish and squash, and cook for another 5 minutes.

6. Add the dashi to the pot with the vegetables. Cover the pot and bring to a boil over high heat. Remove the lid, lower the heat to low, and simmer, uncovered, until all the vegetables are tender and the squash begins to break down, about 30 minutes.

7. Add the crispy tofu to the stew, along with the sliced kombu, shiitakes, and ginger and lemon juices. Simmer until everything is heated through, about 5 minutes. Sprinkle with scallions and serve over rice, if desired.

CHEF'S TIP: Look for burdock root at farmers' markets and specialty Asian grocers.

Bengali Dahl

with Cumin, Fennel, and Mustard Seeds

SERVES 6 TO 8

FOR THE DAHL

1½ cups red lentils (masoor dahl), picked through for stones and rinsed

2 green Thai bird chilies

1½ teaspoons fine sea salt

½ teaspoon ground turmeric

FOR THE TOMATO TARKA

4 tablespoons coconut oil

1 medium yellow onion, finely chopped

4-inch piece of fresh ginger, peeled and chopped

2 plum tomatoes, finely diced

FOR THE FINISHING TARKA

2 tablespoons coconut oil

½ teaspoon cumin seeds

½ teaspoon fennel seeds

½ teaspoon brown mustard seeds

½ teaspoon fenugreek seeds

½ teaspoon black onion seeds

1 dried bay leaf

9 fresh curry leaves

3 dried red chilies

ONE OF THE SECRETS behind the heady, aromatic flavors of Indian cooking is *tarka,* a technique of frying (or "blooming") spices and other aromatics in hot oil, which, when used for sautéing, adds depth to a dish. For even more complexity, we finish the dahl with a drizzle of a second spice-flavored oil.

1. Make the dahl: In a medium pot, combine the lentils, chilies, salt, turmeric, and 4½ cups of water. Bring the mixture to a boil over high heat, reduce the heat to low, and simmer, stirring often, until the lentils are cooked through and broken down, about 20 minutes.

2. While the lentils are cooking, make the tomato *tarka:* Heat a small sauté pan over medium heat, add the oil, and heat until it just starts to shimmer. Add the onion and ginger and sweat, stirring occasionally, until translucent, about 5 minutes. Add the tomatoes and cook until thickened, stirring occasionally, about 8 minutes. Add the tomato *tarka* to the cooked dahl (wipe out the pan from the tomato *tarka* and reserve for later use) and heat over medium heat until the flavors are blended, stirring occasionally, about 5 more minutes.

3. Make the finishing *tarka:* In the same small sauté pan used to make the tomato *tarka,* heat the oil over medium heat. Add the cumin, fennel, mustard, fenugreek, and black onion seeds with the bay and curry leaves and chilies, and cook until fragrant, about 15 to 20 seconds, shaking the pan frequently. Stir the mixture into the dahl and serve.

CHEF'S TIP: If you are unable to find the fenugreek, black onion seeds, or curry leaves available at Indian markets or online, feel free to omit them.

CHAPTER 4

Salads & Sides

Creamy Caesar Salad

SERVES 4

WHILE CRISP ROMAINE LETTUCE leaves and golden, robust croutons are standard in this ubiquitous salad, our vegan Caesar dressing delivers the same savory umami flavors as the original recipe—without the egg yolks or anchovies. We came up with a combination of umeboshi and miso that adds the salty, tangy, savory taste you expect from a Caesar. And in place of Parmesan—nori! Topping the salad with seaweed may be totally unexpected, but the thin, crispy nori strips give a toasted crunch that's flavorful and mineral-rich.

FOR THE CROUTONS

¼ loaf of whole-wheat bread, cut into cubes (about 4½ cups)

2 tablespoons extra-virgin olive oil

¼ teaspoon fine sea salt

Pinch of freshly ground black pepper

FOR THE DRESSING AND SALAD

¾ cup extra-virgin olive oil

2 ounces silken tofu

¼ cup fresh lemon juice (from about 2 lemons)

¼ cup balsamic vinegar

2 large garlic cloves, coarsely chopped

1 teaspoon white or chickpea miso

1 teaspoon Dijon mustard

1 teaspoon umeboshi paste (see page 338 for resources)

2 sushi-size sheets of roasted nori, 1 crumbled and 1 thinly sliced into strips

2 small heads of romaine lettuce, torn into bite-size pieces

1. Preheat the oven to 350°F. On a baking sheet, toss the bread cubes with the oil, salt, and pepper. Bake until golden and crisp, about 10 minutes.

2. Meanwhile, make the dressing: In a blender, combine the oil, tofu, lemon juice, vinegar, garlic, miso, mustard, umeboshi, and sheet of crumbled nori. Purée until creamy.

3. To serve, put the lettuce and croutons in a large bowl and toss with just enough dressing to lightly coat the leaves. Serve with the nori strips on top.

CHEF'S TIP: This recipe makes more dressing than you'll most likely use. Store the extra in an airtight container in the refrigerator for up to 3 days. You may make the dressing in advance as well.

Bitter Greens and Shaved Fennel Salad

with Shallot Vinaigrette and Candied Pistachios

SERVES 8

FOR THE PISTACHIOS

1 tablespoon maple crystals, coconut sugar, or organic raw sugar

1 tablespoon agave syrup

½ teaspoon fennel seeds

½ teaspoon fine sea salt

Pinch of cayenne pepper

½ cup shelled pistachios

FOR THE DRESSING AND SALAD

½ cup extra-virgin olive oil

¼ cup Champagne vinegar or other mild vinegar

2 tablespoons agave syrup

1 small shallot, minced

½ teaspoon fine sea salt, plus more to taste

Freshly ground black pepper to taste

4 cups arugula (4 ounces), torn into bite-size pieces

1 large head of radicchio, cut into bite-size pieces

1 fennel bulb, outer layer and core removed, thinly sliced

IN AYURVEDIC THEORY, BITTER is said to be the most medicinal of all tastes, and bitter greens are considered anti-inflammatory, anti-bacterial, anti-viral, and helpful in detoxifying the body. Bitter is best paired with something sweet and spicy, which makes these candied pistachios the perfect garnish.

1. Make the pistachios: Preheat the oven to 350°F. Line a baking sheet with parchment paper. Combine the maple crystals, agave, fennel seeds, salt, and cayenne in a medium skillet over low heat. When the maple crystals are dissolved, add the pistachios and toss to coat. Transfer the nuts to the prepared baking sheet and roast until golden and fragrant, 5 to 7 minutes. Transfer to a plate and refrigerate to cool completely.

2. Meanwhile, make the dressing: Combine the oil, vinegar, agave, shallot, salt, and pepper in a blender, and purée until smooth.

3. In a large bowl, toss the arugula, radicchio, and fennel with just enough dressing to lightly coat the leaves. Taste and season with more salt and pepper, if needed. Transfer to a serving platter and top with the candied pistachios.

Spinach and Shiitake Salad

with Pine Nuts

SERVES 4

1 tablespoon extra-virgin olive oil

10 ounces shiitake mushrooms, stemmed and thinly sliced

½ teaspoon fine sea salt

5 cups packed baby spinach (5 ounces)

¼ cup toasted pine nuts (see page 56)

½ small red onion, finely minced

¼ cup Sherry Vinaigrette (page 85)

THIS SIMPLE AND VERY popular recipe comes from the brunch presentation class in the Chef's Training Program, where students practice serving a complete three-course brunch menu for about forty guests. We think it's the combination of crunchy pine nuts and umami-rich shiitakes that makes this salad so irresistible.

1. Heat a large skillet over medium heat, add the oil, and heat until it just starts to shimmer. Add the mushrooms and salt, and sauté until the mushrooms are soft and golden, about 8 minutes, stirring frequently to prevent sticking.

2. Transfer the mushrooms to a large bowl and add the spinach, pine nuts, and onion; toss to combine. Dress the salad with the vinaigrette and serve.

Eating the Rainbow BY CHEF ANN NUNZIATA

From creamy green avocados to ruby-red beets, fresh fruits and vegetables are naturally bursting with gorgeous colors. Appearances aside, these brilliant pigments play an important role in a whole-foods diet, due to their antioxidant properties. (Antioxidants are various compounds that protect our cells from damage by neutralizing free radicals, which develop when cells are under stress and can lead to cell damage linked to chronic disease.)

Plants defend themselves from stress by creating phytochemicals. Many of these compounds act as antioxidants and help plants counteract environmental damage. When we eat plant-based foods, we consume these antioxidants, which many believe have the ability to calm inflammation in our own bodies and protect our cells from damage.

Home-cooked meals, made from real ingredients, are inherently more colorful, and therefore more antioxidant-rich, than those that are manufactured. Artificial colors are frequently added to enhance the palatability and aesthetics of premade and prepackaged foods, which often suffer nutrient loss during processing as a result of extensive exposure to high temperatures, light, and oxygen. So during your next visit to the farmers' market, remember that real color means real vitality! Here are a few of the most important and potent antioxidants found in fruits and vegetables.

BETA-CAROTENE: The pigment that gives carrots and sweet potatoes their orange glow. This phytochemical is an antioxidant that our bodies can convert to vitamin A if needed. Beta-carotene is a fat-soluble compound, so be sure to enjoy orange foods with a bit of olive or coconut oil for the most absorption.

LYCOPENE: The red pigment found in tomatoes, watermelon, and pink grapefruit is also in the carotenoid family. Cooking tomatoes increases the bioavailability of lycopene greatly.

CHLOROPHYLL: Green vegetables have this phytonutrient to thank for their emerald color. Chlorophyll is responsible for photosynthesis in plants and for converting water and carbon dioxide into oxygen and carbohydrates. Chemically, chlorophyll is very similar to hemoglobin, which carries oxygen from our lungs to the rest of our cells. (Except chlorophyll contains magnesium, instead of iron.) Chlorophyll also contains beta-carotene, vitamins A, C, E, and K, calcium, and potassium—and is fat-soluble, so be sure to dress your leafy salads with a delicious homemade vinaigrette.

ANTHOCYANINS: Fresh fruits and vegetables that appear dark red, purple, and deep blue, such as blueberries, pomegranates, and beets, are all rich sources of this powerful antioxidant.

Watercress-Fennel Salad

with Citrus

SERVES 4

FOR THE SALAD

1 small fennel bulb (about ¾ pound), outer layer and core removed, thinly sliced

2 blood oranges, supremed (reserve juices; see Chef's Tips)

1 navel orange, supremed (reserve juices)

1 pink grapefruit, supremed (reserve juices)

½ small red onion, cut into thin rings

¼ cup pitted, oil-cured black olives, coarsely chopped

4 ounces watercress, trimmed

FOR THE DRESSING

3 tablespoons extra-virgin olive oil

2 tablespoons reserved combined citrus juices

2 tablespoons brown rice syrup, agave syrup, or maple syrup

2 teaspoons fresh lemon juice (from about ½ lemon)

½ teaspoon white miso

Pinch of dried red pepper flakes

Fine sea salt to taste

Freshly ground black pepper to taste

SUPREMING IS A TECHNIQUE for preparing citrus that reveals the bare fruit slices, sans pith and membrane, making for an impressive presentation. The sweet-sour flavor and juiciness of the mixed citrus make this salad the perfect palate-cleansing first course.

1. Make the salad: Put the fennel into a small bowl and add enough cold water to cover; set aside.

2. Put the oranges, grapefruit, onion, olives, and watercress into another bowl, and set aside.

3. Make the dressing: Combine the oil, citrus juices, rice syrup, lemon juice, miso, and red pepper flakes in a blender and purée until smooth.

4. Drain the fennel and add it to the citrus-watercress mixture. Toss the salad with the dressing and season with salt and pepper.

> **CHEF'S TIPS:** To suprême—or "segment"—citrus, slice off the ends and stand your fruit on one of the flat sides. Run a sharp knife around the fruit, slicing off the skin with all the pith until the juicy flesh is exposed. Hold the fruit in your nondominant hand, positioned over a bowl to catch the juices and, using a sharp paring knife, cut out the segments, cutting around the connecting membranes. Squeeze and reserve the juice from the remaining fruit.
>
> In a pinch, you may slice the citrus fruits into rounds instead of segments: first slice off the skin as outlined above, then cut the fruit lengthwise into ¼-inch rounds.

Massaged Kale Salad

with Spiced Roasted Chickpeas and Pickled Red Onions

SERVES 4 TO 6

1 bunch lacinato kale, stemmed, leaves cut into thin ribbons (chiffonade, see page 47)

1 tablespoon extra-virgin olive oil

1 teaspoon lemon zest

1 tablespoon fresh lemon juice (from about ½ lemon)

½ teaspoon fine sea salt

¼ cup pitted kalamata olives, coarsely chopped

1 batch Spiced Roasted Chickpeas (page 103)

1 batch Pickled Onions (page 67)

THE DIFFERENCE BETWEEN A kale salad and a great kale salad is the delicate art of massage, which softens and wilts the leaves, and releases some of their juices. Massaged kale is easier to chew and digest, and, in our humble opinion, tastier, too. This particular recipe calls for massaging the leaves in the dressing, but in other situations that may not be necessary; you may simply sprinkle the chopped kale with salt before starting the rubdown.

1. Put the kale into a large bowl and add the oil, lemon zest, lemon juice, and salt. Massage the kale for 1 to 2 minutes, until it becomes soft, juicy, and darker in color.

2. Add the olives and roasted chickpeas to the kale. Top with the Pickled Onions and serve.

Warm Pinto Bean Salad

with Shiitakes, Radishes, and Watercress

SERVES 8 TO 10

FOR THE SALAD

1½ cups pinto beans, soaked overnight, drained, and rinsed, or 2 (15-ounce) cans pinto beans, drained and rinsed (see Chef's Tip)

2-inch piece of kombu (optional)

¼ teaspoon fine sea salt

2 teaspoons extra-virgin olive oil

15 shiitake mushrooms, stemmed and thinly sliced

1 small red onion, minced

1 bunch of radishes, thinly sliced

1 bunch of chives, chopped

1 bunch of watercress, torn into bite-size pieces

FOR THE DRESSING

2 tablespoons plus 2 teaspoons shoyu or tamari

2 tablespoons plus 2 teaspoons Dijon mustard

2 teaspoons brown rice syrup, agave syrup, or maple syrup

2 teaspoons brown rice vinegar

¼ cup extra-virgin olive oil

*if made with tamari

ADDING KOMBU, A WIDELY used type of sea vegetable, to bean cooking water enhances the digestibility of beans and adds minerals, too. Tossing the beans with the dressing while they are still warm allows them to absorb it, infusing the beans with flavor throughout. If you purchased radishes with the greens still attached, do not discard them! Radish greens are perfectly edible—and delicious. You can lightly sauté them with olive oil and garlic, or toss them into a pasta dish right before serving.

1. Put the beans, kombu, and salt into a medium pot and add enough water to cover by about 3 inches. Cover, bring to a boil, and simmer with the lid ajar until the beans are cooked through, 30 to 40 minutes.

2. Heat a large skillet over medium heat, add the oil, and heat until it just starts to shimmer. Add the shiitakes and cook until softened, 5 to 7 minutes; set aside.

3. Make the dressing: In a small bowl, combine the shoyu, mustard, rice syrup, and vinegar. While continually whisking, slowly stream in the oil until combined.

4. Drain the beans, discarding the kombu, and transfer to a large bowl, along with the shiitakes, onions, radishes, and dressing. Toss to combine. Gently mix in the chives and watercress right before serving.

CHEF'S TIP: If you're using canned beans, skip to step 2 and warm the beans up before using.

Black Bean–Tarragon Salad

SERVES 4 TO 6 (G)

1 cup dried black beans, soaked, drained, and rinsed (see "About Beans," page 54, and Chef's Tip)

¼ teaspoon ground cumin

¼ teaspoon ground fennel

1 dried bay leaf

1 teaspoon fine sea salt, plus more to taste

¼ cup extra-virgin olive oil

3 tablespoons fresh lime juice (from 2 or 3 limes)

3 radishes, cut into small dice

2 tablespoons minced scallions (white parts only)

1 tablespoon chopped fresh tarragon

Freshly ground black pepper to taste

THE COMBINATION OF FRESH tarragon and ground fennel here lends a hint of anise flavor to this light, refreshing salad. Pair these beans with a grain, such as brown rice or quinoa, for a complete meal.

1. In a medium pot, combine the soaked beans with the cumin, fennel, bay leaf, ½ teaspoon salt, and 4 cups of water, cover and bring to boil over high heat. Reduce the heat to medium-low and simmer with the lid ajar until the beans are tender, about 40 minutes. Remove the bay leaf and drain the beans.

2. In a small bowl, whisk together the oil, the lime juice, and the remaining ½ teaspoon salt. Pour the dressing over the warm beans.

3. When the beans have cooled slightly, toss them together with the radishes, scallions, and tarragon. Season with salt and pepper to taste.

CHEF'S TIP: If you're short on time, you can substitute 3 cups of canned black beans for the cooked beans here. Simply drain and rinse them, then proceed to step 3. No need to heat the beans—just dress, toss, and serve. If you do heat them, though, they'll absorb more of the dressing.

Springtime French Lentil Salad

SERVES 4 TO 6

THE **GOLDEN RULE OF** cooking legumes like lentils is to flavor the cooking water—it is a great opportunity to boost their flavors. Dressing the lentils in the vinaigrette while they are still warm helps absorb flavor, too (this technique holds true for other legumes as well, and even potatoes). We adore this dish because it keeps and travels well, whether for a work lunch or that first springtime picnic in the park. You may also switch out the green beans for asparagus or Brussels sprouts during fall.

FOR THE LENTILS

1 cup French lentils, picked through for stones and rinsed

2 dried bay leaves

¾ teaspoon fine sea salt

6 ounces green beans, trimmed (about 1 generous handful)

½ small red onion, minced

¼ fennel bulb, outer layer and core removed, finely diced

8 sun-dried tomatoes, reconstituted in hot water for 10 minutes, drained, and chopped

¼ cup toasted sliced almonds (see page 56)

2 tablespoons chopped fresh flat-leaf parsley

2 tablespoons chopped fresh tarragon leaves

FOR THE DRESSING

2 sun-dried tomatoes, reconstituted in hot water for 10 minutes and drained

1 small shallot, coarsely chopped

¼ cup plus 2 tablespoons extra-virgin olive oil

3 tablespoons fresh lemon juice (from about 1½ lemons)

1 tablespoon chopped fresh tarragon leaves

2 teaspoons maple syrup

¼ teaspoon Dijon mustard

¼ teaspoon fine sea salt

¼ teaspoon freshly ground black pepper

1. In a medium pot, combine the lentils, bay leaves, ½ teaspoon of salt, and 4 cups of water. Cover, bring to a boil over high heat, reduce the heat to low, and simmer with the lid ajar until the lentils are tender but not mushy, 20 to 25 minutes. Drain the lentils and discard the bay leaves. Transfer the lentils back to the pot and keep covered.

2. Meanwhile, bring a separate medium pot of water to a boil over high heat and season with the remaining ¼ teaspoon of salt. Prepare an ice bath. Boil the green beans for 2 minutes, drain, and immediately transfer them to the ice bath. When cooled, cut the green beans into 1-inch pieces; set aside.

3. Make the dressing: In a blender, combine the sun-dried tomatoes, shallot, oil, lemon juice, tarragon, maple syrup, mustard, salt, and pepper until smooth.

4. In a large bowl, toss together the still-warm lentils, green beans, onion, fennel, sun-dried tomatoes, and dressing. Taste and adjust seasonings, if needed. Sprinkle with the almonds, parsley, and tarragon before serving.

Coleslaw

with Almond Dressing

SERVES 6 TO 8

FOR THE DRESSING

1 head of garlic

2 tablespoons plus 1 teaspoon canola oil

½ cup blanched almonds (see Chef's Tip)

½ teaspoon plus a pinch of fine sea salt

2 tablespoons apple cider vinegar

2 tablespoons fresh lemon juice (from about 1 lemon)

1 scant tablespoon Dijon mustard

1 tablespoon agave syrup

Pinch of freshly ground black pepper

FOR THE COLESLAW

1 small head of cabbage, cored and very thinly sliced

¼ pound red cabbage, cored and very thinly sliced

1 yellow bell pepper, halved, seeded, and cut into matchsticks

1 large carrot, peeled and cut into matchsticks

¼ cup chopped fresh flat-leaf parsley

2 tablespoons chopped fresh dill

TRADITIONALLY, COLESLAW IS DRESSED in a mixture of mayonnaise and vinegar. For this vegan version, we use blanched almonds as a base for the creamy dressing because the skinless nuts easily blend into a silky sauce. Regular unblanched almonds would result in a dressing with a grittier texture and flaky brown bits of skin.

1. Preheat the oven to 375°F.

2. Make the dressing: Slice ¼ inch off the top of the garlic to expose the cloves. Rub with 1 teaspoon of oil, wrap in foil, and roast until the garlic is soft and golden-brown, about 40 minutes. Unwrap and set aside until cool enough to handle, then squeeze out the garlic and discard the skin.

3. Meanwhile, in a medium pot, combine the almonds with ½ cup water and a pinch of salt. Bring to a boil over high heat, cover, remove from the heat, and let the almonds soak for 20 minutes.

4. In a blender, combine the almonds with their soaking water, the roasted garlic, vinegar, lemon juice, mustard, agave, ½ teaspoon of salt, pepper, and the remaining 2 tablespoons of oil. Blend until creamy, gradually adding up to ¼ cup of water until the consistency is similar to mayonnaise. Set aside.

5. Add the cabbages, pepper, and carrot to a large bowl and toss with the dressing. Fold in the parsley and dill, and serve. If you are not planning to eat all the coleslaw at once, keep the vegetables and dressing separate until you're ready to serve; otherwise the coleslaw will get soggy. The dressing can be refrigerated for up to 3 days.

CHEF'S TIP: Blanched almonds are sold in many grocery stores. If you can't find them, you can easily skin almonds yourself using regular raw almonds. Bring a small pot of water to a boil, add your almonds, and boil them for exactly 1 minute. Drain in a colander and run the almonds under cold water until completely cool. Then squeeze the almonds between your fingers and the skins will slip right off.

Jicama Salad

SERVES 6 TO 8 Ⓖ Ⓢ Ⓝ

1 medium jicama (about 1 pound), peeled and cut into medium dice

1 cucumber, seeded and cut into medium dice

½ pineapple, skin removed and cut into medium dice

4 cups baby arugula (4 ounces)

¾ cup canola oil

2 teaspoons lime zest (from 1 or 2 limes), plus more for serving

¼ cup fresh lime juice (from 3 to 4 limes)

2 tablespoons agave syrup

2 tablespoons chopped chives, plus more for serving

Fine sea salt to taste

Freshly ground black pepper to taste

JICAMA (PRONOUNCED HEE-KAH-MAH) IS a tuberous root, indigenous to Mexico and South America. It's large and round with light-brown skin, which, when peeled away, reveals a white flesh that's crispy, like a firm apple or pear. However, the taste is less sweet than that of apples or pears, with a wonderful crunch and juiciness, and it can be eaten raw or cooked. Here we pair the fiber-rich vegetable with cucumber, pineapple, arugula, and a slightly sweet lime dressing for a refreshing salad.

1. In a large bowl, combine the jicama, cucumber, pineapple, and arugula.

2. In a blender, combine the oil, lime zest and juice, agave, and chives, and purée until creamy. Pour the dressing over the salad and gently toss to combine. Season to taste with salt and pepper. Sprinkle with extra chopped chives and lime zest before serving.

Chickpea-Arugula Salad

with Roasted Garlic Tahini Dressing

SERVES 4 TO 6

FOR THE DRESSING

1 head of garlic

¼ cup plus 1 teaspoon extra-virgin olive oil

½ cup unsweetened apple juice or cider

¼ cup fresh lemon juice (from about 2 lemons)

¼ cup tahini

¼ teaspoon fine sea salt

FOR THE SALAD

1 cup dried chickpeas, soaked overnight, drained, and rinsed, or 2 (15-ounce) cans of chickpeas, drained and rinsed (see Chef's Tip)

¼ teaspoon ground cumin

¼ teaspoon fine sea salt, or more to taste

5 cups arugula, coarsely chopped (about 5 ounces)

1 cup pitted kalamata olives, chopped

2 tablespoons fresh flat-leaf parsley, chopped

2 tablespoons fresh basil leaves, chopped

Freshly ground black pepper to taste

HERE IS ONE OF those dishes that gets even better as it sits for a bit, making it perfect for potlucks, picnics, and cookouts. This hearty chickpea salad is bright, thanks to the arugula and fresh herbs, and refreshingly briny, thanks to the olives. The creamy tahini dressing is a great all-purpose condiment to keep on hand as a dip or for drizzling on grain bowls, so feel free to make extra.

1. Start the dressing: Preheat the oven to 375°F. Slice ¼ inch off the top of the garlic to expose the cloves. Rub with 1 teaspoon of oil and wrap in foil. Roast until the garlic is soft and golden-brown, about 40 minutes. Unwrap and, when cool enough to handle, squeeze out the garlic in a blender jar and discard the skin.

2. Meanwhile, cook the chickpeas: In a medium pot, combine the chickpeas, cumin, and salt with 4 cups of water. Cover, bring to a boil over high heat, reduce the heat to medium-low, and simmer with the lid ajar until the chickpeas are tender, 45 to 60 minutes. Drain the chickpeas, transfer them back to the pot, and keep covered.

3. Finish the dressing: In a blender, combine the roasted garlic with the remaining ¼ cup of oil, apple juice, lemon juice, tahini, and salt, and blend until smooth.

4. In a large bowl, toss the warm chickpeas with the dressing and set aside to come to room temperature. Add the arugula, olives, parsley, basil, and pepper. Season with more salt, if needed, and serve.

CHEF'S TIP: You can make this using 3 cups precooked or canned chickpeas instead of boiling dried chickpeas, but note that warm chickpeas will absorb some of the dressing, so warm the chickpeas before using.

Bengali-Style Braised Greens

SERVES 4

1 tablespoon coconut oil

1 teaspoon brown mustard seeds

1 teaspoon cumin seeds

½ teaspoon fennel seeds

¼ teaspoon fenugreek seeds

¼ teaspoon onion seeds

1 medium shallot, minced

1 garlic clove, minced

1½-inch piece of ginger, peeled and minced (about 1 tablespoon)

⅛ teaspoon ground turmeric

6 fresh curry leaves

½ pound mixed braising greens, such as mustard greens, rainbow chard, kale, collards, or beet greens, stemmed and leaves cut into thin ribbons (chiffonade, see page 47)

Fine sea salt to taste

Freshly ground black pepper to taste

HEATING THE SPICES IN the oil before sautéing the greens (a technique called *tarka*, see page 155) allows the flavors to coat and meld nicely with the leaves. You can use this same technique for braising greens with a variety of flavor profiles. In place of the combination we suggest, try any of your favorites to flavor the oil. For a more Southern twist, sub in some crushed red pepper flakes or a dash of chipotle powder; for a French accent, try a premixed spice blend like Herbes de Provence; or even consider using a pinch of cinnamon and a handful of raisins to sweeten the dish.

l. Heat a wok or a large high-sided skillet over medium-high heat, add the oil, and heat until it just starts to shimmer. Add the mustard seeds and cook until they start to pop, about 1 minute. Add the cumin, fennel, fenugreek, and onion seeds, and toast until fragrant, 30 to 60 seconds. Add the shallot, garlic, ginger, and turmeric, and cook for about 1 minute more.

2. Add the curry leaves. As soon as they start to crackle (almost immediately), add the braising greens and season with salt and pepper. Sauté for a couple of minutes, stirring and turning the greens occasionally, until the greens are wilted. Serve immediately.

CHEF'S TIP: A popular ingredient in South Asian cooking, fresh curry leaves (from the same family of plants as citrus fruits) give an aromatic quality to recipes. And don't replace them with dried curry leaves, either; those tend to be flavorless. It's the fresh, shiny, dark leaves you want; they can often be found at specialty Indian grocers. If you are unable to find the fenugreek, onion seeds, or curry leaves, feel free to omit them.

Sautéed Bitter Greens

with Roasted Cipollini Onions, Currants, and Pistachios

SERVES 8

12 cipollini onions, trimmed and peeled

5 tablespoons balsamic vinegar

5 tablespoons extra-virgin olive oil

¾ teaspoon fine sea salt

Pinch of freshly ground black pepper

3 tablespoons brown rice syrup, warmed

4 garlic cloves, thinly sliced

½ head chicory greens (such as escarole or frisée), cut into bite-size pieces

2 small heads of radicchio, halved, cored, and cut into bite-size pieces

1 head of romaine lettuce, cut into bite-size pieces

3 tablespoons dried currants

3 tablespoons toasted pistachios, coarsely chopped (see page 56)

CIPOLLINI ONIONS (PRONOUNCED CHIP-O-LEE-NEE) are a variety of allium that are small, bulbous, and almost squat in appearance. Because of their higher sugar content, they are sweeter than standard yellow onions and are a nice complement to the warm bitter greens in this recipe. We add a head of romaine lettuce, which softens nicely when sautéed while still retaining some of its crunch. The lettuce rounds out the bolder, sharper greens, mellowing the overall flavor of the dish. A combination of balsamic vinegar and brown rice syrup, together with a sprinkling of currants, enhances the sweet-bitter contrast of the onions and greens, too.

1. Preheat the oven to 375°F. Line a baking sheet with parchment paper.

2. In a medium bowl, toss the onions with 3 tablespoons of vinegar, 2 tablespoons of oil, ½ teaspoon of salt, and pepper. Transfer the onions to the prepared baking sheet and roast in a single layer until tender and caramelized, shaking the baking sheet occasionally, 20 to 25 minutes.

3. Meanwhile, in the same bowl you tossed the onions in, whisk together the rice syrup, the remaining 2 tablespoons of vinegar, and the remaining ¼ teaspoon of salt until combined. Set aside.

4. In a large skillet, heat the remaining 3 tablespoons of oil over low heat. Add the garlic and cook just until golden, about 1 minute. Add the chicory, radicchio, and romaine, and cook, stirring occasionally, until just wilted, 1 to 2 minutes. Turn the heat off. Add the rice syrup mixture and toss to combine.

5. Transfer the greens to a serving platter and top with the roasted onions, currants, and pistachios.

Roasted Summer Vegetables

with Mint Pesto, Almonds, and Currants

SERVES 4 TO 6

FOR THE VEGETABLES

2 medium carrots, peeled and cut into ¼-inch cubes

2 medium red potatoes, cut into ¼-inch cubes

1 small eggplant, cut into ¼-inch cubes

1 zucchini, cut into ¼-inch cubes

3 tablespoons extra-virgin olive oil

½ teaspoon fine sea salt

¼ teaspoon freshly ground black pepper

FOR THE PESTO

¾ cup packed mint leaves

¼ cup packed flat-leaf parsley

1 medium garlic clove, coarsely chopped

½ teaspoon grated lemon zest (from about ½ lemon)

½ teaspoon fine sea salt

¼ cup extra-virgin olive oil

¼ cup toasted sliced almonds (see page 56)

¼ cup dried currants

IT MAY SEEM SUPERFLUOUS to parboil the root vegetables before roasting them, but, trust us, it makes a world of difference in unifying the textures of the vegetables and helping them roast evenly. The surprising flavor of the mint makes these vegetables pop, and a bit of sweetness from the currants really rounds out this dish. Double the pesto recipe and use the extra on sandwiches and in grain bowls.

1. Preheat the oven to 400°F. Line a baking sheet with parchment paper and set aside.

2. Bring a medium pot of water to a boil. Add the carrots and potatoes and cook for 90 seconds. Drain and pat completely dry.

3. Transfer the carrots and potatoes to a bowl and toss with the eggplant, zucchini, oil, salt, and pepper. Transfer to the prepared baking sheet, arranging the vegetables into a single layer, and roast until golden-brown, 20 to 25 minutes.

4. Meanwhile, make the pesto: In a food processor, combine the mint, parsley, garlic, lemon zest, and salt, and pulse until everything is broken down. With the motor running, stream in the oil and purée until smooth.

5. In a large bowl, toss the warm vegetables with the pesto, almonds, and currants. Taste and adjust the seasonings, if needed. Serve warm or at room temperature.

Basic Roasted Root Vegetables

SERVES 4 TO 6   (N)

2 to 3 pounds of one or more root vegetables, such as carrots, parsnips, beets, turnips, or sweet potatoes

2 to 3 tablespoons extra-virgin olive oil

¼ teaspoon fine sea salt, or more to taste

Freshly ground black pepper to taste

Fresh or dried herbs and/or spices of your choice (optional)

THERE'S SOMETHING SO WONDERFULLY comforting about a pan of sweet, caramelized vegetables that can be incorporated into other dishes or eaten on their own. The options are numerous with this technique. That said, you may use root vegetables and winter squash in the cooler months, as well as cruciferous favorites, like cauliflower, broccoli, and Brussels sprouts, anytime they are available. The key is that your vegetables must be evenly cut. If the vegetables are not uniform, they will cook at different rates; smaller pieces will cook faster than larger ones. Feel free to experiment by adding different spices as well—we love the combination of smoked paprika and garlic powder, for instance, or a sprinkling of fresh rosemary or thyme leaves.

1. Preheat the oven to 425°F degrees. Wash, peel, and cut the vegetables into 1- or 2-inch pieces or the desired size (again, they just need to be cut uniformly so they cook at the same rate; see headnote above).

2. Put the vegetables on a baking sheet and toss with the oil. The vegetables should be lightly and evenly coated, but not drowning in oil. Sprinkle with salt, pepper, and herbs and/or spices, if using, and toss again, spreading the vegetables in a single layer so they are not crowded. (If they are crowded, divide them between 2 baking sheets.)

3. Roast until fork-tender, tossing the vegetables about halfway through cooking for even browning. To learn cooking times, start checking after about 15 minutes of roasting. Pierce a piece to check for doneness. Roasted vegetables should be soft on the inside and slightly browned on the outside. Continue roasting until the desired doneness is achieved. In general, root vegetables take 20 to 30 minutes to roast.

Broccoli Rabe

with Pine Nuts, Raisins, and Sun-Dried Tomatoes

SERVES 6 TO 8

¼ teaspoon fine sea salt, plus more to taste

2 bunches of broccoli rabe, washed, ends trimmed, and cut into 2-inch pieces

2 tablespoons extra-virgin olive oil

4 garlic cloves, minced

Pinch of freshly grated nutmeg

6 sun-dried tomatoes, soaked in hot water for 10 minutes until softened, drained, and julienned (see Chef's Tip, page 222)

¼ cup golden raisins

2 tablespoons toasted pine nuts (see page 56)

Freshly ground black pepper to taste

DESPITE ITS NAME, BROCCOLI rabe, also known as rapini, is not related to broccoli. In fact, it's more closely related to turnips, while broccoli is part of the cabbage family. Because of its strong, bitter flavor, we blanch the broccoli rabe before sautéing it to mellow the pungent taste. We add sweet and robust sun-dried tomatoes to balance the greens, and the raisins provide a pop of sweetness. The overall combination is stellar, in terms of both taste and nutrition.

1. Bring a large pot of water to a boil over high heat and season with a pinch of salt. Prepare an ice bath and set aside. Add the broccoli rabe to the boiling water, and cook until bright-green and tender but not mushy, 3 to 5 minutes. Drain and transfer to the ice bath, then drain again once cooled.

2. Heat a skillet over medium heat, add the oil, and heat until it just starts to shimmer. Add the garlic and cook until it turns golden, 1 to 2 minutes, then stir in the nutmeg. Add the broccoli rabe, sun-dried tomatoes, and raisins, and stir to combine. Toss in the pine nuts, and season with salt and pepper.

Masala Spiced Potatoes

SERVES 4

MASALA IS A BLEND of various spices popular in South Asian cooking. Here ginger and turmeric are used to season the tender potatoes. Cumin and mustard seed flavor the *tarka* (see page 155) as well, which includes a small amount of raw dahl that is quickly sautéed. This addition gives a textural interest—a wonderful unexpected crunch to this dish. We like to pair these potatoes with Bengali Dahl (page 155) or use them as a filling for Chickpea Crepes (page 275).

FOR THE POTATOES

1 pound red or Yukon gold potatoes, peeled and cut into small chunks

1 tablespoon coconut oil

1 medium yellow onion, finely chopped

1½-inch piece ginger, peeled and minced (about 1 tablespoon)

2 Thai green chilies, seeded and finely chopped (optional)

½ teaspoon ground turmeric

½ teaspoon fine sea salt

FOR THE TARKA

1 tablespoon coconut oil

1 teaspoon brown mustard seeds

1 teaspoon whole cumin seeds

1 teaspoon uncooked urad dahl

1 teaspoon uncooked chana dahl (split Bengal gram dahl)

3 tablespoons fresh cilantro leaves, finely chopped

1. Put the potatoes into a medium pot and add enough water to cover. Bring to a boil over high heat, reduce the heat to low, and simmer until the potatoes are tender and can be pierced with a fork, about 15 minutes. Drain and return the potatoes to the pot. Lightly mash the potatoes until they are chunky; set aside.

2. In a large skillet, heat the oil over medium heat until it just starts to shimmer and sauté the onion until it turns translucent, 5 to 7 minutes. Add the ginger and green chilies, if using, and sauté until fragrant, 2 to 3 minutes more. Add the potatoes, turmeric, salt, and ¼ cup water, and stir to combine. Cover and cook over low heat until the potatoes are warmed through, about 8 to 10 minutes.

3. Make the *tarka:* In a small sauté pan, heat the oil over medium heat. Add the mustard seeds and cook until they begin to crackle, 1 to 2 minutes. Add the cumin seeds, urad dahl, and chana dahl, and cook, stirring, until the dahl turns golden-brown, 1 to 2 minutes. Mix the *tarka* into the potato mixture. Sprinkle with cilantro leaves and serve.

CHEF'S TIP: If you do not already have urad dahl and chana dahl on hand, fry the spices without the dahl and mix them in with the potatoes. There's no need to buy a large bag of each dahl for just the 1 teaspoon of each for this recipe.

Coconut Basmati Rice

with Lime Zest and Pistachios

SERVES 4

1 cup canned full-fat coconut milk

¾ cup store-bought vegetable stock or homemade Carrot-Onion Stock (page 75)

1 cup brown basmati rice, rinsed (see page 51)

1 teaspoon coconut oil

2 whole cloves

2 green cardamom pods

1 cinnamon stick

1½-inch piece of ginger, peeled and minced (1 tablespoon)

½ teaspoon fine sea salt

1 tablespoon lime zest (from about 2 limes)

1 tablespoon fresh lime juice (from about 1 lime)

¼ cup shelled toasted pistachios (see page 56)

2 scallions (white and green parts), thinly sliced

BROWN BASMATI RICE IS naturally aromatic, and when you add just a few spices for flavor, it becomes incredibly fragrant. Another favorite hack for transforming rice from boring to brilliant: coconut milk. Cooking any type of rice in the creamy liquid adds a touch of sweetness. This dish is distinct enough to stand alone, but also works well as a mellow side to a robust main, like Seared Tofu with Cilantro-Orange Dressing (page 209).

1. In a small pot, combine the coconut milk and stock and bring to a simmer over medium-high heat.

2. Toast the rice in a medium pot over medium-low heat until it is dry and just starts to turn golden, about 2 minutes. Add the oil and toss to coat the rice, stirring for another minute. Add the hot coconut milk mixture, as well as the cloves, cardamom, cinnamon, ginger, and salt. Cover and gently simmer until all the liquid is absorbed, about 30 minutes. Discard the spices and stir in the lime juice.

3. To serve, sprinkle with the lime zest and juice, pistachios, and scallions.

Traditional Bulgur Tabouli

SERVES 4

1 cup bulgur, cooked, still warm (see Grains-at-a-Glance Cooking Guide, page 52)

½ cup fresh lemon juice (from about 4 lemons)

¼ cup extra-virgin olive oil

½ teaspoon fine sea salt, plus more to taste

2 plum tomatoes, halved, seeded, and cut into small dice

1 bunch of fresh flat-leaf parsley, minced (about 1 cup)

4 scallions (white and green parts), thinly sliced

2 celery stalks, cut into small dice

½ bunch of fresh mint leaves, chopped (about ½ cup)

Freshly ground black pepper to taste

THERE ARE MANY VERSIONS of tabouli on menus around the world. Typically, this Middle Eastern salad is composed of herbs and bulgur wheat, which is made by cracking whole-wheat grains and partially cooking them. For ours, we like to dress the salad just enough to coat the grains and vegetables so they're not left dry, but also not overly dressed. There's a nice crunch from the celery, too. Serve this with Traditional Muhammara (page 117) and Baked Falafel Bowl (page 201) for a hearty mezze spread.

1. In a large bowl, toss the warm bulgur with the lemon juice, oil, and ½ teaspoon of salt. Set aside until it reaches room temperature.

2. Add the tomatoes, parsley, scallions, celery, and mint to the seasoned bulgur, and gently toss until well combined. Season with more salt and pepper.

CHEF'S TIP: For a gluten-free version, replace the bulgur with quinoa or riced cauliflower, which you can make by pulsing florets in a food processor until they are the size of rice pieces (or you can simply grate the cauliflower on a box grater). Use the riced cauliflower raw or sauté it for a few minutes before incorporating it into the salad.

Curried Couscous Salad

with Almonds and Raisins

SERVES 4

2 tablespoons refined coconut oil or another neutral oil

1 cup whole-wheat couscous (see Grains-at-a-Glance Cooking Guide, see page 52)

1 cup boiling water

¼ teaspoon fine sea salt, plus more to taste

2 tablespoons extra-virgin olive oil

1 small yellow onion, finely diced

1½ teaspoons curry powder (preferably Madras)

½ cup toasted almonds, coarsely chopped (see page 56)

½ cup golden raisins

2 tablespoons chopped fresh cilantro or flat-leaf parsley

1 to 2 tablespoons fresh lemon juice (from about 1 lemon)

Freshly ground black pepper to taste

WE FEEL STRONGLY ABOUT toasting grains, and this recipe is a great example why. Cooking the couscous in oil until it is golden-brown brings out a fantastic nutty fragrance that will make your whole kitchen smell heavenly. It also helps the grains stay separate and fluffy after the couscous is finished cooking. You may serve this salad as is or dressed in Sherry Vinaigrette (page 85).

1. Heat the coconut oil in a small pot over medium-low heat. Add the couscous and toast, stirring frequently, until it smells really nutty, 3 to 4 minutes. Turn the heat off and add the boiling water (careful—the water may sputter) and ¼ teaspoon salt. Cover and let stand until all the water is absorbed, 5 to 10 minutes. Fluff the couscous with a fork, and set aside to cool.

2. Meanwhile, heat a medium skillet over medium heat, add 1 tablespoon of olive oil, and heat until it just starts to shimmer. Add the onion and curry powder, and sweat until the onion is soft but not browned, about 5 minutes.

3. Transfer the onion mixture to a large bowl, along with the couscous, almonds, raisins, cilantro, lemon juice, and the remaining tablespoon of olive oil. Season to taste with salt and pepper, and serve.

Broiled Polenta

with Garlic and Rosemary

SERVES 8

1 cup coarse or medium-grain cornmeal, preferably stone-ground (see Grains-at-a-Glance Cooking Guide, page 52)

¼ teaspoon fine sea salt, plus more to taste

2 tablespoons extra-virgin olive oil, plus more for greasing the pan

1 tablespoon chopped fresh rosemary leaves

1 large garlic clove, minced

THESE SQUARES OF CREAMY polenta are crispy and golden on the outside and soft and tender on the inside. Eat the cornmeal cakes alone or top them with Tempeh Bolognese (page 228) or fresh tomatoes and olive oil for a complete meal. Use this recipe as a base for other herb and aromatic combinations, such as basil and oregano or chives and parsley. You can even try whisking a small amount of miso into a few tablespoons of soy sauce and brushing this mixture on top of the polenta before broiling.

1. In a small saucepan over high heat, whisk together the cornmeal and salt with 2 cups of water. Bring the mixture to a boil, whisking constantly, until it has thickened and there are no lumps, 2 to 3 minutes. Add 1 more cup of water, a little at a time, stirring well between each addition to mix thoroughly. Reduce the heat to low and simmer, stirring occasionally, until the grains are cooked through and no longer taste starchy, 20 to 30 minutes. If the mixture becomes too thick to stir, add a little extra water. The consistency should be that of a thick porridge.

2. Pour the hot polenta onto a parchment-lined baking sheet and spread with a lightly oiled spatula to a ½-inch thickness. Set aside at room temperature until the polenta is firm, 45 minutes to 1 hour (at this point, you may also refrigerate it for up to several days).

3. Lightly oil a baking sheet and set aside. Adjust an oven rack to the upper-middle position (about 5 inches from the heating element) and preheat the broiler to high.

4. In a small bowl, combine the oil, rosemary, garlic, and a pinch of salt.

5. Cut the set polenta into 8 squares. Transfer the squares to the prepared baking sheet and brush the top with half of the garlic oil.

6. Broil the polenta until golden and crisp, 6 to 8 minutes, then flip, brush the other side with the remaining garlic oil, and continue to broil until golden, about another 5 minutes more. Serve hot.

CHAPTER 5

Weeknight Dinners

Pressure Cooker Brown Rice Risotto

with Asparagus

SERVES 4 TO 6 (G)   (N)

THIS CREAMY, COMFORTING, AND easy dish is a perfect weeknight meal and is elegant enough to serve at any dinner party. Instead of making risotto from traditional white Arborio rice, we substitute short-grain brown rice for its health benefits and slightly nutty taste. As you may know, traditional risotto requires about 20 minutes of constant stirring, which means brown rice takes twice as long. Enter the pressure cooker. Simply lock on the lid, bring up the pressure, and walk away while the creamy risotto develops inside. If ever there was a time to dust off your pressure cooker, this is it. (Full disclosure: We soak the rice overnight, which shortens the cooking time as well. If you don't have a pressure cooker, soaking will most definitely still shorten the process. See the Chef's Tips below for how to make this dish without a pressure cooker.)

2 tablespoons extra-virgin olive oil

1 large yellow onion, finely diced

4 garlic cloves, minced

2 cups short-grain brown rice, soaked overnight, drained, and rinsed (see page 51)

4 cups store-bought vegetable stock or homemade Carrot-Onion Stock (page 75), plus more if needed

2 pounds asparagus, trimmed and cut into ¼-inch-thick rounds

⅛ teaspoon saffron threads, dissolved in a bit of warm stock or water

1 teaspoon fine sea salt

1 to 2 teaspoons umeboshi paste, or to taste (see page 338 for resources)

Freshly ground black pepper to taste

Chopped flat-leaf parsley, for serving

SPECIAL EQUIPMENT

Pressure cooker

1. Heat a pressure cooker over medium heat, add the oil, and heat until it just starts to shimmer. Add the onion and sauté, stirring frequently, until translucent, about 5 minutes. Stir in the garlic and cook for 1 minute more.

2. Add the rice and stir to coat it in the oil. Cook until the rice starts to become translucent around the edges, about 3 minutes.

3. Add the stock, set the lid on top and lock it in place, and bring up to pressure. Cook for 35 minutes.

4. Remove from the heat and allow the pressure to come down completely before opening. Open the pressure cooker and stir in the asparagus, saffron with its liquid, salt, 1 teaspoon of umeboshi, and pepper. Cook uncovered on low heat, stirring often, until the asparagus is tender and the rice is creamy, 5 to 10 minutes. Add more stock or water, if needed. Taste and season with more umeboshi, if needed. Sprinkle with parsley before serving.

CHEF'S TIPS: If you don't have a pressure cooker, you may bake the risotto, incorporating the following changes: (1) add 4 cups boiling stock to the rice after you sauté it and before you cover it with a lid; (2) bake in an oven-safe pot or Dutch oven at 375°F for 1 hour, or until the rice is tender; (3) stir in an additional cup of stock to the rice when you remove it from the oven (you'll need 5 cups of stock total) and continue to step 4.

In fall and winter, when asparagus is not in season, substitute 2 cups (about 5 ounces) of sliced porcini mushrooms.

Yuca Focaccia

with Zucchini, Tomatoes, and Red Onion

SERVES 4

NATIVE TO SOUTH AMERICA and the Caribbean, yuca (pronounced YOO-ka, also known as cassava) is a food staple for millions in many of the world's tropical and subtropical regions. The large, tapered roots have a thick brown skin that, when sold in the United States, is often waxed to preserve it (that skin should always be peeled before using; see the Chef's Tip). When cooked and mashed, yuca becomes very starchy, almost glue-like, and helps create a wonderfully smooth dough that makes a deliciously chewy, gluten-free bread. We like to top it with tomatoes and zucchini in the summer, but you can use this crust for any of your favorite toppings year-round.

¼ cup plus 1 tablespoon extra-virgin olive oil, plus more for greasing

1 medium yuca (about 1 pound), peeled, cored (see Chef's Tip), and cut into 1-inch cubes (about 2 cups)

1 teaspoon fine sea salt, plus more for sprinkling

½ cup cassava flour (also known as yuca flour), plus more if needed

2 teaspoons minced fresh rosemary

1 teaspoon garlic powder

¼ teaspoon freshly ground black pepper, plus more for sprinkling

2 plum tomatoes, thinly sliced lengthwise

1 small zucchini, sliced into thin rounds

½ small red onion, thinly sliced

2 tablespoons pitted black olives, coarsely chopped (optional)

1. Preheat the oven to 350°F. Line a baking sheet with parchment paper and lightly grease with oil; set aside.

2. Place the yuca and ¼ teaspoon salt in a medium pot and add enough water to cover by about 2 inches. Cover, bring to a boil, reduce the heat to low, and simmer the yuca until it is tender and can be easily pierced with a fork, about 20 minutes.

3. Drain the yuca and place it in a food processor. Purée until the yuca turns into a sticky purée, and transfer it to a bowl. Add the cassava flour, rosemary, garlic powder, pepper, ¼ cup of the oil, and the remaining ¾ teaspoon of salt. Using a wooden spoon, stir the mixture to form a smooth dough, adding a bit more flour if the dough is sticky.

4. Transfer the dough onto the prepared baking sheet and, using your fingers, spread it into a 9-inch square, about ¼ inch thick. Arrange the tomatoes, zucchini, onion, and olives in an overlapping pattern on the dough square, leaving a 1-inch border around the edges. Drizzle with the remaining tablespoon of oil and sprinkle with pinches of salt and pepper. Bake until lightly golden, 30 to 40 minutes. Slice the focaccia into squares and serve immediately.

CHEF'S TIP: To peel yuca, use a sharp knife and cut the root crosswise into 3 or 4 pieces. When you cut into the root, the flesh should be white. If you see spots or discoloration throughout, or detect a strong acidic aroma, it has gone bad and should be discarded. Carefully wedge the knife between the flesh and the skin and peel the skin away, loosening it as you move the knife around the piece of root. Repeat this with each piece. Next, cut the peeled pieces lengthwise into batons to reveal a woody core (you may not see it, but it is there). Slice away a ¼-inch piece of the core and discard. *Then* you can cut it into cubes and cook as directed.

Kimchi Fried Rice

SERVES 4

1 cup long-grain brown rice, rinsed
(see page 51)

1¾ cups boiling water

2 tablespoons sesame oil or
another neutral oil

1 small yellow onion, finely diced

½ teaspoon fine sea salt

2 garlic cloves, minced

¾ cup drained kimchi, coarsely
chopped

½ cup mung bean sprouts
(see Chef's Tip, opposite)

1 tablespoon toasted sesame oil

3 scallions (white and green parts),
thinly sliced, plus more for serving

UNLIKE MOST TAKE-OUT FRIED rice, our version features whole grains, kimchi (a great source of gut-friendly probiotics), and mung bean sprouts, which contain protein, fiber, folate, and many other micronutrients. Feel free to toss in extra vegetables with the cooked rice, and finish the dish with toasted sesame seeds, fresh cilantro, or Thai basil.

1. Place the rice in a small saucepan over medium heat and toast until completely dry, 4 to 6 minutes. Add the boiling water, cover, reduce the heat to low, and cook until all the water is absorbed, about 30 minutes. Turn the heat off and let stand, covered, for an additional 10 minutes to steam. Fluff with a fork before using.

2. Meanwhile, heat the sesame oil in a wok or a large skillet over medium heat. Add the onion and salt. Cook until the onion is softened, about 4 minutes. Add the garlic, kimchi, and sprouts, and cook for 2 minutes, stirring frequently. Add the rice and cook for 1 to 2 minutes, stirring frequently. Mix in the toasted sesame oil and scallions, and turn the heat off.

3. Divide the rice among 4 bowls and sprinkle with scallions.

CHEF'S TIP: Sprouted legumes, such as mung bean sprouts, are easier to digest for many than conventionally cooked beans. Sprouting also boosts beans' nutritional content, and gives us an extra source of freshness and crunch. It is very simple to sprout your own mung beans at home (see page 56), and you can often find them fresh in Asian markets.

Meal Planning 101

Life is demanding and sometimes leaves little time for things like meal prep, which can make midweek meals the most challenging to prepare. Whether you are new to cooking or a seasoned home cook looking to incorporate more health-supportive recipes into your routine, one of the best ways to guarantee healthy weekday meals is with thoughtful planning. An investment of time early in the week or over the weekend can have big payoffs later on. Start with recipes that appeal to you at first glance. Then look at them practically: Do you have the ingredients on hand? Do you need to shop for special items? Can components of the dish be made ahead? Can you prep some items in the morning or the night before? Or even double up on prep, chopping two onions instead of one to help prepare two meals in half the time? Is the time commitment realistic? Will the dish keep well in the fridge, or does it need to be eaten immediately?

If undertaking a whole recipe seems overwhelming, consider whether you can deconstruct it and perhaps make just one element. Take the Quinoa-Stuffed Tomatoes (page 225), for instance. If it seems too time-consuming to hollow out and roast tomatoes, just make the quinoa filling to enjoy on its own or with a handful of cherry tomatoes. Mastering grain prep is key to a plant-based diet, so practice with an easy recipe like Broiled Polenta (page 190), pair it with a side of Basic Roasted Root Vegetables (page 182), and you've got a veg-centric dinner on the table.

At the bare minimum, you can start with prepping a grain, a bean, and a variety of vegetables—whether roasting a large batch of broccoli or simply cutting some carrots into matchsticks so they're ready to go. Mix up the dressing in advance, too, like the Avocado Green Goddess Dressing (page 85) or the Sherry Vinaigrette (page 85), so your Tuesday night salads or grain bowls are much easier to assemble. And you can't go wrong with a large batch of soup or stew, like our cozy Cauliflower Rice Curry with Sweet Potatoes (page 217), which can be easily reheated. Don't forget to think seasonally, listen to your body and follow its directive (see "Finding Balance with Intuitive Eating," page 256), and try to include different colors (see "Eating the Rainbow," page 161) for nutritional and flavor variety as well.

Weekends are a great time to prep for the week ahead, from shopping, washing, and precutting vegetables, to batch-cooking a week's worth of lunches and dinners. Weekends are also a good time to try your hand at slightly more time-consuming recipes, like Black Rice–Black Bean Burgers with Fresh Mango Salsa (page 218); make the whole batch and freeze some patties for an in-a-pinch weeknight healthy dinner solution.

Once you're comfortable with the basics, make them your own. Tweak the recipes in this book with herbs, spices, and variations you love or have on hand. No matter how skilled you are, look at each meal as practice—a chance to better your culinary skills, build your confidence, and broaden your repertoire. Taking a mindful approach toward meal prep can be a game changer for health-supportive living.

Baked Falafel Bowl

with Red Quinoa and Preserved Lemon Cucumbers

SERVES 4   (G)*

FOR THE FALAFEL

1 cup dried chickpeas, soaked overnight, drained, and rinsed, or 3 cups canned chickpeas, drained and rinsed

1¼ teaspoons fine sea salt

⅓ cup extra-virgin olive oil, plus more for brushing

1 small red onion, minced

1 tablespoon ground cumin

2 teaspoons sweet paprika

½ teaspoon freshly ground black pepper

⅓ cup packed flat-leaf parsley leaves, minced

¼ cup packed fresh dill, minced

1 tablespoon finely grated lemon zest (from about 3 lemons)

3 tablespoons fresh lemon juice (from about 1½ lemons)

¼ cup plain dried bread crumbs

FOR THE QUINOA

¼ teaspoon fine sea salt

1 cup red quinoa, rinsed

4 teaspoons white balsamic or Champagne vinegar

4 teaspoons extra-virgin olive oil

1 cup pitted kalamata olives, coarsely chopped

2 tablespoons store-bought za'atar

*if made with tamari and gluten-free bread crumbs

THOUGH IT MAY SEEM like there is a long list of ingredients for this Moroccan-flavored bowl, all the elements, apart from the cucumbers, can be made in advance and reheated as needed. We like to peel the cucumbers partially, leaving behind a few strips of dark-green skin for extra flavor, texture, and nutrients.

1. Cook the chickpeas for the falafel: Place the chickpeas in a medium pot, add ¼ teaspoon salt and enough water to cover the chickpeas by about 2 inches. Cover, bring to a boil over high heat, reduce the heat to low, and simmer with the lid ajar until tender, about 45 minutes. Drain and set aside.

2. Meanwhile, make the quinoa: Bring 1¾ cups of water to a boil in a small pot. Reduce the heat to low, add the salt and quinoa, cover, and simmer until all the water is absorbed, 10 to 15 minutes. Remove from the heat and let stand, covered, for an additional 10 minutes to steam before stirring in the vinegar and olive oil; set aside.

3. Make the falafel: Transfer the chickpeas to a food processor and pulse until a coarse paste forms; set aside.

4. Heat a medium skillet over medium heat, add the olive oil, and heat until it just starts to shimmer. Add the onion, cumin, paprika, pepper, and the remaining teaspoon of salt. Sauté until the onion is soft, about 4 minutes.

5. Preheat the oven to 350°F. Line a baking sheet with parchment paper and lightly brush it with oil; set aside.

6. In a bowl, combine the chickpeas paste, the onion-spice mixture, the parsley, dill, lemon zest and juice, and bread crumbs, and stir. Using an ice cream scoop, form the mixture into about 1 dozen small patties and place them on the prepared baking sheet. Bake until golden-brown, about 20 minutes.

ingredients and recipe continue

CHEF'S TIP: If you are unable to find preserved lemons, toss the cucumbers in a bit of fresh lemon zest and juice instead.

FOR THE CUCUMBERS

2 English cucumbers, partially peeled and cut into ¼-inch-thick slices

1 preserved lemon, seeded and finely chopped (see tip, page 201)

1 tablespoon extra-virgin olive oil

FOR THE TAHINI DRESSING

¼ cup tahini

2 tablespoons toasted sesame oil

2 tablespoons white balsamic or Champagne vinegar

1 tablespoon shoyu or tamari

1 tablespoon maple syrup

½ teaspoon fine sea salt

7. Meanwhile, prepare the cucumbers: In a bowl, toss the cucumbers with the preserved lemon and oil; set aside.

8. Make the tahini dressing: In a bowl, whisk together the tahini, sesame oil, vinegar, shoyu, maple syrup, salt, and ½ cup of water until smooth. Set the dressing aside.

9. Divide the quinoa among 4 bowls and top with the falafel, cucumbers, and olives. Sprinkle with the za'atar and serve with the tahini dressing.

General Tso's Broccoli Bowl

with Black Rice and Spicy Edamame

SERVES 4 *

THE SWEET AND SALTY flavor of General Tso's is a crowd-pleaser. We have adapted the beloved Chinese take-out order for a healthier dinner alternative (no deep-frying here!) featuring chewy black rice (also known as forbidden rice in China because it was once reserved only for nobles and emperors), edamame (which boasts about 8 grams of protein per half cup), and crunchy, bright-green, steamed broccoli. With a slightly more toothsome and sticky texture, black rice is a luxurious alternative to brown.

FOR THE RICE

1 cup black rice, rinsed (page 51)

1½ teaspoons toasted sesame oil

¼ teaspoon fine sea salt

1¾ cups hot store-bought vegetable stock or homemade Carrot-Onion Stock (page 75)

FOR THE EDAMAME

1½ cups shelled frozen edamame, thawed

⅓ cup unsalted roasted peanuts, finely chopped

1 small garlic clove, grated

2 teaspoons toasted sesame oil

1 tablespoon sriracha, or to taste

2 teaspoons shoyu or tamari

FOR THE SAUCE AND BROCCOLI

3 tablespoons shoyu or tamari

2 tablespoons brown rice vinegar

1 tablespoon maple syrup

1 tablespoon mirin

1 tablespoon organic arrowroot

2 garlic cloves, minced

1½-inch piece ginger, peeled and minced (about 1 tablespoon)

¼ teaspoon red pepper flakes

1 head of broccoli, cut into florets

3 scallions (white and green parts), thinly sliced on a diagonal

¼ cup toasted sesame seeds, for serving (see page 56)

Fresh cilantro, for serving

1. Make the rice: Put the rice in a medium pot over medium heat and toast, stirring frequently, until the rice is dry, 3 to 5 minutes. Add the oil and salt, and toast the rice for 2 minutes more. Pour in the stock, cover, increase the heat to high, and bring to a boil. Reduce the heat to low and simmer, covered, until all the stock is absorbed and the rice is cooked through, about 25 minutes. Remove from the heat and let stand, covered, for an additional 10 minutes to steam.

2. Meanwhile, make the edamame: In a medium bowl, combine the edamame, peanuts, garlic, oil, sriracha, and shoyu. Taste and adjust seasonings, if needed, and set aside at room temperature until ready to serve.

3. Make the sauce: In a small saucepan, combine the shoyu, vinegar, maple syrup, mirin, arrowroot, garlic, ginger, and red pepper flakes. Stir to dissolve the arrowroot. Bring to a simmer over medium-low heat and cook until the mixture is slightly thickened, 2 to 4 minutes. Set aside.

4. Make the broccoli: Fill a medium pot with 2 inches of water, fit it with a steamer basket, and bring the water to a boil over high heat. Add the broccoli to the steamer insert, cover the pot with a lid, and steam the broccoli until it is bright-green and slightly tender, about 3 minutes. Stir the broccoli and scallions into the sauce.

5. Divide the rice among 4 bowls and top with the broccoli and edamame. Sprinkle with the sesame seeds and cilantro before serving.

*if made with tamari

Tempeh Reuben

MAKES 4 SANDWICHES

THIS IS OUR OWN take on the traditional Reuben sandwich. You won't find any Russian dressing or Swiss cheese here, and tempeh (tofu's hearty cousin, long praised for its high protein, fiber, and vitamin B12 content) replaces the traditional corned beef. A quick marinade and fry gives the tempeh a savory flavor that contrasts nicely with the briny sauerkraut. This sandwich is a legacy at our school.

¼ cup shoyu or tamari

2 cloves garlic, smashed

1 dried bay leaf

8 ounces tempeh, cut horizontally into ¼-inch-thick strips

3 to 4 tablespoons refined coconut oil, for frying

2 cups sauerkraut

2 ripe avocados, halved, pitted, peeled, and mashed

8 slices of homemade Spelt Bread (page 286) or store-bought rye bread, toasted

1 large tomato, thinly sliced

1. Make the tempeh: In a medium pot, combine the shoyu, garlic, and bay leaf with 2 cups of water, and bring to a boil. Add the tempeh, reduce the heat to low, and simmer, uncovered, for 30 minutes. Drain the tempeh, discard the marinade, and pat completely dry.

2. Meanwhile, heat a medium skillet over medium-high heat, add the oil, and heat until it just starts to shimmer. Gently slide the tempeh into the skillet and cook until browned, about 2 minutes, then flip and brown the other side, about 2 minutes more. Transfer the cooked tempeh to a paper towel–lined plate to drain the excess oil.

3. Meanwhile, place the sauerkraut in a small pot over low heat to warm through.

4. To serve, divide the mashed avocado among 4 pieces of bread and top with tomato slices. Divide the tempeh and sauerkraut over the tomatoes and place the remaining slices of bread on top. Slice the sandwiches in half on a diagonal (we like to secure the sandwich halves with wooden toothpicks) and serve.

Seared Tofu

with Cilantro-Orange Dressing

SERVES 4 *

BECAUSE AROMATIC SPICES ARE central to flavoring the tofu in this dish, we like to grind them fresh (see "Herbs and Spices," page 58). These fragrant seasonings, combined with the bright flavors of the orange juice and ginger, create a fresh dish that comes together quickly, yet is extremely satisfying. The tofu, which develops an irresistible caramelized crust, has a nice soft interior bite and pairs well with leafy greens for a textural contrast.

FOR THE DRESSING

¼ cup freshly squeezed orange juice

3 tablespoons brown rice vinegar

1 tablespoon canola oil

1 teaspoon toasted sesame oil

1½-inch fresh ginger, peeled and grated (about 1 tablespoon)

1 tablespoon finely chopped fresh cilantro, plus more for serving

¼ teaspoon fine sea salt

FOR THE TOFU

1 (14-ounce) package extra-firm tofu, drained

3 tablespoons canola oil

2 teaspoons coriander seeds, ground

2 teaspoons cumin seeds, ground

2 tablespoons shoyu or tamari

3 generous handfuls mixed salad greens (about 3 ounces), for serving

*if made with tamari

1. Make the dressing: In a small bowl, whisk together the orange juice, rice vinegar, canola oil, sesame oil, ginger, cilantro, and salt. Refrigerate while you prepare the rest of the dish.

2. Prepare the tofu: Cut the tofu block lengthwise into eight ½-inch-thick slices, and cut each slice lengthwise on the diagonal into 2 triangles to make 16 triangles in total.

3. Heat a large nonstick skillet over medium-high heat, add the oil, and heat until it just starts to shimmer. Add the coriander and cumin, and swirl the spices around until they become fragrant, about 1 minute. Add the tofu—in batches, if needed, so as not to overcrowd the pan—and cook until golden-brown, 3 to 4 minutes. Then flip and cook for 3 to 4 minutes more. Return all the browned tofu to the pan and add the shoyu and 1 cup of water. Increase the heat to high and cook until all the water has evaporated, 7 to 8 minutes, flipping the tofu halfway through cooking and gently tilting the pan occasionally so that the tofu cooks evenly.

4. In a medium bowl, toss the salad greens with some of the cilantro-orange dressing and transfer to a serving platter. Place the tofu on top of the greens, drizzle with the remaining dressing, and sprinkle with cilantro.

Vegetable Tempeh Wraps

with Avocado Cream

SERVES 4 TO 6

FOR THE WRAPS

1 small red onion, thinly sliced

1 (8-ounce) package of tempeh

2 tablespoons extra-virgin olive oil

1 teaspoon ground cumin

¼ teaspoon ground coriander

¼ teaspoon fine sea salt, or more to taste

Freshly ground black pepper to taste

8 to 10 round 8-inch rice paper sheets

1 red bell pepper, halved, seeded, and cut into thin strips

1 medium zucchini, cut into 3-inch matchsticks

1 English cucumber, peeled, seeded, and cut into 3-inch matchsticks

1 carrot, peeled and cut into 3-inch matchsticks

FOR THE AVOCADO CREAM

2 ripe avocados, halved, pitted, and peeled

½ cup packed fresh cilantro leaves (from about ½ bunch)

2 tablespoons extra-virgin olive oil

1 teaspoon brown rice vinegar

¼ teaspoon fine sea salt

¼ teaspoon freshly ground black pepper

EDIBLE RICE PAPER—THE TYPE used for Vietnamese spring rolls—becomes pliable and almost translucent when dipped in water, which makes it a great wrapper for a variety of foods. We like to show off thinly cut fresh vegetables under the thin rice skin for a colorful presentation.

1. Put the onion in a small bowl and cover with water. Set aside while you prepare the rest of the ingredients.

2. Using a box grater, coarsely grate the tempeh. In a medium nonstick skillet, heat the oil and lightly sauté the tempeh until browned, 4 to 5 minutes. Stir in the cumin, coriander, salt, and pepper, and cook until fragrant, about 3 minutes. Transfer the mixture to a large bowl and set aside to cool.

3. To roll the wraps: Place a medium bowl of warm water next to your cutting board. Dip 1 rice paper sheet in the water for a few seconds (it will be hydrated but still a bit stiff—you don't want it to lose its shape entirely as the sheet will continue to soften as you fill it). Gently place it on a clean, dry towel. Spoon about a tablespoon of the tempeh on the lower part of the wrap and place a few pieces of each vegetable lengthwise on top of it. Fold the bottom of the wrap over the mixture, then fold in the left and right sides to meet in middle. Finish rolling the wrap forward as tightly as you can to form the shape of a spring roll. Repeat with the remaining rolls. Cover the rolls with a damp paper towel to keep them from drying out.

4. Make the avocado cream: In a food processor, combine the avocado, cilantro, oil, vinegar, salt, and pepper, and purée until smooth.

5. Slice each wrap in half on a diagonal and serve with the avocado cream.

CHEF'S TIP: Most large grocery stores carry rice paper wraps in the international foods aisle; they are also available online or in specialty Asian food markets. If you prefer a less crunchy texture, try blanching the vegetables (see "Blanching and Shocking," page 57) before wrapping.

Tofu Teriyaki

SERVES 4 *

1 (14-ounce) package extra-firm tofu, drained

1 cup shoyu or tamari

½ cup maple crystals, coconut sugar, or raw organic sugar

¼ cup brown rice vinegar

¼ cup brown rice syrup

2 tablespoons fresh ginger juice from about a 6-inch piece (see page 74)

1 large garlic clove, minced

½ teaspoon toasted sesame oil

About ¼ cup refined coconut oil

2 tablespoons toasted sesame seeds, for serving (see page 56)

*if made with tamari

MASTERING THE TECHNIQUE OF searing—browning food on all sides over high heat—is essential for any cook. A good sear can create a pleasing, crispy crust on foods. The key: patience! It may be tempting to flip foods before they've had a chance to brown, but if you wait, a chemical reaction happens between the proteins and sugars in food that creates distinctive flavors and aromas. Tofu is a great food to practice searing because you can get a beautiful golden-brown crust—and here we finish it off with a simple teriyaki sauce. This deliciously glazed tofu is so satisfying, it's sure to become part of your regular weeknight rotation. We recommend making your own sauce so you can control the quality of the ingredients used, as well as the amount of sweetness. Serve this tofu with brown rice or soba noodles, and stir-fried vegetables.

1. Slice the tofu in half horizontally. Place the halves on a plate and top with another plate. Weigh down with cans or pie weights for 20 to 30 minutes to remove excess water, draining off the water periodically.

2. Meanwhile, in a bowl, whisk together the shoyu, maple crystals, rice vinegar, rice syrup, ginger juice, garlic, and toasted sesame oil with 1 cup of water; set aside.

3. Pat the tofu completely dry with paper towels and cut lengthwise into ½-inch-thick slabs.

4. Heat a large skillet over medium heat, add enough coconut oil to generously coat the bottom, and heat until it just starts to shimmer. Cook the tofu in batches, if needed, so as not to overcrowd the pan, until golden-brown, 3 to 4 minutes. Then flip and cook for 3 to 4 minutes more. Set the tofu aside once it is browned, adding more oil to the pan, as needed, to brown the remaining tofu.

5. Drain any excess oil and return all the tofu to the skillet. Add the shoyu mixture, reduce the heat to low, and cook for about 15 minutes, until the teriyaki sauce is thick and syrupy. Sprinkle with the sesame seeds and serve.

Lentils

with Caramelized Fennel and Onions

SERVES 4

2 medium yellow onions

1 cup French or green lentils, picked through for stones and rinsed

½ teaspoon ground turmeric

¼ teaspoon ground fennel

3 cups store-bought vegetable stock or homemade Carrot-Onion Stock (page 75)

½ teaspoon fine sea salt, plus more to taste

3 tablespoons extra-virgin olive oil

2 fennel bulbs, outer layer removed, cored, and finely diced, and ¼ cup reserved fennel fronds, for serving

Freshly ground black pepper to taste

2 scallions (white and green parts), thinly sliced on a diagonal

GENTLY CARAMELIZING FENNEL BRINGS out its natural sweetness. After separating the bulbs from the stalks, reserve the stalks and use them to flavor vegetable stock, or finely chop and use in place of celery in *mirepoix* (a classic French aromatic consisting of onions, carrots, and celery) that's destined for a soup or stew. Fennel fronds (the green feathery shoots on top) taste a bit like dill and can be used as a garnish or in salads.

1. Quarter the onions and thinly slice all but one quarter; set aside the sliced onions.

2. In a medium pot, combine the remaining quarter of the onion, lentils, turmeric, ground fennel, stock, and ¼ teaspoon salt. Cover the pot and bring to a boil over high heat. Reduce the heat to low, and simmer, uncovered, until the lentils are tender, 20 to 25 minutes. Remove the onion and discard. Drain off any remaining cooking liquid through a strainer and set the lentils aside.

3. Meanwhile, heat a large skillet over medium heat, add the oil, and heat until it just starts to shimmer. Add the sliced onions with ¼ teaspoon of salt and sweat until translucent, stirring occasionally, 5 to 6 minutes. Add the diced fennel and continue to cook until the vegetables soften and turn brown, stirring often to prevent burning, 20 to 25 minutes.

4. Add the cooked lentils to the vegetables, reduce the heat to low, and cook until all the remaining liquid is absorbed, 1 to 2 minutes. Taste and season with salt and pepper, if needed.

5. To serve, sprinkle with scallions and the reserved fennel fronds.

CHEF'S TIP: Be sure to start checking the lentils after about 20 minutes, as they can overcook quickly and turn to mush. However, if your lentils are on the older side, they may take upwards of an hour to cook through.

Bean and Root Vegetable Cassoulet

SERVES 6 TO 8

1 large carrot, peeled and cut into medium dice

1 large parsnip, peeled and cut into medium dice

5 tablespoons extra-virgin olive oil

1 teaspoon fine sea salt

Freshly ground black pepper to taste

1 medium yellow onion, thinly sliced

3 medium garlic cloves, minced

4 plum tomatoes, finely diced

1½ cups store-bought vegetable stock or homemade Brown Vegetable Stock (page 76)

1 rosemary sprig, leaves picked and minced

3 cups cooked or canned Great Northern beans

¾ cup whole-wheat panko bread crumbs

2 tablespoons chopped flat-leaf parsley

1 thyme sprig, leaves picked and minced or ¼ teaspoon dried thyme

*if made with gluten-free bread crumbs

SOUTHERN FRENCH CASSOULET IS a thick, long-simmered stew of white beans, duck confit, sausages, and/or pork. We've lightened up the dish and made it weeknight-friendly by using hearty root vegetables and precooked beans. We also love the satisfying crunch of the toasted panko bread crumbs on top. File this under "Recipes for a Snow Day."

1. Preheat the oven to 400°F.

2. On a baking sheet, toss the carrot and parsnip with 2 tablespoons of oil, ¼ teaspoon salt, and a pinch of black pepper. Spread the vegetables into an even layer and roast until lightly browned, stirring once halfway through cooking, 15 to 20 minutes. Remove from the oven and set aside.

3. Meanwhile, heat a large high-sided skillet over medium heat, add 1 tablespoon of oil, and heat until it just starts to shimmer. Add the onion and sauté until softened and starting to brown, stirring occasionally, 5 to 7 minutes. Add the garlic and cook for 1 minute more. Add the tomatoes, stock, rosemary, and the remaining ¾ teaspoon of salt. Bring to a boil, cover, reduce the heat to low, and simmer for 10 minutes.

4. Stir in the beans and simmer, uncovered, for another 5 minutes.

5. Meanwhile, in a small bowl, combine the bread crumbs, parsley, thyme, and the remaining 2 tablespoons of oil. Rub the mixture together with your fingertips to incorporate the oil.

6. Stir the roasted vegetables into the bean mixture and transfer to an 8 × 8-inch baking dish. Top with the bread crumb mixture. Reduce the oven temperature to 375°F, and bake until the bread crumbs are golden-brown, about 25 minutes.

CHEF'S TIP: This cassoulet can be made several days in advance—just hold off on adding the bread-crumb topping until reheating the dish in the oven to serve.

Cauliflower Rice Curry

with Sweet Potatoes

SERVES 4 TO 6

1 tablespoon unrefined coconut oil

1 medium yellow onion, diced

¾ teaspoon fine sea salt, plus more to taste

1 medium sweet potato, peeled and cut into ½-inch dice

1 (13.5-ounce) can full-fat coconut milk

3 tablespoons tomato paste

4 teaspoons curry powder

¾-inch piece of ginger, peeled and grated (about 2 teaspoons)

1 large head of cauliflower, cut into florets

1½ cups cooked or canned chickpeas

4 teaspoons fresh lime juice (from 1 to 2 limes), plus more to taste

Chopped cilantro, for serving

Lime wedges, for serving

WE LOVE HOW BEAUTIFUL, fragrant, and full of vegetables this cozy curried stew is. It's perfect for any season, since these ingredients are typically available—and affordable—year-round. If you do not have a food processor, you may finely chop the cauliflower instead (or buy it prericed in the produce department or freezer section of your supermarket).

1. Heat the oil in a large saucepan over medium heat. Add the onion with a ¼ teaspoon of salt and sauté, stirring occasionally, until it is soft and translucent, about 5 minutes. Add the sweet potato and cook, stirring occasionally, until it is starting to soften and brown, about 8 minutes.

2. Stir in the coconut milk, tomato paste, curry powder, ginger, ½ teaspoon of salt, and 1 cup of water. Simmer over low heat until the mixture thickens and the potatoes are soft, about 10 minutes.

3. Meanwhile, in a food processor, pulse the cauliflower in 2 batches until it is similar in size to rice grains. Transfer the cauliflower rice to a bowl and pulse the other half.

4. Add the cauliflower rice and chickpeas to the curry, and cook for another 5 minutes. Stir in the lime juice, taste, and season with more salt and/or lime juice if needed. Serve with cilantro and with lime wedges on the side.

Black Rice–Black Bean Burgers

with Fresh Mango Salsa

MAKES 12 BURGERS

FOR THE BURGERS

1 cup short-grain black rice, rinsed and drained (page 51)

1¾ teaspoons fine sea salt

¼ cup plus 1 tablespoon extra-virgin olive oil

1 medium yellow onion, finely diced

2 teaspoons ground cumin

2 teaspoons chipotle chili powder

4 garlic cloves, minced

½ to 1 jalapeño, seeded and minced

2 tablespoons flaxseed meal

¼ cup fresh lime juice (from 4 limes)

3 cups cooked or canned black beans

2 scallions, thinly sliced

½ cup brown rice flour

FOR THE SALSA AND SERVING

2 ripe plum tomatoes, finely diced

1 ripe mango, peeled, pitted, and finely diced

1 jalapeño, halved lengthwise, seeded, and minced

1 small shallot, minced

1 tablespoon fresh lime juice

1 tablespoon chopped fresh cilantro

½ teaspoon fine sea salt

Store-bought or homemade Vegan Mayonnaise (page 66) for serving (optional)

12 burger buns, toasted

1 head romaine lettuce, shredded, for serving (optional)

TO GIVE THIS VEGAN burger a satisfying texture, we started with black beans and black rice, puréeing half the rice into the mixture and stirring in the rest for a toothsome bite. We also added plenty of seasonings, opting for the Mexican-influenced route with cumin, chipotle powder, jalapeño, and lime. Enjoy these in a bun, as suggested below, or on a bed of lettuce. The uncooked burgers freeze beautifully—simply wrap the patties in plastic and freeze until hard, then transfer to an airtight container or a reusable freezer bag for up to 6 months. Thaw completely before cooking.

1. In a small pot, combine the black rice with 2 cups of water and ¼ teaspoon of salt. Cover and bring to a boil over high heat. Reduce the heat to low and simmer until all the water is absorbed, about 25 minutes.

2. Heat a large nonstick skillet over medium-low heat, add 1 tablespoon of oil, and heat until it just starts to shimmer. Add the onion, cumin, chipotle powder, and a pinch of salt. Sweat until the onion is soft, about 5 minutes. Add the garlic and jalapeño, and cook for 1 minute more.

3. Meanwhile, in a small bowl, stir together the flaxseed meal and lime juice. Chill until the mixture is thickened, 5 to 10 minutes

4. Transfer the onion mixture to a food processor (reserve the skillet) along with the beans, scallions, rice flour, the remaining 1½ teaspoons of salt, 1 cup of the cooked rice, and the flaxseed–lime juice mixture. Purée until smooth, stopping the food processor to scrape down the sides as needed. Transfer the mixture to a large bowl and stir in the remaining rice. Set the mixture to cool to room temperature.

5. Meanwhile, make the salsa: In a medium bowl, combine the tomatoes, mango, jalapeño, shallot, lime juice, cilantro, and salt. Chill until ready to serve.

6. Wipe clean the skillet you used to cook the onion and heat enough oil to cover the bottom of the pan. Heat over medium-low heat until the oil just starts to shimmer. Using a ⅓-cup measure, scoop and shape the burger mixture into ½-inch-thick patties. Cook the patties in batches until nicely browned, 3 to 4 minutes, then flip and cook the other side for 3 to 4 minutes more.

7. To serve, spread a bit of mayo on the buns and top with lettuce, a burger patty, and mango salsa.

CHEF'S TIP: In place of brown rice flour, feel free to use black rice flour. To make your own, grind black rice in a high-speed blender until it is very finely ground.

Baked Millet Croquettes

with Herbs

SERVES 4

1 cup millet, rinsed and drained
(see About Grains, page 51)

½ teaspoon fine sea salt

½ cup toasted sunflower seeds
(see page 56)

3 scallions (white and green parts),
thinly sliced on a diagonal

2 tablespoons minced parsley

1 small carrot, peeled and grated

2 to 4 tablespoons shoyu or tamari
to taste

ˇif made with tamari

MILLET IS A GLUTEN-FREE seed—or "pseudograin," like quinoa or amaranth—that comes from North Africa and is a great source of protein, fiber, and magnesium. After it's cooked and lightly kneaded, millet becomes sticky, which makes it perfect for these crispy, chewy croquettes. We like to serve these with a blended vinaigrette like the Sherry Vinaigrette (page 85), Basic Basil Pesto (page 88 and at left), or some Vegan Mayonnaise (page 66).

1. In a medium pot, dry-roast the millet over medium heat, stirring constantly, until it smells nutty and fragrant, about 10 minutes. Add the salt and 2 cups of water (careful—the water may sputter). Cover, bring to a boil over high heat, and then reduce the heat to low and simmer until all the water is absorbed, about 30 minutes. Transfer the millet to a large bowl and cool completely.

2. Meanwhile, preheat the oven to 350°F. Line a baking sheet with parchment paper.

3. Place the sunflower seeds in a food processor and grind to a fine meal. Add the ground sunflower seeds to the cooled millet, along with the scallions, parsley, carrot, and shoyu. Using your hands, toss the mixture together and then knead it until it becomes soft and sticky, about 1 minute.

4. Using a ¼-cup measure, form the mixture into 2- to 3-inch round patties (you should get about 12) and place on the prepared baking sheet. Bake until golden, about 30 minutes, and serve warm.

No-Cook Summer Squash Pappardelle

with Fresh Tomato Sauce and Vegan Ricotta

SERVES 4

FOR THE PAPPARDELLE

3 medium zucchini, ends trimmed

3 medium yellow squash, ends trimmed

1 teaspoon extra-virgin olive oil

½ teaspoon fine sea salt

Freshly ground black pepper to taste

FOR THE TOMATO SAUCE AND SERVING

¼ cup sun-dried tomatoes, soaked in hot water for 10 minutes and drained (see Chef's Tips)

1 medium tomato, seeded and coarsely chopped

1 red bell pepper, halved, seeded, and coarsely chopped

1 garlic clove, minced

1 tablespoon white balsamic vinegar

1 tablespoon extra-virgin olive oil

Pinch of dried red pepper flakes

½ small shallot, minced

12 fresh basil leaves, chopped, plus more for serving

1 cup homemade Vegan Ricotta (page 67) or store-bought vegan ricotta cheese

FRESH AND LIGHT, THIS raw "pasta," made from wide ribbon-like strands of zucchini and yellow squash, sings of summer. The chunky tomato sauce, which gets depth from rich sun-dried tomatoes, has a hint of heat from the red pepper flakes and complements the cool and delicate squash noodles. A few dollops of vegan ricotta, plus a handful of basil, and dinner is done—without even having to boil water!

1. For the pappardelle: Using a mandoline, a spiralizer, a vegetable peeler, or a sharp knife, slice the zucchini and squash lengthwise into paper-thin strips, then stack the strips and slice lengthwise to make ½-inch thin ribbons. Place them in a bowl and drizzle with the oil, salt, and pepper, and set aside to soften.

2. Make the tomato sauce: Put the drained sun-dried tomatoes in a food processor and pulse a few times to coarsely chop. Add the fresh tomato, bell pepper, garlic, and vinegar, and pulse a few times until just combined. With the motor running, slowly stream in the oil, being careful not to overprocess the mixture, as the sauce should be thick and remain a bit chunky. Transfer to a bowl and fold in the red pepper flakes, shallot, and basil.

3. Transfer the squash pappardelle to a paper towel–lined plate and, using another paper towel, blot it dry. Divide the noodles among 4 bowls. Top with dollops of the tomato sauce and the ricotta and serve.

CHEF'S TIPS: You may use either dry or oil-packed sun-dried tomatoes for the sauce. If you're using oil-packed, there's no need to reconstitute the tomatoes since they're already soft—be sure to drain off the excess oil.

If you like truffle oil, add a tablespoons to the ricotta for an extra umami note.

Stir-Fried Soba Noodles

with Vegetables

SERVES 4 TO 6 *

½ teaspoon fine sea salt, plus more to taste

8 ounces soba noodles

2 tablespoons sesame oil

4 large garlic cloves, minced

¾-inch piece of ginger, peeled and minced (about 2 teaspoons)

¾ cup shelled edamame (thawed if frozen)

1 head of bok choy, stems and leaves separated, sliced into thin ribbons (chiffonade, page 47)

1 red bell pepper, halved, seeded, and cut into thin strips

1 bunch of scallions (white and green parts), cut into 2-inch pieces

1½ cups mung bean sprouts (see page 56)

1 jalapeño pepper, halved, ribs and seeds removed, and minced

¼ cup shoyu or tamari

1 tablespoon toasted sesame oil

*if made with tamari and gluten-free noodles

SOBA NOODLES ARE MADE of buckwheat flour and are easily recognizable by their earthy brownish-gray color. Soba can be made with 100 percent buckwheat flour, which makes it naturally gluten-free; sometimes soba is made with half wheat flour and half buckwheat (if you are sensitive to gluten, be sure to look closely at the ingredient label). This recipe is a great example of the importance of *mise en place* (see page 42). Since all the ingredients are added in quick succession, be sure to prep them entirely before heating up your wok. Leftovers reheat nicely for desk lunches or quick dinners.

1. Bring a large pot of water to a boil and add the salt. Cook the soba according to the package directions until al dente. Drain and rinse under cold running water until the noodles are cool; set aside.

2. Heat a large wok or nonstick high-sided skillet over high heat until it is very hot, about 3 minutes. Add the sesame oil, garlic, and ginger, and cook until fragrant, about 1 minute. Add the edamame, bok choy stems, red pepper, and scallions, and sauté just until the pepper is tender, 1 to 2 minutes. Mix in the bok choy leaves, bean sprouts, jalapeño, shoyu, and toasted sesame oil. Add the noodles and toss to coat evenly. Taste and season with salt, if needed.

Quinoa-Stuffed Tomatoes

SERVES 4

¾ cup tricolor quinoa, rinsed (see Grains-at-a-Glance Cooking Guide, page 52)

1½ cups store-bought vegetable stock or homemade Carrot-Onion Stock (page 75)

4 large, ripe yet firm heirloom or beefsteak tomatoes

¼ teaspoon fine sea salt

3 tablespoons extra-virgin olive oil

1 medium red onion, finely chopped

2 garlic cloves, minced

⅓ cup pitted kalamata olives, chopped

¼ cup toasted pine nuts (see page 56)

2 tablespoons chopped fresh parsley leaves

2 tablespoons balsamic vinegar

Freshly ground black pepper to taste

¼ to ⅓ cup Basic Basil Pesto (page 88), for serving (optional)

ACCORDING TO OUR SEVEN Principles of Food Selection (pages 22 to 23), the flavor of our meals is significantly enhanced if we cook with seasonal produce. Here, choosing ripe, juicy tomatoes certainly has a profound effect on the final dish. We stuff those sweet, tender, summer delicacies with a Mediterranean-influenced quinoa that's tossed with olives and pine nuts. When the flavors of the fresh tomatoes meld with the filling, the result is brilliant. They can easily be made ahead and quickly reheated, or eaten at room temperature for a no-fuss warm-weather meal. For a simpler alternative to stuffing the tomatoes, make the quinoa filling to enjoy on its own and throw in a handful of cherry tomatoes.

1. In a medium pot, combine the quinoa and stock. Cover, bring to a boil over high heat, reduce the heat to low, and simmer until all the liquid is absorbed, about 15 minutes.

2. Meanwhile, line a baking sheet with paper towels and place a wire rack on top. Hollow out the tomatoes by cutting a large circle downward around the stem (almost to the rim of the tomato, as you would a pumpkin). Remove the top and scoop out the pulp (reserve for another use). Salt the insides of the hollowed-out tomatoes and turn them upside down on the prepared wire rack. Let them stand for 10 minutes.

3. Preheat the oven to 375°F.

4. Make the filling: Heat a medium skillet over medium-high heat, add 2 tablespoons of oil, and heat until it just starts to shimmer. Add the onion and sweat until slightly softened, about 5 minutes. Add the garlic and continue to cook for 1 minute more. Remove the pan from the heat and stir in the cooked quinoa, olives, pine nuts, parsley, vinegar, pepper, and the remaining tablespoon of oil and toss to combine.

5. Remove the tomatoes from the baking sheet, discard the paper towels, and line with parchment paper. Return the rack to the pan, turn the tomatoes cut-side up, and stuff with the quinoa filling. Bake until warmed through and the tomatoes start to look juicy, about 25 minutes. Top with a spoonful of pesto, if using, before serving.

Chili Beet Tacos

with Creamy Cabbage-Pineapple Slaw

SERVES 4

DO YOU KNOW THAT 85 billion corn tortillas are eaten annually in the United States alone? (And that doesn't include hard corn chips.) While we are huge fans of Homemade Corn Tortillas (page 95), you can often find freshly made ones for sale at taquerias or Mexican grocers. We like to fill the soft, pliable shells with hearty vegetable fillings like these smoky roasted beets, which develop a complex flavor from a dusting of chipotle chili powder and—yes!—coffee. A bit of ground coffee adds a gentle bitterness and toasty aroma that complement the sweet beets. We like to top the earthy combination with a bright and zesty cabbage-pineapple slaw and toasted sunflower seeds for crunch.

FOR THE BEETS

1 teaspoon finely ground coffee

½ teaspoon chipotle chili powder

½ teaspoon ground cumin

½ teaspoon fine sea salt

Freshly ground black pepper to taste

2 pounds red beets, scrubbed, trimmed, peeled, and cut into ½-inch dice

2 tablespoons extra-virgin olive oil

FOR THE SLAW AND SERVING

½ cup dairy-free plain yogurt

2 teaspoons extra-virgin olive oil

1 tablespoon Dijon mustard

2 teaspoons lime zest (from about 1 lime)

1 tablespoon fresh lime juice (from about 1 lime)

¼ teaspoon fine sea salt

Freshly ground black pepper to taste

¼ head small green cabbage, finely shredded (about 2 cups)

1 cup finely diced fresh pineapple

8 (6-inch) gluten-free corn tortillas, warmed

¼ cup toasted sunflower seeds, for serving (see page 56)

Fresh cilantro leaves, for serving

1. Preheat the oven to 400°F. Line a baking sheet with parchment paper.

2. In a small bowl, stir together the coffee, chili powder, cumin, salt, and pepper.

3. Place the beets in a large bowl, drizzle with the oil, sprinkle with the coffee-spice mixture, and toss to coat. Transfer to the prepared baking sheet and roast until tender, about 30 minutes, tossing once halfway through cooking.

4. Meanwhile, make the slaw: In a medium bowl, whisk together the yogurt, oil, mustard, lime zest and juice, salt, and pepper. Stir in the cabbage and pineapple. Taste and adjust seasonings, if needed.

5. To serve, fill the tortillas with the slaw and roasted beets, and sprinkle with sunflower seeds and cilantro.

CHEF'S TIP: Toasting nuts and seeds elevates their flavor tenfold. We highly recommend taking the extra time to toast the sunflower seeds in this recipe for a more complex flavor.

Roasted Spaghetti Squash

with Tempeh Bolognese

SERVES 4

1 large spaghetti squash, cut in half lengthwise and seeded

5 tablespoons extra-virgin olive oil

1 to 2 teaspoons fine sea salt, plus more to taste

Freshly ground black pepper to taste

1 (8-ounce) package tempeh, grated on the large holes of a box grater

1 Spanish onion, finely diced

4 medium garlic cloves, minced

1 teaspoon dried oregano

1 cup dry red wine

1 (28-ounce) can tomato purée

2 tablespoons brown rice syrup (optional)

3 tablespoons fresh basil leaves, chopped

IF YOU'VE NEVER USED tempeh, this is the perfect recipe to give it a go. Unlike classic slow-simmered beef or pork versions of Bolognese that require extra time to tenderize the meat, this easy vegan sauce comes together in less than 30 minutes. First you grate the tempeh, which is a whole food made from fermented soybeans, then give it a quick sauté before adding the red wine and tomato purée. You can serve this all-purpose sauce over pasta, polenta, grilled eggplant or, as we do, with gluten-free roasted spaghetti squash.

1. Preheat the oven to 400°F and line a baking sheet with parchment paper.

2. Brush the insides of the squash with 1 tablespoon of oil, sprinkle with salt and pepper, and place cut-side down on the prepared baking sheet. Add enough water to the pan to just barely cover the bottom and roast until the squash feels soft when pressed, about 50 minutes. Remove from the oven and, when it's cool enough to handle, use a fork to scrape the stringy flesh into a medium bowl; set aside.

3. Meanwhile, make the Bolognese: Heat a medium skillet over medium-high heat, add 3 tablespoons of oil, and heat until it just starts to shimmer. Add the tempeh and sauté until it starts to turn golden, stirring occasionally, 8 to 10 minutes.

4. Add the remaining tablespoon of oil, the onion, and 1 teaspoon of salt to the tempeh and stir to combine. Sauté, stirring occasionally, until the onions are soft, about 5 minutes. Add the garlic and oregano and cook until fragrant, 2 to 3 minutes more. Add the red wine and stir, making sure to deglaze the pan by scraping off the stuck-on bits on the bottom of the pan. Raise the heat to medium-high and simmer until the liquid is nearly evaporated, about 4 minutes.

5. Add the tomato purée and cook, covered, until thickened, 15 to 20 minutes.

6. Season with salt, pepper, and the rice syrup, if using. Stir in the basil and serve over the roasted spaghetti squash.

Baked Tempeh Polpette

with Tomato-Basil Sauce

SERVES 6

FOR THE POLPETTE

1 pound tempeh, quartered

½ cup shoyu or tamari

2 tablespoons extra-virgin olive oil

4 medium shallots, minced

¼ teaspoon plus 1 pinch fine
sea salt

2 large garlic cloves, minced

1 teaspoon ground fennel

1 teaspoon dried oregano

½ teaspoon ground sage

Pinch of cayenne pepper

Freshly ground black pepper
to taste

2 tablespoons oat or sorghum
flour

¼ cup chopped fresh flat-leaf
parsley

¼ cup canola oil

FOR THE TOMATO-BASIL SAUCE

1 tablespoon extra-virgin olive oil

1 large garlic clove, minced

Pinch of dried red pepper flakes

1 (14-ounce) can crushed tomatoes

¼ cup packed basil leaves, torn

Fine sea salt to taste

Freshly ground black pepper
to taste

*if using tamari

THIS VEGETARIAN ALTERNATIVE TO classic Italian meatballs is sure to become a Sunday supper staple at your house—it's that good. The polpette (the Italian word for "meatballs") are simple to make but require about an hour of inactive time for simmering the tempeh and then chilling the polpette before baking, so plan accordingly. Simmering the tempeh in a shoyu bath helps tame its slight bitterness and season it throughout. Serve the polpette over creamy polenta or spaghetti.

1. Make the polpette: In a medium pot, combine the tempeh, shoyu, and 4 cups of water. Cover and bring to a boil over high heat. Reduce the heat to low and simmer with the lid ajar for 20 minutes. Drain the tempeh and set aside.

2. Heat a large skillet over medium heat, add the oil, and heat until it just starts to shimmer. Add the shallots and a pinch of salt. Sauté until the shallots are soft and translucent, 1 to 2 minutes. Add the garlic, fennel, oregano, sage, and cayenne. Cook until fragrant, about 1 minute.

3. Transfer the shallot mixture to a food processor, add the tempeh, the remaining ¼ teaspoon of salt, and a pinch of pepper, and pulse until the mixture is homogenous but still has some texture. Scrape the mixture into a bowl. Fold in the oat flour and parsley.

4. Using your hands, portion out the mixture into small balls about 1 inch in diameter, rolling them between your palms. Refrigerate the polpette for 30 minutes.

5. Meanwhile, make the tomato-basil sauce: In a medium saucepan, heat the oil over medium-low heat. Add the garlic and red pepper flakes, and cook until fragrant, about 1 minute. Add the tomatoes and simmer the mixture until it thickens a bit, about 10 minutes. Turn the heat off. Stir in the basil, and season with salt and pepper.

6. Place a baking sheet into the oven and preheat it to 375°F. Once the oven comes to temperature, remove the hot baking sheet from the oven and pour in the ¼ cup of canola oil. Carefully transfer the chilled polpette onto the baking sheet and bake them for 20 to 25 minutes, shaking the pan about every 5 minutes, until the polpette are browned on all sides.

7. Serve the polpette hot with the sauce.

CHEF'S TIP: Do not forget to shake the baking sheet once the polpette are baking—this helps them get crispier.

Baked Mac and Cheese

SERVES 6 TO 8 Ⓢ

2 cups blanched almonds, soaked for 8 hours or overnight, drained

1 pound elbow macaroni

1 teaspoon fine sea salt, plus more for salting the pasta water

¼ cup plus 2 tablespoons canola oil, plus more for greasing the pan

¼ cup unbleached all-purpose flour

¼ cup nutritional yeast

1 teaspoon garlic powder

½ teaspoon smoked paprika

Pinch of freshly grated nutmeg

⅓ cup whole-wheat panko bread crumbs

SPECIAL EQUIPMENT

Nut milk bag or mesh strainer lined with cheesecloth

THE RICH, HOMEMADE ALMOND milk made from blanched almonds is the key to making this mac and cheese creamy and satisfying (to make your own blanched almonds, see page 173). This recipe uses the traditional French roux method (cooking fat and flour together to form a thickener) for the béchamel sauce but instead of cheese, we use nutritional yeast, garlic powder, and smoked paprika to achieve a cheesy, smoky flavor. Reserve the almond pulp for the Almond Pulp Crisps (page 103) or the Almond Pulp Cookies (page 104).

1. In a high-speed blender, combine the almonds and 6 cups of water. Blend until the almonds are pulverized and the mixture resembles milk, 1 to 2 minutes. Strain through a nut milk bag or a mesh strainer lined with cheesecloth, squeezing out as much liquid as possible. Reserve the almond pulp for other uses.

2. Meanwhile, cook the macaroni in salted water according to package directions until it is 1 minute shy of al dente; drain and set aside.

3. Preheat the oven to 350°F. Grease a 9 × 13-inch baking dish with canola oil and set aside.

4. Heat ¼ cup of the oil in a large pot over medium-low heat. Add the flour and cook, whisking constantly, until the flour is fully incorporated into the oil and starts to turn a light blond color, 1 to 2 minutes. Gradually whisk in the almond milk and bring the liquid to a simmer over medium-high heat, whisking frequently to avoid lumps and prevent the mixture from burning. Simmer the sauce until it is thick enough to coat the back of a wooden spoon, about 10 minutes. Whisk in the nutritional yeast, 1 teaspoon sea salt, garlic powder, paprika, and nutmeg. Taste and adjust seasonings, if needed.

5. Place the bread crumbs in a small bowl and drizzle with the remaining 2 tablespoons of oil. Rub the mixture together with your fingertips to incorporate the oil.

6. Stir the cooked macaroni into the sauce. Transfer the mixture to the prepared baking dish and sprinkle with the bread crumb topping. Bake until the mac and cheese is bubbly and golden, 20 to 25 minutes.

7. Let stand for 5 minutes before serving.

A Friday Night Dinner Like No Other BY CHEF OLIVIA ROSZKOWSKI

Historically, on Friday nights we'd set the tables, light the candles, and turn our classrooms into a pop-up restaurant—a Natural Gourmet tradition that predated that very concept by decades. Each week featured a new three-course, plant-based menu, prepared by our students under the guidance of seasoned chef instructors. Years ago, before the descent of "vegetable-forward" eateries upon every corner of New York City, our Friday Night Dinner was one of the only destinations where the city's vegans and vegetarians could enjoy a sophisticated plant-based meal, and it was cherished as a best-kept secret among the then–modest-sized community.

The Chef's Training Program (CTP, for short) would culminate with a Friday Night Dinner prepared by the graduating class. The students would spend weeks writing, testing, tasting, and retesting the menu, so when a plate finally reached a guest's table, it was a truly special moment. The dinner would exemplify how far the students had come since their first-day introductions, or since attending a dinner as a guest before they decided to enroll in the 619-hour, 6-month program.

Friday Night Dinner was also a fantastic illustration of all the culinary and nutrition principles taught throughout CTP, since "three-course" and "plant-based" were far from the only criteria. In fact, each menu had to pass upwards of twenty checkpoints before being deemed complete. Curious about those standards? Here are a few key points:

- The menu must include all five flavors: sweet, salty, sour, bitter, and spicy.
- It must be seasonally appropriate.
- The meal must have a hearty protein base, utilizing legumes, tofu, tempeh, or seitan.
- The menu must include a whole grain or another healthy starch. It may not, however, be too starchy, or include refined carbohydrates, such as white pasta or rice.
- It must include some raw foods and leafy greens, with some of the greens cooked.
- The menu should limit fried food to a garnish or a small component of one course.

Try using some of these criteria to create your own delicious and balanced weekend feasts!

Sweet Potato Sushi Rolls

with Homemade Pickled Ginger and Dynamite Sauce

SERVES 6

FOR THE PICKLED GINGER

½ cup brown rice vinegar

¼ cup agave syrup

1 teaspoon fine sea salt

5 ounces fresh ginger, peeled and very thinly sliced using a mandoline, food processor, or sharp knife

FOR THE SUSHI

2 cups short-grain brown rice, soaked overnight, drained, and rinsed (see page 51)

½ teaspoon fine sea salt

1 large sweet potato (about 1 pound), peeled and cut into 2-inch-long and ¼-inch-thick matchsticks

2 tablespoons canola oil

¼ cup brown rice vinegar

½ teaspoon maple syrup

1 English cucumber, peeled, seeded, and cut into 2-inch-long and ¼-inch-thick matchsticks

3 scallions (white and green parts), finely chopped

6 to 8 nori sheets

About ¼ cup shoyu or tamari, for serving

*if using tamari

NORI ROLLS ARE A great vehicle for consuming your whole grains and vegetables—whether cooked, raw, or pickled. They're also a fun way to get kids involved in the kitchen, letting them assemble and roll the nori logs. While sushi mats make the rolling easier, they are not necessary; roll directly in the nori if desired. Hold on to any leftover dynamite sauce and pickled ginger to use in grain bowls or stir-fries.

1. Make the pickled ginger: In a small pot, combine the rice vinegar, agave, salt, and ½ cup water. Bring to a boil over high heat and turn the heat off. Stir in the ginger and let sit at room temperature until completely cooled, about 1 hour. (Refrigerate leftover pickled ginger in its brine in an airtight container for up to 2 weeks).

2. Preheat the oven to 350°F. Line a baking sheet with parchment paper and set aside.

3. Make the rice: Put the rice and ¼ teaspoon of the salt in a medium pot and add 2 cups water. Cover and bring to a boil over high heat. Reduce the heat to low, and simmer until all the water is absorbed, about 35 minutes. Turn the heat off and let the rice sit, covered, to steam for 15 minutes.

4. Meanwhile, toss the sweet potatoes with the oil and arrange on the prepared baking sheet in a single layer. Roast until tender, tossing once halfway through cooking, about 20 minutes. Set aside to cool.

5. Uncover the rice and use a wooden spoon to stir in the rice vinegar, maple syrup, and the remaining ¼ teaspoon salt. Cover the pot with a damp kitchen towel and set aside for 10 minutes.

6. Make the dynamite sauce: In a blender, combine the tofu, sriracha, lemon juice, salt, and 2 tablespoons of water, and purée until creamy. With the motor running, slowly stream in the canola oil until creamy. Taste and adjust seasonings, if needed. Transfer the sauce to a bowl, and chill until ready to serve.

7. To assemble, place the rice, fillings, dynamite sauce, and a bowl of water near your work surface. Place a nori sheet on the bottom edge of a sushi mat, if using, shiny side down. Spread about ½ cup of rice on the nori sheet and spread it evenly with your fingers—dipping your fingers in the bowl of water when the rice starts to stick—leaving a 1-inch border at the top edge of the nori. Spread a thin stripe of dynamite sauce across the rice near the bottom end. Arrange a few pieces of sweet potato, cucumber, and scallions lengthwise on top of

ingredients and recipe continue

FOR THE DYNAMITE SAUCE

7 ounces soft tofu (half a standard package)

2 tablespoons sriracha

1 tablespoon fresh lemon juice, or to taste (from about ½ lemon)

1 teaspoon fine sea salt, or to taste

2 tablespoons canola oil

the sauce. Roll the bottom edge of the mat up and snugly over the vegetables. Continue tightly rolling forward, withdrawing the mat as you go. Moisten the top border of the nori with wet fingertips. Continue to roll forward to seal the roll. Repeat with the remaining ingredients.

8. To serve, use a sharp chef's knife to cut the rolls in half crosswise, then each half into 3 pieces crosswise. Serve with the pickled ginger and shoyu for dipping. Store refrigerated in an airtight container for up to 1 day.

Black Bean–Mushroom Enchiladas

with Mole Negro

SERVES 4 TO 6

FOR THE MOLE SAUCE

3 dried ancho chilies

2 dried guajillo chilies

⅓ cup toasted almonds
(see page 56)

⅓ cup toasted sesame seeds
(see page 56)

¼ cup refined coconut oil or
another neutral high-smoke-
point oil

2 garlic cloves, halved lengthwise

½ medium yellow plantain, peeled
and cut into ½-inch-thick rounds
(see Chef's Tips)

1 (14-ounce) can fire-roasted
tomatoes

½ cup raisins, soaked in hot water
for 10 minutes and drained

1 teaspoon ground cinnamon

1 ounce vegan dark chocolate,
chopped

2 to 3 cups store-bought
vegetable stock or homemade
Brown Vegetable Stock (page 76)

2 tablespoons fine sea salt,
or to taste

MOLE REFERS TO A number of traditional Mexican sauces, as well as the dishes in which they are used. One such variety, *mole negro*, is a smoky, nutty sauce that utilizes dark chocolate to round out all its rich flavors. Traditionally, making mole is an all-day, if not several-day, event, and the dish may contain upwards of forty ingredients. Ours only calls for about a third of that—and the end result is still deeply satisfying. (Both the filling and the sauce can be made in advance.)

1. Make the mole sauce: In a medium cast-iron skillet over medium heat, toast the ancho and guajillo chilies until they are flexible, using tongs to turn them occasionally and being careful not to burn them, 2 to 3 minutes. Transfer the chilies to a cutting board, cut in half, and remove the seeds and ribs. Place the chilies in a medium pot with enough water to cover them by a few inches. Bring to a simmer over medium-high heat and cook until the chilies are softened, about 5 minutes. Remove the chilies from the pot; set aside and discard the liquid.

2. In a food processor, grind the almonds to a fine powder; set aside. In a mini food processor or a spice grinder, grind the sesame seeds to a fine powder; set aside.

3. Heat a medium skillet over medium heat, add the oil, and heat until it just starts to shimmer. Add the garlic and cook just until golden, about 1 minute. Using a slotted spoon, transfer the garlic to a small bowl and set aside. Reserve the oil in the skillet. Raise the heat to medium-high and fry the plantains until golden on both sides, about 4 minutes total. Transfer the plantains to a paper towel–lined plate to drain excess oil. (Reserve the oil in the skillet for later.)

4. In a food processor, combine the plantains, chilies, ground almonds, ground sesame seeds, garlic, tomatoes, and raisins. Purée until a thick paste forms. Transfer the paste to the pan used for frying the plantains and cook over medium heat until it is bubbling, about 2 minutes. Stir in the cinnamon and chocolate. Add the stock ½ cup at a time, stirring between each addition, until the mixture is the consistency of heavy cream. Strain the mixture through a fine-mesh sieve and return it to the skillet. Simmer the sauce until it thickens slightly, 2 to 3 minutes. Season to taste with salt and set the sauce aside.

1 cup dried black beans, soaked for 8 hours or overnight, drained and rinsed, or 2 (15-ounce) cans black beans, drained and rinsed (see Chef's Tips)

1 small Spanish onion, coarsely diced

1 small carrot, scrubbed and halved crosswise

1 dried bay leaf

2 tablespoons extra-virgin olive oil

3 garlic cloves, minced

1 small jalapeño pepper, halved, ribs and seeds removed, and minced

1½ teaspoons ground cumin

1 pound cremini mushrooms, stemmed and sliced

1 teaspoon salt, or to taste

8 (6-inch) corn tortillas, warmed

¼ cup chopped fresh cilantro

2 limes, cut into wedges

5. Make the enchiladas: (If using canned beans, move on to step 6.) In a medium pot, combine the beans, half of the diced onion, the carrot, bay leaf, and enough water to cover by 2 inches. Cover and bring to a boil over high heat. Reduce the heat to medium-low and cook at a brisk boil with the lid ajar until the beans are soft, 50 to 60 minutes. Drain the beans, reserving ¼ cup of the cooking liquid.

6. Heat a large skillet over medium heat, add the oil, and heat until it just starts to shimmer. Add the garlic and cook for 30 seconds. Add the remaining half of the diced onion and cook, stirring occasionally, until softened, 7 to 10 minutes. Stir in the jalapeño and cumin and cook for 1 minute more. Add the mushrooms and the reserved bean liquid (see Chef's Tips if you're using canned beans) and cook until the mushrooms are cooked through, about 7 minutes. Add the beans and partially mash the mixture using a potato masher or a fork; the texture should be chunky but creamy enough to hold together. Season to taste with salt.

7. Preheat the oven to 375°F.

8. Pour about a cup of the mole sauce into a 9 × 13-inch baking dish, spreading it to coat the bottom. Fill each tortilla with about ⅓ cup of the bean mixture, roll it up, and place it seam-side down in the baking dish. Pour about a cup of the mole sauce over the rolled tortillas. (Refrigerate leftover mole sauce in an airtight container for up to 5 days, or in the freezer for up to 3 months.) Cover the baking dish with foil and heat in the oven for 15 minutes. Serve hot with cilantro and lime wedges.

CHEF'S TIPS: If you can't find a sweet plantain at your market, use a roasted sweet potato instead. To roast, pierce the sweet potato with a fork and place it on a baking sheet. Roast it in a 400°F oven until tender, about 40 minutes. When cool enough to handle, peel the potato and use in place of the fried plantain.

If using precooked or canned beans instead of dried, use ¼ cup mushroom or vegetable stock instead of the bean cooking liquid.

Pulled Barbecue Mushroom Sandwiches

with Kale Slaw

MAKES 8 SANDWICHES

FOR THE SLAW AND DRESSING

1 bunch lacinato kale, stemmed, leaves sliced into thin ribbons (chiffonade, about 4 cups; see page 47)

¼ head of a small red cabbage, shredded (about 2 cups)

1 teaspoon lemon zest (from about ½ lemon)

3 tablespoons fresh lemon juice (from about 1½ lemons)

¼ teaspoon fine sea salt

½ cup raw cashews, soaked overnight, drained, and rinsed

1 tablespoon brown rice vinegar

1 garlic clove, coarsely chopped

1 teaspoon maple syrup

1 teaspoon Dijon mustard

½ teaspoon fine sea salt

Pinch of cayenne pepper

1 small red onion, halved, thinly sliced, and soaked in cold water until ready to use

1 carrot, peeled and cut into matchsticks

IF YOU'RE LOOKING TO elevate your vegan barbecue offerings from the typical veggie burgers and grilled vegetable skewers, we've got you covered. Smoking the king trumpet and oyster mushrooms before roasting and shredding deeply infuses them with barbecue flavor and does wonders in terms of umami. The texture and flavor of these mushrooms will delight both vegans and omnivores alike. The preparation is lengthy, but it is definitely worth it. Save time by making the slaw dressing and barbecue sauce a day in advance. We like to soak the raw onions for the slaw in cold water to tame their spicy bite.

1. Start the slaw: In a large bowl, combine the kale, cabbage, lemon zest and 2 tablespoons of the juice, and salt. Massage until some of the moisture is released and the kale begins to soften, about 1 minute. Transfer to a colander (set the bowl aside for later), top with a plate and a heavy weight (such as a can of tomato sauce), and let drain for 30 minutes.

2. Make the dressing: In a high-speed blender, combine the cashews, ½ cup of water, vinegar, garlic, maple syrup, mustard, salt, cayenne, and the remaining tablespoon of lemon juice, and blend until smooth and creamy. Chill until ready to serve.

3. Make the mushrooms: Preheat the oven to 375°F. In a large bowl, toss the mushrooms with the oil and salt. Place the wood chips into an indoor smoker. Arrange half the mushrooms in a single layer in the smoker. Closer the smoker and set over medium heat. After smoke appears, smoke the mushrooms for 8 minutes. Transfer the mushrooms to a baking sheet and repeat with the other half. When they're cool enough to handle, shred the king trumpet mushrooms, using a fork, and thinly slice the oyster mushrooms. Arrange all the mushrooms in a single layer on the baking sheet and roast for about 15 minutes, until they are slightly dried out.

4. Finish the slaw: Return the kale-cabbage mixture to the bowl and add the onion, carrot, and dressing. Toss to combine. Taste and adjust seasonings, if needed.

5. Toss the mushrooms with the barbecue sauce. Divide the mushrooms among the buns, top with kale slaw, and serve.

FOR THE MUSHROOMS

1 pound king trumpet mushrooms, cleaned and trimmed

1 pound oyster mushrooms, cleaned and trimmed

¼ cup extra-virgin olive oil

½ teaspoon fine sea salt

4 tablespoons indoor wood chips (see Chef's Tip)

About 1 cup store-bought or Homemade Barbecue Sauce (page 84), or more to taste

8 potato, brioche, or gluten-free buns, toasted

SPECIAL EQUIPMENT

Indoor smoker (See Chef's Tip)

CHEF'S TIP: If you do not own an indoor smoker, no worries—you can make your own. Line the bottom of a large pot with foil. Place the indoor wood chips on top and cover with another piece of foil. Using a toothpick, poke holes all over the top piece of foil. Place a steamer basket on top, arrange the mushrooms inside the basket, and close the pot tightly with a lid. For indoor smoking, look for smaller wood chips, as opposed to big chunks, as they burn more easily. You will find them online in a variety of hardwoods—cherry, apple, mesquite, pecan—and at many hardware stores. Experiment with woods to see what flavors you prefer.

Pear and Leek Spelt Pizza

with Pesto

MAKES FOUR 10-INCH PIZZAS

FOR THE DOUGH

1 tablespoon dry active yeast

1 tablespoon maple syrup

3¼ cups spelt flour, plus more for kneading

⅔ cup plus ½ cup warm water (90°F to 100°F)

2 tablespoons extra-virgin olive oil, plus more for greasing the bowl

1 tablespoon fine sea salt

½ cup fine cornmeal or semolina flour, plus more for kneading and dusting the pans

FOR THE PEAR-LEEK TOPPING

3 tablespoons extra-virgin olive oil

4 leeks (white and light-green parts), trimmed, halved lengthwise, and sliced crosswise into half-moons (see page 125)

2 Bartlett pears, peeled, halved, cored, and thinly sliced

1 teaspoon fine sea salt

½ teaspoon freshly ground black pepper

1 tablespoon fresh thyme leaves, chopped

1 cup Basic Basil Pesto (page 88)

2 Almond Mozzarella rounds (page 62), sliced, or your favorite store-bought dairy-free cheese (optional)

SPELT, AN ANCIENT WHOLE grain, is slightly higher in protein than conventional wheat and, although not gluten-free, many people with gluten sensitivities can tolerate spelt better than modern wheat. We love the nutty bite it offers this tomato-less pizza. With pears and leeks, it's perfect for fall feasts.

1. Make the dough: In a medium bowl, whisk together the yeast, maple syrup, ¼ cup spelt flour, and ⅔ cup warm water. Cover with plastic wrap and set aside in a warm place until the mixture is doubled in size and bubbly, 20 to 30 minutes.

2. Add another ½ cup warm water, the oil, and salt, and stir to combine. Mix in the remaining flour in ½-cup increments until the dough forms a ball that pulls away from the sides of the bowl (you may not need to use all the flour). Transfer to a well-floured surface and knead until the dough is smooth and pliable, about 10 minutes, adding small amounts of flour whenever the dough gets sticky.

3. Place the dough into a lightly oiled large bowl, cover with plastic wrap, and leave it in a warm spot until it has doubled in size, about 40 minutes.

4. Meanwhile, make the pear-leek topping: Heat a large skillet over medium heat, add the oil, and heat until it just starts to shimmer. Add the leeks, pears, and salt and cook, stirring often, until the leeks start to become translucent and the pears pliable, 5 to 7 minutes. Remove from the heat and stir in the pepper and thyme; set aside.

5. Preheat the oven to 475°F. Adjust the oven racks to the upper-third and lower-third positions. Place 2 baking sheets in the oven to heat them up.

6. Punch down the dough to release the gas and reshape the dough into a ball. Divide the dough into 4 equal portions. Roll 2 of the portions into 12-inch circles about ⅛ inch thick.

7. Remove the baking sheets from the oven and sprinkle with cornmeal. Place the dough circles directly on the baking sheets and bake until lightly golden around the edges, 5 to 7 minutes. Remove from the oven and top with a thin layer of pesto, some of the pear-leek mixture, and the Almond Mozzarella, if using. Return to the oven and bake until the crust is deeply golden, 5 to 7 minutes more. Remove from the oven and repeat with the remaining dough and toppings. Serve immediately.

Grilled Spelt Flatbreads

with Caramelized Onions and Oyster Mushrooms

MAKES EIGHT 5-INCH FLATBREADS (S)* (N)*

FOR THE FLATBREADS

1 cup warm water
(about 90°F to 100°F)

1 teaspoon maple syrup

2 teaspoons active dry yeast

1 cup spelt flour

1 teaspoon fine sea salt

2 tablespoons extra-virgin olive oil, plus more for greasing the bowl

½ to 1 cup unbleached all-purpose flour, plus more for kneading

FOR THE TOPPINGS

4 tablespoons extra-virgin olive oil

3 large yellow onions, thinly sliced

1 teaspoon dried thyme and/or rosemary

¾ teaspoon fine sea salt, plus more to taste

1 tablespoon balsamic vinegar

¾ pound oyster mushrooms, stems removed

Freshly ground black pepper to taste

Pepita Blue Cheese Spread (page 68) or Almond Mozzarella (page 62), for serving (optional)

*without Pepita Blue Cheese Spread

*without Almond Mozzarella

TIME AND PATIENCE CAN do wonders for simple ingredients, and onions are a prime example. If you simply sauté them for 10 minutes, the result is tasty enough, but when you continue to cook them for another half hour or so, the result is a sweet and savory topping. Unfortunately, there's no rushing the process, which also goes for homemade flatbreads. Sure you could buy premade pizza dough to save time, but we contend that scratch is the best way to go. The spelt (see page 243) imparts a nutty flavor to the soft, chewy bread that's worth every second.

1. Make the flatbreads: In a medium bowl, stir together the warm water and the maple syrup. Whisk in the yeast until it's completely dissolved, then whisk in 2 tablespoons of the spelt flour. Set the mixture aside until it becomes foamy, 5 to 10 minutes.

2. Stir in the salt and oil. Add the remaining spelt flour and use a wooden spoon to stir to combine. Gradually mix in enough of the all-purpose flour to get the mixture to come together (it shouldn't be sticky). Turn the dough out onto a lightly floured surface and knead the dough to form a round, smooth ball, about 5 minutes. Place the dough in a lightly oiled bowl and cover with a kitchen towel. Set aside to rise until the dough has doubled in size, 30 to 40 minutes, then punch down the dough to release the gas and let the dough rise a second time until it almost doubles again, about 15 minutes.

3. While the dough rises, make the toppings: Heat a large skillet over medium heat, add 2 tablespoons of oil, and heat until it just starts to shimmer. Add the onions, thyme and/or rosemary, and ½ teaspoon of salt, and stir to coat the onions in oil. Cover the skillet with a lid and let the onions sweat until they start to soften and release their moisture, 5 to 7 minutes. Remove the lid, turn the heat down to medium-low, and cook, stirring frequently, until the onions turn a caramel-brown color and become a little jammy, 40 to 50 minutes (if the onions start to dry out, add 1 to 2 tablespoons of water). Add the balsamic vinegar and, using a wooden spatula, scrape up and stir in the browned bits from the bottom of the skillet. Turn the heat off, taste, and season with more salt, if needed.

Oyster mushrooms can be pricey (and are often unavailable), in which case you may use a mix of chanterelles, creminis, and/or shiitakes. You can also purchase dried mushrooms and reconstitute them in warm water before using.

If you do not have a grill, use a griddle, a cast-iron skillet, or a regular nonstick skillet to cook the flatbreads.

4. While the onions cook, sauté the mushrooms: Leave the small mushrooms whole and tear the bigger mushrooms into 2 or 3 pieces. Heat a separate skillet over medium-high heat, add the remaining 2 tablespoons oil, and heat until it just starts to shimmer. Add the mushrooms and toss to coat in the oil. Cook over medium-high heat, stirring frequently, until the mushrooms are reduced in size and browned in places with a few crispy edges, 10 to 12 minutes. Season with the remaining ¼ teaspoon of salt and pepper, and turn the heat off.

5. Punch down the dough once more and transfer it to a lightly floured surface. Roll it into a 12-inch log, sprinkling the surface with a little all-purpose flour if it sticks to your hands. Cut the dough crosswise into 8 equal pieces and roll each piece into a ball. Using a rolling pin, roll each ball into a 5-inch circle, dusting the dough, the work surface, or the rolling pin with more flour if the dough is sticky. The rounds will be quite thin. Place the flatbreads in a single layer on a baking sheet and cover them with a kitchen towel. Let them rest for about 5 minutes and up to 15 minutes (much longer and they'll start to dry out).

6. Heat a grill (or a grill pan) to medium heat. Cook the flatbreads until grill marks appear, 2 to 4 minutes. Then flip the flatbreads and cook the other side for 2 to 4 minutes more. (Alternatively, you can bake the flatbreads in a 400°F oven, flipping them once halfway through cooking, until they are browned, about 20 minutes.)

7. Divide the onions and mushrooms evenly among the flatbreads, top with the Pepita Blue Cheese Spread or Almond Mozzarella, if using, and serve immediately.

Quinoa and Tempeh– Stuffed Poblanos

SERVES 4

8 poblano peppers

3 tablespoons extra-virgin olive oil, plus more for greasing

½ cup unsweetened apple juice

2 tablespoons shoyu or tamari

2 teaspoons Dijon mustard

1 dried bay leaf

4 ounces tempeh, cut into 4 slices

½ bunch scallions (white parts only), minced (2 to 3 tablespoons)

½ medium carrot, peeled and cut into small dice

2 teaspoons ground cumin

2 teaspoons smoked paprika

1 teaspoon fine sea salt, or to taste

1 plum tomato, finely diced

2 large garlic cloves, minced

¼ cup cooked quinoa (see Grains-at-a-Glance Cooking Guide, page 52)

Freshly ground black pepper to taste

CHEF'S TIP: Wear gloves when handling the peppers, and don't touch your eyes or mouth with your hands after working with them.

WHEN FILLED WITH QUINOA, tempeh, and sautéed vegetables, stuffed poblano peppers make a comforting, satisfying meal. Generally the size of a smallish standard bell pepper but with a tapered bottom, poblanos are considered quite mild. Sometimes, though, they can be unpredictably hot—so keep that in mind when serving to people with heat sensitivity! Don't be tempted to skip roasting the peppers—it deepens their flavor, and steaming them makes the skins easy to remove, too (don't forgo removing the skins, either, as they are quite tough).

1. Preheat the oven to 350°F. Line a baking sheet with parchment paper. Rub the poblanos with a little bit of oil. Put them on the baking sheet and roast until the skins blister and pucker, 15 to 20 minutes.

2. Transfer the poblanos to a bowl. Cover the bowl tightly with plastic wrap and let the poblanos steam for 10 minutes.

3. When the poblanos are cool enough to handle, using your hands, slide off the skins, rinsing the chilies under running water, if necessary, to remove any charred bits. Using a paring knife, cut a vertical slit into each poblano from stem to tip, making an opening large enough for stuffing. Use a spoon to gently remove the seeds and set the poblanos aside.

4. In a medium skillet over medium heat, whisk together the apple juice, shoyu, mustard, and bay leaf. Slide the tempeh into the skillet, bring the liquid to a simmer, reduce the heat to low, and simmer until the liquid is reduced to a few tablespoons, about 20 minutes.

5. Transfer the tempeh to a paper towel–lined baking sheet to cool. Then crumble the tempeh and set aside.

6. To make the filling: Heat a medium skillet over medium heat, add 1 tablespoon of oil, and heat until it just starts to shimmer. Add the scallions, carrot, cumin, paprika, and salt. Sweat until the carrot begins to soften, stirring occasionally, about 8 minutes. Add the tomato and garlic and cook until the tomato is slightly broken down, 1 to 2 minutes more. Transfer the mixture to a large bowl.

7. Return the same pan to medium heat, add the remaining 2 tablespoons of oil and the crumbled tempeh. Cook until the tempeh is browned, 8 to 10 minutes. Transfer the tempeh to the bowl with the cooked vegetables. Add the quinoa and pepper and toss to combine. Taste and adjust the seasonings, if needed. Stuff each poblano with about ¼ cup of the filling. Warm the stuffed poblanos briefly in the oven before serving.

Butternut Squash and Pepita Blue Cheese Cannelloni

in White Bean Broth

SERVES 6 TO 8

FOR THE BROTH

1 cup dried navy beans, soaked overnight, drained, and rinsed (see page 51), or 2 (15-ounce) cans navy beans

1 dried bay leaf

1½ teaspoons fine sea salt

2 tablespoons extra-virgin olive oil

1 medium yellow onion, diced

2 garlic cloves, minced

1 teaspoon fresh thyme leaves

Pinch of dried red pepper flakes

FOR THE DOUGH

7 ounces silken tofu

¼ cup extra-virgin olive oil, plus more for greasing

¼ teaspoon fine sea salt, plus more for salting the pasta water

1 cup whole-wheat bread flour

1 cup unbleached all-purpose flour, plus more for kneading

1 teaspoon freshly ground black pepper

TRADITIONALLY, FRESH PASTA IS made with eggs. For our vegan version, we use silken tofu instead. Once the pasta dough is made, it gets formed into sheets using either a pasta machine, a pasta attachment on a mixer, or by hand with a rolling pin—then we cut the sheets to the desired size. The steps required here are numerous, from making the broth to rolling out the pasta dough, not to mention the option of making your own vegan blue cheese. However, the sum of the parts makes one amazingly delicious whole; after you've mastered each component, you'll have some great additions to your repertoire. And the pasta dough is versatile as well—the tofu makes it soft, so it doesn't hold shapes too well, but it works wonderfully for ravioli, cannelloni, and lasagna sheets.

1. If you're using dry beans, make the broth: In a medium pot, combine the beans, bay leaf, and ½ teaspoon of salt with enough water to cover by about 2 inches. Cover, bring to a boil, reduce the heat to low, and simmer with the lid ajar until the beans are very tender, about 50 minutes. Reserve 3 cups of the cooking liquid, then drain the beans and discard the bay leaf; set aside.

2. Meanwhile, make the pasta dough: In a food processor, combine the tofu, oil, and salt with ½ cup water, and purée until smooth. Transfer the mixture to a bowl and set aside. Wipe out the bowl of the food processor and add the bread flour, all-purpose flour, and pepper, and pulse a few times to combine. Return the tofu mixture to the food processor and process until a dough forms, 15 to 30 seconds.

3. Turn the dough out onto a lightly floured surface and gather it into a ball. Knead the dough while rotating it in quarter-turns until smooth and no longer sticky, about 1 minute. Wrap in plastic and let sit at room temperature for 30 minutes or refrigerate for up to 3 days.

4. Make the butternut squash filling: Preheat the oven to 375°F. Toss the butternut squash with the oil, thyme, and salt, and arrange on a baking sheet in a single layer. Bake until tender, 25 to 30 minutes; set aside.

5. Finish the bean broth: Heat a large skillet over medium heat, add the oil, and heat until it just starts to shimmer. Add the onion and sweat until translucent, stirring frequently, about 5 minutes. Add the garlic, thyme, red pepper flakes, and the remaining ¾ teaspoon of salt and cook for 1 minute. Add the cooked beans and reserved cooking liquid (or, if you're using canned beans, the entire contents of both cans) and simmer for 2 minutes. Transfer to a blender and blend until the mixture is puréed but is still a bit chunky.

1 medium butternut squash, peeled, halved lengthwise, seeded, and cut into ¾-inch cubes

2 tablespoons extra-virgin olive oil

1 teaspoon fresh thyme leaves

¼ teaspoon fine sea salt

½ batch Pepita Blue Cheese Spread (page 68), or 2 cups store-bought dairy-free blue cheese

1 batch Pickled Onions (page 67)

6. Bring a large pot of salted water to a boil. Lightly grease a baking sheet with oil and set up your pasta machine. On a lightly floured surface, divide the pasta dough into 4 equal portions. Working with 1 portion at a time (while keeping others covered with a damp kitchen towel), pass the dough through the floured pasta machine until it reaches a ⅛-inch thickness, or alternatively, roll it out using a rolling pin. When using a pasta machine, start with the rollers at the widest setting. Form the dough into a rectangular shape and insert it, using the shortest side of the rectangle slab, through the machine. After the dough has come through the rollers, fold it in thirds, and pass it through the rollers again. Roll the dough through the machine 3 times at the widest setting (continuing to lightly flour the dough with each pass). Then adjust the rollers to the next narrow setting, and repeat the process (no need to fold the pasta into thirds at this point). Repeat until you've reached the narrowest setting on the pasta machine and the dough is ⅛ inch thick (there are usually 7 to 10 settings on a machine, so you'll likely pass it through that many times).

7. Using a sharp knife, slice each sheet widthwise into 3- to 4-inch-square pieces. Boil the pasta in batches until al dente, 2 to 3 minutes. Transfer the cooked pasta to the prepared baking sheet and drizzle lightly with oil to prevent it from sticking. Continue with the rest of the sheets.

8. To serve, dollop a few tablespoons of the blue cheese in the center of each pasta sheet, top with some roasted butternut squash, and roll it up. Ladle some puréed bean broth mixture in a shallow dish, place the cannelloni on top, and finish with Pickled Onions.

CHAPTER 7

Weekday Breakfasts

Blueberry Beet Smoothie

SERVES 2

THE WOODY TEXTURE OF raw beets gives this scrumptious smoothie a naturally pulpy texture, which we think of as an added fiber bonus. For an extra-smooth smoothie, strain it through a fine-mesh sieve.

1½ cups coconut water

1 small red beet, scrubbed, peeled, and cut into small pieces

1 apple, cored and cut into chunks

½ cup frozen blueberries

¼ cup frozen pitted cherries

2 tablespoons shelled hemp seeds

1 to 2 teaspoons fresh lime juice (from about ½ lime)

¼ teaspoon freshly grated ginger

¼ to ½ cup ice

Put all the ingredients in a blender, starting with the coconut water, and purée until smooth, about 1 minute. Taste and add more ice if an icier texture is desired. Divide among 2 glasses and enjoy immediately.

CHEF'S TIP: If you don't have a high-powered blender, you may want to steam the beet before blending for a creamier consistency.

Chocolate-Hazelnut Smoothie

SERVES 2

GOT OVERLY RIPE BANANAS on your counter? Banana bread is not the only answer. Instead, slice the peeled bananas into 1-inch pieces, wrap them in plastic, and freeze. Frozen bananas are the perfect base for indulgent smoothies like this one, thanks to their creamy texture and natural sweetness. Plus: They eliminate the need to water down your smoothie with ice.

2 cups unsweetened dairy-free milk

2 frozen bananas

¾ cup roasted, skinned hazelnuts

2 tablespoons shelled hemp seeds

2 tablespoons cocoa powder

1 teaspoon pure vanilla extract

1 pitted Medjool date, or 1 tablespoon maple syrup (optional)

½ to 1 cup ice (optional)

Put all the ingredients in a blender, starting with the milk, and purée until smooth, about 1 minute. Taste and add ice if an icier texture is desired. Divide among 2 glasses and enjoy immediately.

*may be (S) or (N) depending on the milk

Tropical Green Smoothie

SERVES 2

Making smoothies at home allows you to control the quality of your ingredients (think organic and natural!), as well as the amount of added sugar, which in this case is none. The pineapple and mango give a natural sweetness, and adding oats, seeds, and/or avocado to your smoothies takes them from snack to meal territory. Oats are a great source of fiber and protein, which help you feel full longer. Hemp seeds (sometimes labeled "hemp hearts") and avocado are both high in healthy fats, which also help keep you feeling satiated. You're getting a lot in one glass here, plus a sweet and refreshing start to your day. Feel free to switch out the spinach for kale and the mango for bananas.

2 cups coconut water

2 cups cubed pineapple
(about ½ medium pineapple)

2 cups packed baby spinach

1 mango, peeled, cored, and cubed

1 ripe avocado, peeled, halved, and pitted

½ cup old-fashioned rolled oats

4 teaspoons shelled hemp seeds

½ teaspoon ground turmeric

1 to 2 cups ice

Put all the ingredients in a blender, starting with the coconut water, and purée until smooth, about 1 minute. Taste and add more ice if an icier texture is desired. Divide among 2 glasses and enjoy immediately.

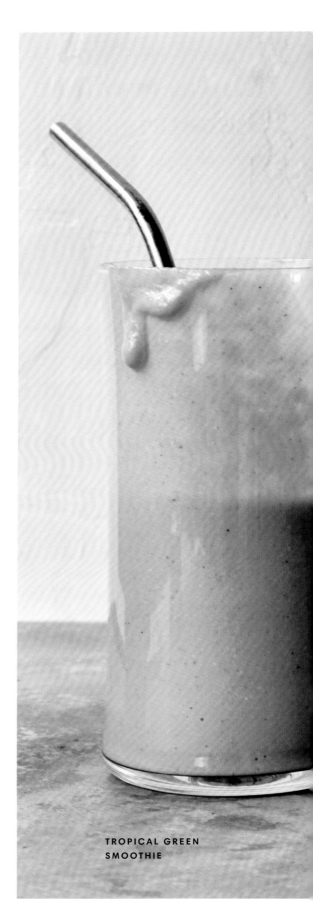

TROPICAL GREEN
SMOOTHIE

CHEF'S TIP: To make weekday mornings easy, cut up the fruits, portion out the ingredients (minus the coconut water and ice), divide among freezer-safe containers or bags, and freeze until ready for use. Simply add your liquid, ice, and blend— breakfast is ready.

BLUEBERRY BEET SMOOTHIE
page 253

CHOCOLATE-HAZELNUT SMOOTHIE
page 253

Finding Balance with Intuitive Eating BY CHEF JILL BURNS AND CHEF ELLIOTT PRAG

One of the school's principal tenets—balance—suggests that no one diet or approach (vegetarian, vegan, paleo, etc.) is inherently better or healthier than another. Instead, it emphasizes that too much or too little of any one food can create cravings or another imbalance, which reflects the innate intelligence of our bodies. When you listen to your body, it will tell you what, how, and when to eat. This is intuitive eating: forging a stronger relationship between your food choices and their effects on your well-being.

No one knows your body better than you. Intuitive eaters know that true intuition only exists in the present. Thinking about food as "right" versus "wrong" or "good" versus "bad" removes us from the present and robs us of insight and freedom. By contrast, the intuitive eater listens to what the body is communicating in the moment: Does this food make me feel nourished? Grounded? Satiated? How does this food affect my mood? My energy? Do I have enough energy for my activities and appropriate mental focus and clarity?

Intuitive eaters quiet the barrage of conflicting dietary chatter in their minds, recognizing that fad diets and trends often offer false or misleading claims. Embracing intuition in eating involves an integration of mind, body, and spirit—in short, a more holistic approach to eating.

Intuitive eating accesses right-brain input (intuition) to enhance left-brain input (logic). We use the sensory aspects of eating—quality, color, texture, flavor, aroma, how food makes us feel—to balance and inform left-brain concepts, such as measurements, calories, and macro- and micronutrient content. Eating whole foods as nature provides them, with all their edible parts intact, unifies our knowledge, perceptions, and intuition about food. The balance of sweet, salty, sour, and savory flavors, plus a variety of textures, such as creamy or crunchy, can keep our palates satisfied. For example, if you drink sweet smoothies for three meals a day, you may find yourself craving something crunchy or salty.

Honoring and enjoying the process of eating also makes a difference in your relationship with food. Sitting down to meals without the distraction of phones, laptops, or TV, and taking adequate time to eat and chew food thoroughly can facilitate and enhance intuition. These practices also create a more fulfilling experience of eating, digestion, and satiety.

Intuitive eating is challenging in a society whose heavy focus is on dieting and rigid rules about eating. Remember that intuition is fluid: Your food choices over time change and evolve, just as you do.

Amaranth Porridge

with Ginger Peaches and Pistachios

SERVES 4 TO 6

FOR THE PORRIDGE

1 cup amaranth, soaked for
at least 6 hours or overnight

1½ cups unsweetened
dairy-free milk

¼ teaspoon fine sea salt

⅓ cup roasted shelled pistachios,
coarsely chopped

FOR THE PEACHES

3 ripe peaches (about 1½ pounds),
halved, pitted, and thinly sliced

1 tablespoon fresh lemon juice
(from about ½ lemon)

1 tablespoon maple syrup, maple
crystals, or another sweetener
of your choice

¼ teaspoon ground ginger

Pinch of fine sea salt

WE PREFER TO STEER clear of the term *superfood*—because, in our opinion, all plant-based whole foods are super!—so we'll just say that amaranth, a gluten-free grain that also happens to be a complete protein, is a really good option for breakfast, or any meal, really. Its nutty flavor and slightly viscous texture make it a great base for roasted nuts and fruit. For the topping, use the best peaches you can find—preferably local ones when they're in season. In the colder months, serve the porridge with pear sauce (page 126) instead.

1. Drain the amaranth in a nut milk bag or fine-mesh sieve lined with cheesecloth and put the grains in a medium pot. Add the milk, salt, and 1½ cups of water. Cover, bring to a boil over high heat, reduce the heat to low, and simmer until the grains are chewy and no starchy aftertaste remains, stirring frequently to keep it from sticking to the bottom, about 30 minutes. If the porridge starts to look dry, stir in another ½ cup of water.

2. Meanwhile, prepare the peaches: In a large saucepan, combine the peaches, lemon juice, maple syrup, ginger, and salt. Place over medium-low heat and bring to a gentle simmer. Cook until the peaches are soft and syrupy, about 5 minutes. Taste and adjust the seasonings if needed.

3. Divide the amaranth among bowls and top with the warm peaches and pistachios.

CHEF'S TIP: The amaranth can be made up to 4 days in advance. Reheat it on the stove with a splash of liquid to reconstitute it to its original consistency.

Spiced Overnight Muesli

with Pecans and Pomegranate Seeds

SERVES 4

2 cups dairy-free yogurt

1 cup dairy-free milk

2 tablespoons maple syrup

¼ teaspoon ground cinnamon

⅛ teaspoon ground cardamom

Pinch of fine sea salt

1 cup old-fashioned rolled oats

¼ cup flaxseed meal

¼ cup toasted unsweetened coconut flakes

1 apple, cored and coarsely grated

½ cup coarsely chopped toasted pecans (see page 56)

⅓ cup fresh pomegranate seeds

PACKED WITH WHOLE FRESH fruits, seeds, and nuts, this version of muesli, also known as bircher muesli, offers a health-supportive start to the day. This preparation hails back to the early 1900s when a Swiss doctor developed this way of eating oats to get more raw fruit and fiber into his patients' diets. And this recipe does exactly that—the ingredients are left whole, unlike most store-bought cereals whose ingredients are processed and stripped of their nutrition, which is then added back in as fortified vitamins and minerals. More than anything, we like this bowl of goodness for its varying tastes and textures, which partially result from soaking the oats and fruit overnight. The grains soften, and together with the pecans and pomegranate, satisfy morning cravings for crunch, creaminess, and even a bit of sweetness. The end result is a bit like a granola pudding.

1. In a medium bowl, whisk together the yogurt, milk, maple syrup, cinnamon, cardamom, and salt. Stir in the oats, flaxseed, coconut, and apple. Cover the bowl and chill for several hours or overnight.

2. Stir the muesli before serving and divide it among 4 bowls. Sprinkle with the pecans and pomegranate, and serve.

Vanilla-Balsamic Buckwheat Granola

with Dried Cherries

MAKES 6 CUPS

½ cup maple syrup

¼ cup melted coconut oil

3 tablespoons balsamic vinegar

2 tablespoons pure vanilla extract

1 teaspoon almond extract (optional)

¾ teaspoon fine sea salt

1 cup raw buckwheat groats

1 cup old-fashioned rolled oats

1 cup sliced almonds

½ cup quinoa

¼ cup chia seeds

1 cup dried cherries

GRANOLA MAY BE CRUNCHY by default, but this recipe really ups the ante on the texture front. While buckwheat groats and quinoa are partially responsible, the other element that contributes to this highly satisfying crunch is baking the granola using the "low-and-slow" method. Whereas many granolas are baked around 375°F for 20 minutes or so, this one roasts at a lower temperature for a longer period, which allows the ingredients to dehydrate. The balsamic vinegar coats the grains, giving them a darker hue and lending a sweet-and-sour flavor to the granola. If you don't have dried cherries, use dried cranberries instead.

1. Preheat the oven to 225°F. Line a baking sheet with parchment paper.

2. In a large bowl, whisk together the maple syrup, oil, balsamic vinegar, vanilla, almond extract (if using), and salt. In a separate bowl, combine the buckwheat, oats, almonds, quinoa, and chia seeds. Using a rubber spatula, stir the buckwheat mixture into the maple syrup mixture to coat evenly.

3. Transfer to the prepared baking sheet and bake until golden, about 1 hour, stirring every 15 to 20 minutes during baking.

4. Toss in the cherries, and let cool. Store in an airtight container in a cool, dry place for up to 2 weeks.

Breakfast as Self-Care BY CHEF ANN NUNZIATA

Self-help expert Louise Hay said, "How you start your day is how you live your day. How you live your day is how you live your life."

If you are looking to eat more healthfully, but don't know how to begin, why not start from the moment you wake up? Eating a nutritious breakfast is a simple yet powerful form of self-care. After not eating all night, breakfast is the fuel that helps kick-start our metabolism, body, and mind into functioning optimally throughout the day. Research also shows that eating a satisfying breakfast can tame mindless snacking between meals and help maintain a healthy weight. Lastly, since we can't always predict how and when our lunch and dinner will happen, breakfast is the perfect opportunity to do right by our bodies. Here are a few tips for adding a self-care breakfast to your routine.

PLAN AHEAD: Decide what your breakfast will be before you go to bed. The night before, tidy up your kitchen and check that you have your ingredients on hand—you can even place them on your counter so everything is ready to go. The last thing you need in the morning is another problem to solve.

START HYDRATED: Upon getting up, have a glass of water. We all wake up experiencing some level of dehydration. During sleep, our bodies are busy repairing muscles and other tissues; a tall glass of water is the first thing our bodies need. It can be room temperature, warm, or cool, depending on what you enjoy. If you had a heavy meal the night before, add a splash of lemon juice or raw apple cider vinegar to refresh your digestive system.

MAKE IT COUNT: A nourishing breakfast will put you on the right track for the whole day. If you find yourself running on caffeine alone, polishing off a glazed doughnut, or skipping breakfast altogether, you may find it impossible to resist cravings for sweet or rich foods throughout the rest of the day. A balanced, whole-foods meal should include carbohydrates (from fruit or whole grains), as well as protein (from legumes), and fat (from nuts, seeds, or avocados). Check the labels of your cereals and pastries, which may be mostly refined carbohydrates and chemicals; their high sugar content will give you a quick surge of energy followed by a plummeting crash an hour or so later.

KEEP IT SIMPLE: Toast, smoothies, and oatmeal are all quick and easy to make. You can also get creative and repurpose leftovers from last night's dinner. Warm up brown rice with some milk, ginger, and a spoonful of agave syrup for an instant rice pudding, or mash some cooked beans on sourdough toast.

MAKE IT FUN: Eat something that makes you happy and brings you comfort (i.e., don't suffer through an icy smoothie on a cold winter morning). Serve it in your favorite bowl or buy yourself a pretty mug. Eat outside or by a big window to get some natural light. Avoid checking your email or social media; instead, crack open an inspirational book or listen to a favorite podcast.

Savory Yogurt Bowl

with Roasted Carrots, Chickpeas, and Spiced Pumpkin Seeds

SERVES 4

2 large carrots (about 1 pound), peeled and cut into ¼-inch-thick half-moons

1 (15-ounce) can chickpeas, drained, rinsed, and patted dry

2 tablespoons plus ½ teaspoon extra-virgin olive oil, plus more for drizzling

1 teaspoon ground fennel

¾ teaspoon garlic powder

½ teaspoon ground cumin

½ teaspoon fine sea salt

Freshly ground black pepper to taste

½ cup hulled pumpkin seeds

¼ teaspoon smoked paprika

2 cups dairy-free yogurt

¼ cup cilantro leaves, for serving

Zest of 1 lime, for serving

Lime wedges, for serving (optional)

MOST OF US ARE well-versed in the concept of a yogurt bowl with fresh fruit and sweet, crunchy granola. But the idea of a savory yogurt bowl is a little less common. We love the combination of cooling yogurt, sweet carrots, and crunchy, spiced pumpkin seeds (also called pepitas). Feel free to roast the carrots and chickpeas, and toast the pumpkin seeds, in advance for a speedy assembly on busy mornings. Make this savory breakfast extra special by toasting whole fennel and cumin seeds and grinding them yourself (see page 56). You may also switch out the carrots for sweet potatoes, parsnips, or butternut squash.

1. Preheat the oven to 400°F. On a large baking sheet, combine the carrots and chickpeas. Add 2 tablespoons of oil, the fennel, ½ teaspoon of garlic powder, cumin, ¼ teaspoon of salt, and a pinch of pepper. Toss to coat evenly. Spread the mixture into an even layer and bake until the carrots are lightly browned and some chickpeas are starting to split, tossing occasionally, about 25 minutes. Set aside.

2. Meanwhile, put the pumpkin seeds in a small skillet and toast over a medium-low heat until they start gently crackling, are slightly puffy, and smell nutty, tossing occasionally, about 4 minutes. Turn the heat off. Add the remaining ½ teaspoon of oil and toss to coat the seeds. Season with the paprika, the remaining ¼ teaspoon of garlic powder, and the remaining ¼ teaspoon of salt. Toss to combine.

3. To serve, divide yogurt among 4 bowls, top with about ½ cup of the carrot mixture, the spiced pumpkin seeds, cilantro, and lime. Drizzle with oil and serve with lime wedges, if desired.

Weekday Rice Flour Pancakes

with Caramelized Bananas

SERVES 4 (G) (S) (N)

2 cups brown rice flour

2 tablespoons flaxseed meal

1 tablespoon plus 1¾ teaspoons baking powder

2 teaspoons maple crystals, coconut sugar, or organic raw sugar

1 teaspoon sea salt

2¼ cups unsweetened dairy-free milk

About ¼ cup melted coconut oil

1 teaspoon pure vanilla extract

2 bananas, cut into ⅓-inch-thick rounds

2 tablespoons maple syrup, plus more to serve (optional)

CHEF'S TIP: Be sure to form small, thin pancakes when adding the batter to the skillet—otherwise they won't cook through. And be patient while they're cooking—they need a full 2 to 3 minutes per side to become golden brown.

THESE CRISP, GLUTEN-FREE PANCAKES could not be any easier to make. The rice flour lends a slightly nutty taste and chewier texture, but the pancakes' flavor is not that different from their classic all-purpose-flour counterparts. Their light, airy texture makes them a blank canvas for myriad toppings, and the complete opposite of those giant weekend flapjacks you need a nap after eating.

1. In a large bowl, whisk together the flour, flaxseed meal, baking powder, maple crystals, and salt. In another bowl, whisk together the milk, 2 teaspoons of coconut oil, and vanilla. Stir the wet ingredients into the dry just until combined.

2. Heat a large nonstick skillet over medium-low heat and add enough oil to lightly coat the bottom. Add scant ¼ cup scoop of the batter to the skillet (you should hear sizzling), making 2 or 3 small, thin pancakes at a time. Cook until the pancakes start to look dry on top and lightly golden on the bottom, 2 to 3 minutes, then flip and cook until the other side is browned, an additional 2 to 3 minutes. Transfer the pancakes to a platter and continue cooking the rest of the batter, adding more oil to the skillet as needed. (You'll end up with about 8 to 10 pancakes.)

3. After cooking the rest of the batter, wipe down the skillet with a paper towel, and return to medium-low heat. Add 2 tablespoons of oil and place the bananas in the skillet in a single layer. Cook until the bananas are golden-brown, about 1 minute, flip, and cook until the other side is browned, about 1 minute more. Drizzle in the maple syrup, if using, and cook until bananas start to become sticky and shiny, about 1 minute.

4. Serve the pancakes topped with bananas.

Tomato Tofu Scramble

SERVES 4

1 pound firm tofu, drained

3 tablespoons extra-virgin olive oil

1 small yellow onion, finely chopped

2 tablespoons pine nuts

1 garlic clove, minced

½ teaspoon ground cumin

½ teaspoon ground turmeric

¼ teaspoon dried red pepper flakes

1 large ripe tomato, seeded and diced

1 teaspoon fine sea salt, or to taste

2 tablespoons fresh lime juice (from 1 to 2 limes)

Whole-wheat toast, to serve (optional)

CRUMBLED TOFU GETS A golden yellow glow thanks to a spoonful of turmeric in this vegan take on scrambled eggs. We pair tofu with tomatoes, but it can be cooked up with almost any vegetable, such as leftover roasted potatoes, sautéed mushrooms, or roasted bell peppers. For a fluffier scramble, we recommend pressing the tofu prior to crumbling it to remove excess water—this takes about 20 minutes of inactive time. If you're in a pinch, you can skip the pressing step for a less defined, slightly softer-textured scramble.

1. Line a plate with paper towels and place the tofu on top. Place another paper towel on the tofu then top with another plate. Weigh it down with cans or pie weights for 20 to 30 minutes to remove excess water, draining off the water periodically. Using a fork or your hands, crumble the tofu into small bits.

2. Heat a medium skillet over medium heat, add the oil, and heat until it just starts to shimmer. Add the onion and cook until just softened, 2 to 3 minutes.

3. Stir in the pine nuts, garlic, cumin, turmeric, and red pepper flakes, and continue to cook until fragrant, about another 2 minutes.

4. Stir in the crumbled tofu, tomato, salt, and lime juice. Increase the heat to medium-high and cook until the tofu is heated through, about 5 minutes, stirring occasionally. Divide among plates and serve.

Rice Congee

with Ginger, Scallions, and Gomasio

SERVES 6

4 cups store-bought vegetable stock or homemade Carrot-Vegetable Stock (page 75)

1 cup Japanese sweet short-grain rice, soaked overnight and drained (see page 51)

2 teaspoons fine sea salt

1 cup raw sesame seeds

2 scallions (white and green parts), minced

1 tablespoon toasted sesame oil

½-inch piece of ginger, peeled and minced (about 1 teaspoon)

1 piece nori, sliced into thin strips

CHEF'S TIP: A *suribachi*, or mortar, used with a *surikogi*, or pestle, is often used for grinding sesame seeds in Japan. If you don't have a mortar and pestle to make the gomasio, you can use a spice grinder.

CONGEE IS A CREAMY rice porridge of Asian origin—a risotto of the East, if you will. It is made by simmering sweet short-grain rice in a large volume of liquid and stirring it frequently to release the starch. Served sweet or savory, this comforting dish is traditionally eaten for breakfast in China but works for any meal on chilly winter days. It's a good dish for those feeling under the weather or experiencing digestive issues, as it is easy on the stomach. It can take upwards of 2 hours from start to finish, but it may be kept in the refrigerator and reheated for breakfast throughout the week. Gomasio is a toasted sesame seed salt commonly used in macrobiotic cooking (see page 27); this mixture is believed to offer relief from motion sickness, general nausea, and even hangovers.

1. In a large pot, combine the stock, rice, and 1 teaspoon of salt. Cover and bring to a boil over medium heat. Reduce the heat to low and cook, covered, stirring frequently, until the rice is thick and creamy, 1½ to 2 hours.

2. Meanwhile, make the gomasio: In a medium skillet, toast the sesame seeds over medium-low heat until fragrant, tossing frequently and being careful not to burn them, 3 to 4 minutes. Transfer to a plate and let cool for a few minutes. Transfer the seeds to a *suribachi* (see Chef's Tip), add the remaining teaspoon of salt, and grind until about half of the seeds are powdered and the other half remain whole. Set aside.

3. Remove the congee from the heat, and stir in the scallions, oil, and ginger. Serve the congee in bowls sprinkled with nori and gomasio.

Raspberry Chia Jam

MAKES ABOUT 1½ CUPS

12 ounces raspberries

2 tablespoons maple syrup

¼ teaspoon lemon zest

1 tablespoon fresh lemon juice
(from about ½ lemon)

1 teaspoon pure vanilla extract

2 tablespoons chia seeds

THIS QUICK SUMMER JAM is a great way to utilize the abundance of local berries in early summer, especially if you subscribe to a CSA. Note that you may have to adjust the amount of lemon juice and maple syrup, based on the fruits' inherent sugar-acid balance. The chia seeds help the jam thicken and also add fiber and various minerals. Serve the jam over Light and Crisp Gluten-Free Belgian Waffles (page 281), Weekday Rice Flour Pancakes (page 264), or on Spelt Bread (page 286) with coconut butter.

1. In a small saucepan, combine the raspberries, maple syrup, lemon zest and juice, and vanilla. Bring to a simmer over medium heat, crushing the berries with a fork to help release the juices. Reduce the heat to low and simmer until the liquid reduces a bit, stirring occasionally, 5 to 7 minutes. Taste and add more lemon juice or maple syrup, if needed. Stir in the chia seeds and turn the heat off.

2. Set the jam aside to come to room temperature, about 30 minutes. Transfer to a medium bowl and chill in the fridge until the jam thickens, about 1 hour. The jam will keep in the fridge in an airtight container for up to 10 days.

Weekend Brunches

Fried Cornmeal Squares

with Steamed Greens

SERVES 4

WE ARE BIG FANS of cornmeal for its versatility. Ground corn can be used for baking and thickening stews, and cooked on its own to make polenta. Here we form a loaf using cooked cornmeal that we cut into squares and fry until it's lightly browned. There's something very satisfying about the mildy sweet, soft grain, especially after it's seared to form a nice crispy crust—a definite comfort food. Because you can prep it in advance, this dish is great to serve for brunch. You can make the cornmeal loaf the night before, and trim and wash the greens, too. You can even get the table set. The following day, heat up the cornmeal squares and greens shortly before guests arrive, and keep them warm in the oven on a baking sheet, covered with foil.

FOR THE CORNMEAL SQUARES

½ teaspoon fine sea salt

1 cup coarse cornmeal

3 tablespoons canola oil, or more as needed

FOR THE STEAMED GREENS

4 cups dandelion greens, trimmed and washed

1 to 2 teaspoons shoyu or tamari to taste

1 teaspoon fresh lemon juice

Fine sea salt to taste

Freshly ground pepper to taste

*if using tamari

> **CHEF'S TIP:** If dandelion greens aren't in season, try Swiss chard or spinach.

1. Line a 9 × 5-inch loaf pan with a piece of parchment so it hangs over the long sides. In a medium pot, bring 3½ cups of water and the salt to a boil over medium-high heat. While continually whisking, gradually add the cornmeal in a steady stream, continuing to whisk until smooth and no lumps remain, about 2 minutes. Cover, reduce the heat to low, and cook, stirring occasionally, until the mixture is thick, creamy, and no longer has a raw grainy taste, about 20 minutes. Scrape the cooked cornmeal into the prepared pan, cover with plastic wrap, and chill in the refrigerator until a solid loaf forms, at least 1 hour or up to 24 hours.

2. Cut the cornmeal loaf into ½-inch slices crosswise. Heat a medium skillet over medium-high heat, add the oil, and heat until it just starts to shimmer. Gently slide the polenta into the hot oil, being careful not to overcrowd the pan, and cook until crispy and golden-brown, 4 to 5 minutes, then flip and crisp up the other side, 4 to 5 minutes more, adding more oil as needed if the pan becomes dry. Be patient and don't flip the squares too soon to ensure that each side browns.

3. Meanwhile, steam the greens: Place the slightly wet greens (still damp from washing them) in a medium pot. Cover and place over medium-low heat. Steam until wilted, 2 to 3 minutes.

4. Turn off the heat and sprinkle with the shoyu, lemon juice, salt, and pepper.

5. Transfer the greens to a platter and serve warm with cornmeal squares.

Chickpea Crepes

with Curry Filling and Mango Sauce

SERVES 6

FOR THE CREPES

1 cup chickpea flour

1 cup unbleached all-purpose flour

1 teaspoon fine sea salt

¼ teaspoon finely ground black pepper

1½ cups warm water, or more as needed

1 tablespoon chopped fresh chives

1 tablespoon chopped fresh cilantro leaves

2 tablespoons extra-virgin olive oil or coconut oil, plus more for greasing the pan

FOR THE CURRY FILLING

2 tablespoons coconut oil

1 medium onion, cut into small dice

1 tablespoon Madras curry powder

2 medium carrots, cut into small dice

1 medium potato, peeled and cut into small dice

2 large garlic cloves, minced

1 teaspoon fine sea salt

½ cup store-bought vegetable stock, homemade Carrot-Onion Stock (page 75), or water

1 (13.5-ounce) can full-fat coconut milk

1 cup cooked or canned chickpeas (see page 54)

2 small bunches of spinach (about 1 pound), stemmed and coarsely chopped

ELEGANT, CRISP, AND LACE-THIN, these savory pancakes are the perfect vessel for the fragrant coconut curry filling that gets wrapped inside. The slightly sweet mango sauce gives just the right balance to the chickpeas, which get a kick from a sprinkle of jalapeño. Sunny and bright, these crepes make a pretty presentation on the plate, too, which makes them ideal to serve as an alternative to pancakes or waffles for Sunday brunch.

1. Make the crepes: In a large bowl, whisk together the chickpea flour, all-purpose flour, salt, and pepper. Add the water, chives, cilantro, and coconut oil, and whisk until completely smooth (this may also be done in a blender). Allow the batter to rest at room temperature for at least 30 minutes or up to 1 hour. After resting, the batter should be the consistency of light cream; if necessary, thin with a bit more water.

2. While the batter rests, make the curry filling: Heat a large skillet over medium-low heat, add the coconut oil, and heat until it just starts to shimmer. Add the onion and sweat, stirring frequently, until translucent, about 4 minutes. Add the curry powder and cook until fragrant, about 2 more minutes.

3. Add the carrots and potato, stirring often to prevent sticking (the mixture will be dry). Continue to sweat until the vegetables are starting to soften, about 5 minutes. Add the garlic and salt, and cook for 1 more minute.

4. Add the stock, coconut milk, and chickpeas, increase the heat to high, and bring the mixture to a boil. Reduce the heat to low and simmer until the potato pieces are fork-tender, about 8 minutes. Add the spinach, in 2 or 3 batches if necessary, and stir to combine, cooking just until wilted, about 2 minutes. Taste and season with salt, if needed. The mixture should be spoonable and creamy; if it looks too thick, add a bit more stock.

5. Make the sauce: In a blender, combine the mango, tomatoes, shallot, canola oil, lime juice, and salt. Blend until smooth. Taste and adjust the seasonings, if needed.

ingredients and recipe continue

1 ripe mango, peeled, pitted, and coarsely chopped

2 ripe plum tomatoes, coarsely chopped

1 shallot, coarsely chopped

2 tablespoons canola or another neutral oil

2 to 3 teaspoons fresh lime juice (from about ½ lime)

1 teaspoon fine sea salt

1 or 2 jalapeño peppers, seeded and minced

3 tablespoons fresh cilantro leaves, chopped

6. Cook the crepes: Lightly oil a crepe pan or a small nonstick pan, and place over medium heat. Pour in about ¼ cup of the batter, tilting the pan so the batter evenly covers the bottom. Cook until the crepe is golden-brown on the bottom, about 30 seconds, then flip and cook until browned on the other side, another 30 seconds or so. Stack the cooked crepes on a plate and lightly cover them with a kitchen towel while you cook the remainder of the batter.

7. To serve, divide the filling among the crepes and gently roll them up. Top with the mango sauce and sprinkle with jalapeño and cilantro. Serve hot.

Orange Currant Drop Scones

MAKES 10 SCONES

1 cup whole-wheat pastry flour

1 cup unbleached all-purpose flour

3 tablespoons maple crystals, coconut sugar, or turbinado sugar

1 tablespoon baking powder

1 tablespoon orange zest (from 2 oranges)

½ teaspoon fine sea salt

7 tablespoons cold, solid virgin or refined coconut oil (see Chef's Tip)

¼ cup dried currants

¾ cup unsweetened dairy-free milk

CHEF'S TIP: To get the oil appropriately cold, you may place it in the freezer for a few minutes.

THE DOUGH FOR THESE scones is the sweet version of our Peppery Biscuits (page 278). Instead of rolling out and folding the dough several times, these scones take the hassle-free route of simply being dropped onto a baking sheet, resulting in a more free-form appearance. Feel free to use lemon zest instead of orange, as well as other dried fruits like cranberries or chopped apricots.

1. Preheat the oven to 375°F. Line a baking sheet with parchment paper and set aside.

2. In a food processor, combine the whole-wheat and all-purpose flours, maple crystals, baking powder, orange zest, and salt, and pulse to combine. Add the coconut oil and pulse until the fat is crumbly and coated in flour, 8 to 10 times (the crumbles should be about the size of small peas). Transfer the mixture to a large bowl and toss in the currants. Using a rubber spatula, gently toss the mixture while gradually adding the milk just until a shaggy dough forms, being careful to not overmix the dough.

3. Drop large spoonfuls of the dough onto the prepared baking sheet, making about 10 scones and setting them about 1 inch apart. Bake until lightly golden, 15 to 20 minutes. Transfer to a cooling rack to cool slightly. These scones are best served warm.

Peppery Biscuits

with Mushroom Gravy

SERVES 4 Ⓢ* Ⓝ*

HERE IS A VEGAN riff on the classic Southern breakfast of biscuits and gravy. The biscuits are made with coconut oil instead of butter, and cremini mushrooms and almond milk are used in place of sausage and cream in the peppery gravy (feel free to use your favorite dairy-free milk here in place of the almond!). These biscuits are best eaten warm, straight out of the oven, while they are still airy on the inside and crisp on the outside. Be sure to thoroughly brown the mushrooms before adding the liquid, as caramelizing brings out their natural umami.

FOR THE BISCUITS

1 cup whole-wheat pastry flour

1 cup unbleached all-purpose flour, plus more for dusting

1 tablespoon baking powder

¾ teaspoon fine sea salt

¼ teaspoon coarsely ground black pepper

7 tablespoons cold, solid refined coconut oil (see Chef's Tip, page 277)

¾ cup unsweetened almond milk or other dairy-free milk

FOR THE GRAVY

3 tablespoons extra-virgin olive oil

1 medium shallot, finely diced

¼ teaspoon fine sea salt, or more to taste

1 medium garlic clove, minced

¼ teaspoon fennel seeds

10 ounces cremini mushrooms, finely diced

1 tablespoon plus 1 teaspoon unbleached all-purpose flour

1 cup store-bought mushroom or vegetable stock, or homemade Brown Vegetable Stock (page 76)

1 cup unsweetened almond milk or other dairy-free milk

Coarsely ground black pepper to taste

2 tablespoons chopped chives

1. Preheat the oven to 375°F. Line a baking sheet with parchment paper and set aside.

2. Make the biscuits: Sift the whole-wheat and all-purpose flours, baking powder, and salt into a medium bowl. Add the pepper and whisk to combine. Transfer to a food processor, add the coconut oil, and pulse until the fat is crumbly and coated in flour, 8 to 10 times (the crumbles should be about the size of small peas). Transfer the mixture back to the bowl and sprinkle in the almond milk. Using a rubber spatula, gently toss the mixture just until a shaggy dough forms, being careful not to overmix.

3. Transfer the dough to a lightly floured surface and gather it into a disk. Gently roll it out into a 12-inch long, ¼-inch-thick rectangle, dusting the surface of the rolling pin with more flour if the dough is sticky. With the long edge facing you, fold in the short ends to meet in the middle and then fold the dough one more time in half (see Chef's Tip, page 280). Gently roll to a ¾-inch thickness and fold the short ends to meet in the middle. Roll again into a ¾-inch-thick rectangle and cut the dough into 12 squares. Transfer to the prepared baking sheet, placing the biscuits about 1 inch apart.

4. Bake for 6 minutes, then rotate the pan and continue baking until the biscuits are lightly golden, 10 to 12 minutes more. Transfer the biscuits to a cooling rack.

5. Meanwhile, make the gravy: Heat a large skillet over medium-low heat, add 1 tablespoon of olive oil, and heat until it just starts to shimmer. Add the shallot and salt, and sweat, stirring occasionally, until softened, 2 to 3 minutes. Add the garlic and fennel and cook until fragrant, 1 minute more. Increase the heat to medium-high and add the remaining 2 tablespoons of olive oil and the mushrooms. Cook, stirring occasionally, until the mushrooms are fragrant and browned all over, 5 to 7 minutes.

*can be Ⓢ or Ⓝ depending on the milk

recipe continues

6. Add the flour and stir to incorporate. Add the stock and stir to deglaze the skillet. Simmer until the sauce thickens a bit, about 1 minute. Then add the milk and return to a simmer. Reduce the heat to low and cook, stirring frequently, until the sauce thickens, 3 to 5 minutes. Taste and season with more salt, if needed. Finish the gravy with a few pinches of pepper.

7. Split the biscuits in half widthwise and divide them among 4 plates. Divide the gravy among the plates. Sprinkle with chives and extra black pepper, if desired.

Food Is Community

One of our goals in writing this book was to inspire people to "eat food, not nutrients." What we mean is this: People often get so caught up with consuming specific nutrients or "superfoods," they begin to see food as fuel and lose sight of all the other facets of the rituals of eating. While food is certainly about nourishment, it's also about joy, gratitude, celebration, culture, and community.

Ever since fire was first discovered, people have been gathering around it—to connect, exchange stories, celebrate, mourn, and to cook and share food. Breaking bread with friends and neighbors is an undeniably powerful means of strengthening interpersonal bonds. In fact, the French word for "friend," *copain*, literally translates to someone you share bread with.

Oftentimes when people embark on the path to a healthier lifestyle, they feel they have to give up many of their favorite foods—and food rituals—in order to achieve their health goals. However, that doesn't have to be the case. If forsaking certain foods means saying no to a work party, a taco night with friends, or your aunt's famous pumpkin pie, can you really call that "healthy"? Or, more importantly, will you feel good about making that choice? Arguably not. Because food is about more than just fuel and nutrients—it's about togetherness.

If you think of your food choices throughout your entire lifetime as a whole, a beloved indulgence here and there is unlikely to derail your long-term health goals. So next time you're at a birthday party, remember that a slice of cake can be part of a healthy diet, too.

Light and Crisp Gluten-Free Belgian Waffles

SERVES 4

3 tablespoons flaxseed meal or ground chia seeds

1¾ cups store-bought gluten-free flour mix

2 teaspoons baking powder

½ teaspoon fine sea salt

2 tablespoons plus 1 teaspoon maple crystals, coconut sugar, or turbinado sugar

1¼ cups full-fat canned coconut milk

¼ cup melted coconut oil, plus more for greasing the waffle iron

1 teaspoon pure vanilla extract

SPECIAL EQUIPMENT

Waffle iron

OUR GOLDEN GLUTEN-FREE WAFFLES are the perfect blank canvas for myriad toppings—whether sweet (like the ginger peaches on page 257) or savory (looking at you, Shiitake Crumble [page 72]). There are many gluten-free flour mixes on the market today, and as with all products, some are better than others—some result in a grainy texture while others have a strong nutty flavor. It's best to test a few until you find one you like. For this recipe, you'll find the best success using a 1:1 gluten-free substitute for all-purpose flour.

1. Put the flaxseed meal in a small bowl, stir in 9 tablespoons of water, and set aside for 10 minutes, or until thickened.

2. Meanwhile, in a large bowl, whisk together the flour, baking powder, salt, and maple crystals. In a separate bowl, whisk together the milk, oil, vanilla, and flaxseed mixture. Stir the wet ingredients into the dry ingredients until the batter is smooth.

3. Preheat a waffle iron and cook the batter according to the manufacturer's instructions until golden and crispy, about 5 minutes (if it feels like the waffles are stuck when you try to open the iron, continue cooking them for another minute or two.) Repeat with the rest of the batter, keeping the waffles warm in a low-temperature oven, if desired.

Sweet Potato Waffles

SERVES 4

1 large sweet potato, peeled and cut into large chunks

1 cup plus 2 tablespoons whole-wheat pastry flour

2 tablespoons cornmeal

2 tablespoons maple crystals, coconut sugar, or turbinado sugar

1 teaspoon baking powder

½ teaspoon fine sea salt

3 tablespoons flaxseed meal

¾ cup dairy-free milk

¼ cup melted coconut oil, plus more for the waffle iron

Maple syrup, for serving (optional)

SPECIAL EQUIPMENT

Waffle iron

IS THERE ANYTHING THAT says, "It's the weekend!" more than a batch of waffles sizzling away in the iron? The smell of these crispy waffles is so irresistible, you'll have zero trouble getting your family out of bed on Saturday morning. These waffles are light, airy, and moist inside. The gentle aroma of the sweet potato lends just enough sweetness that you don't even need to serve them with syrup.

1. Put the sweet potato chunks into a small pot, cover with water, and bring to a boil over high heat. Reduce the heat to low and simmer until the sweet potatoes are tender and can be easily pierced with a fork, about 15 minutes.

2. Meanwhile, in a medium bowl, whisk together the flour, cornmeal, maple crystals, baking powder, and salt. Set aside.

3. Put the flaxseed meal into a large bowl, stir in 9 tablespoons of water, and chill for about 10 minutes.

4. Drain the potatoes and mash with a fork until smooth (you may also use a food processor). Measure out ½ cup of the purée and save the rest for another use.

5. Add the sweet potato purée to the flax mixture along with the milk and oil and stir to combine. Add the flour mixture to the sweet potato mixture and gently stir until just combined.

6. Preheat a waffle iron, generously brush it with oil, and cook the batter according to the manufacturer's instructions until brown and very crispy, about 7 minutes.

CHEF'S TIPS: Use the leftover sweet potato purée in a smoothie, grain bowl, or sandwich.

You can double the recipe and freeze leftover waffles for up to a month. To reheat, pop them in the toaster or heat in an oven preheated to 350°F for about 8 minutes, or until crisp and warm.

Johnnycakes

(Cornmeal Pancakes)

MAKES TEN 4-INCH CAKES (S) (N)

1 tablespoon flaxseed meal

1 cup fine or medium-grind cornmeal

1 tablespoon maple crystals, coconut sugar, or turbinado sugar

¾ teaspoon fine sea salt

1 cup boiling water

½ cup dairy-free milk

2 tablespoons melted coconut oil, plus more for greasing the pan

½ cup whole-wheat pastry flour

2 teaspoons baking powder

ONCE UPON A TIME, johnnycakes, or cornmeal flatbreads, were to early North America what tortillas are to Central America—you could find people cooking these traditional cakes up and down the East Coast. Today there are debates over what a "real" johnnycake is, from the kind of corn used to the ratio of liquid to corn. We don't know that ours resemble the original johnnycakes, but we love our light and fluffy version that uses whole-wheat pastry flour in addition to the cornmeal for added whole grains. Be careful not to overmix the batter. You want to stir just until all the ingredients are incorporated. We like to serve with a drizzle of another North American favorite—maple syrup.

1. Put the flaxseed meal in a small bowl and stir in 3 tablespoons of water. Chill while you prepare the rest of the ingredients.

2. In a large bowl, whisk together the cornmeal, maple crystals, and salt. Gradually stir in the boiling water. Let stand for 10 minutes.

3. To the cornmeal, add the milk, coconut oil, and flaxseed mixture, and whisk to combine. In another bowl, whisk together the flour and baking powder and stir it into the cornmeal mixture with a few swift strokes.

4. Heat a large nonstick or cast-iron skillet over medium-low heat, add just enough oil to lightly coat the bottom, and heat until it just starts to shimmer (the pan should be hot enough that a drop of water sizzles in the pan). Add scant ¼ cup scoops of the batter to the skillet, making 2 or 3 pancakes at a time. Cook until the pancakes start to look dry around the edges and golden on the bottom, about 2 minutes, then flip and cook until the other side is browned, about 2 minutes more. Transfer the pancakes to a platter and continue cooking the rest of the batter, adding more oil to the skillet as needed.

Whole-Wheat Focaccia

MAKES ONE 10-INCH
ROUND LOAF (S) (N)

1 medium white potato, peeled and cut into large chunks

1 tablespoon active dry yeast

1 tablespoon brown rice syrup or maple syrup

½ cup whole-wheat bread flour

⅔ cup plus ½ cup warm water (about 110°F)

¼ cup extra-virgin olive oil, plus more for oiling the bowl and brushing on the bread

1 tablespoon fine sea salt

1 cup semolina flour

2 to 3 cups whole-wheat pastry flour

1 to 2 tablespoons coarsely chopped rosemary leaves

Flaky sea salt, for sprinkling

CHEF'S TIP: If you want to get fancy, serve the focaccia with rosemary oil (page 115) and a splash of balsamic vinegar.

WARM FROM THE OVEN, this soft and tender bread nearly melts in your mouth. In the Puglia region of Italy, using a potato in the dough is traditional to this style of bread, which makes the crumb moist, and allowing the dough to rise twice contributes to a finer texture. Adding olive oil to the dough gives it a delicate, almost fruity flavor. Be sure to have some extra olive oil handy for dipping the warm bread into.

1. Put the potato in a small pot and add enough water to cover by about 2 inches. Bring to a boil over high heat, reduce the heat to low, and simmer until the potato can be easily pierced with a fork, 15 to 20 minutes. Drain, return the potato to the pot, gently mash with a fork, and set aside.

2. In a medium bowl, combine the yeast, rice syrup, bread flour, and ⅔ cup of warm water and whisk until smooth. Cover the bowl with plastic wrap and set aside in a warm place until the mixture becomes bubbly and thick, 20 to 30 minutes.

3. Add ¾ cup of the mashed potato, the remaining ½ cup warm water, oil, and salt to the bowl with the yeast mixture, and stir well. Add the semolina and pastry flours in ½-cup increments, stirring until the dough starts to form a ball (you may only use 2 cups of flour at this point). The dough should be soft and a little sticky.

4. Turn the dough out onto a floured surface and knead until smooth, 8 to 10 minutes. If the dough sticks to your hands, use more flour as needed. Place it in a lightly oiled bowl, cover the bowl with plastic wrap, and place it in a warm place until the dough is doubled in size, about 1 hour.

5. After the dough has risen, transfer it to a parchment-lined baking sheet and use your hands to flatten it. Press the dough into a 5-inch square and then fold each corner into the center. Turn the dough over so the seam is on the bottom, shape the dough into a ball, and place it in the center of the baking sheet, covered with a damp towel. Allow it to rise until it's doubled in size again, 15 to 20 minutes.

6. Preheat the oven to 475°F.

7. Using a pastry brush, brush the surface of the dough generously with the oil and sprinkle with the rosemary and flaky salt. Using your fingers, dimple the surface of the focaccia, gently creating a 10-inch round.

8. Bake until golden-brown, 20 to 25 minutes. Allow the loaf to cool for at least 20 minutes before cutting.

Spelt Bread

MAKES ONE 1½-POUND LOAF

1¼ cups warm water (about 110°F)

¼ cup maple syrup

1 tablespoon active dry yeast

3½ cups spelt flour, plus more for kneading

1½ teaspoons fine sea salt

2 tablespoons extra-virgin olive oil

A VERSATILE, EVERYDAY BREAD, the light texture of this loaf makes it perfect for sandwiches, avocado and nut butter toasts, and even French toast on the weekends. For this particular recipe we like to use spelt flour, derived from an ancient grain, because it's better tolerated by some with gluten sensitivities than all-purpose flour, but feel free to use that if you'd like; white whole-wheat flour is another great option. (White whole-wheat flour is the same as whole wheat flour in the sense that it's ground from the entire wheat kernel—unlike all-purpose white flour, which is bleached and the bran and germ removed. The difference is that it is ground from a hard white wheat berry that results in a lighter, milder tasting flour.) Make sure to use active dry yeast and not instant. The difference is that instant yeast is mixed directly into the dry ingredients, while active dry yeast needs to be activated in warm water before using (otherwise the two yeasts are essentially interchangeable). Active dry yeast does have a longer shelf life, though, and is what we tend to use at the school—and therefore in this recipe.

1. In a small bowl, combine the warm water and maple syrup, then sprinkle with the yeast and stir until it's dissolved. Allow it to sit until the mixture is foamy, about 10 minutes.

2. Meanwhile, stir together the flour and salt in a large bowl. Add the foamy yeast mixture and the oil, and stir well to combine. The dough may seem a little dry, but when you gather it with your hands, it should all stick together, even if it's a little shaggy.

3. Transfer the dough to a floured surface and knead until it becomes smooth, 8 to 10 minutes—you'll know it's properly kneaded when it's springy and bounces back when you press your finger into it. Place the dough in a large, lightly oiled bowl and cover with plastic wrap. Set aside in a warm place until the dough has doubled in size, 45 to 60 minutes.

4. Meanwhile, line a large (12¼ × 4½-inch) Pullman loaf pan with parchment paper. Punch down the dough by placing your fist in the middle of the dough and pushing down gently (despite the term *punch*!), then gather up the sides of the dough to the top center to form a ball and pinch together to form a seam. Place the dough ball seam-side down in the prepared pan. Loosely cover the dough with a damp kitchen towel and set aside in a warm place. Allow it to rise until the dough has doubled in size, about 40 minutes more.

5. Preheat the oven to 375°F.

6. Bake the bread until it is golden and firm to the touch, 40 to 50 minutes. Allow it to cool for 10 minutes before removing it from the pan and cool completely before slicing. Store at room temperature for 2 to 4 days or freeze for up to 1 month.

CHEF'S TIP: If you don't have a loaf pan, you can form the dough into a free-form loaf on a parchment-lined baking sheet.

TEMPEH REUBEN
page 206

CHAPTER 9

Desserts

Strawberry-Rhubarb Crumble

SERVES 6 TO 8

THE CLASSIC COMBINATION OF sour rhubarb and sweet strawberries is what early summer harvest dreams are made of. We've replaced the generous amount of sugar typically found in the filling and crumble topping with a fraction of the amount of maple crystals, and switched out the white flour for the almond flour to make the recipe gluten-free. This summer dessert is virtually foolproof, making it perfect for the baking-averse among us. (Yes, not all chefs love to bake.)

FOR THE FILLING

Coconut oil, for greasing the pan

2 tablespoons arrowroot starch

¾ pound rhubarb, cut into medium dice (about 3 cups)

¼ cup maple crystals, coconut sugar, or raw turbinado sugar

1 pint strawberries, hulled and coarsely chopped

FOR THE TOPPING

1 cup almond flour

¼ cup maple crystals, coconut sugar, or raw turbinado sugar

¼ teaspoon ground cinnamon

Pinch of fine sea salt

¼ cup coconut oil, melted

1. Preheat the oven to 375°F. Grease an 8 × 8-inch baking dish with the oil and set aside.

2. Make the filling: In a small bowl, dissolve the arrowroot in 2 tablespoons water, stirring to combine. Transfer to a large pot set over low heat and add the rhubarb, maple crystals, and ¼ cup water. Simmer until the rhubarb begins to soften, 5 to 7 minutes, then stir in the strawberries and turn off the heat. Transfer the mixture to the prepared baking dish and set aside.

3. Make the topping: In a medium bowl, combine the almond flour, maple crystals, cinnamon, and salt. Using a wooden spoon, mix in the oil until the mixture is shaggy. Crumble the topping evenly over the fruit mixture and bake until the topping is golden-brown and the filling is bubbly, about 20 minutes. Serve hot or warm.

Maple Almond Fudge

MAKES SIXTEEN 2-INCH PIECES

2 cups blanched almonds (see page 173)

2 tablespoons unsweetened almond milk

¾ cup maple crystals, coconut sugar, or raw turbinado sugar

Pinch of fine sea salt

2 tablespoons coconut oil, melted

½ teaspoon edible gold powder (optional)

THIS RECIPE COMES FROM the Indian cuisine class in the Chef's Training Program, and is inspired by *doodh peda* (dood PE-dah)—Indian milk fudge. Traditionally, this sweet treat is made by reducing dairy milk until virtually all the liquid is evaporated and only a thick mass of fat solids, known as *khoya*, remains. The *khoya* is then sweetened and flavored with saffron and/or cardamom and sometimes garnished with pistachios or almonds. In place of reduced milk fat, this version uses ground blanched almonds for a similar richness; of course, they also add healthy fats, protein, and fiber.

1. Line a baking sheet with parchment paper and set aside. Put the almonds in a food processor, grind them to a powder similar in texture to coarse cornmeal (be careful not to not overprocess or the meal may turn to butter), and set aside.

2. In a medium pot, briefly warm the almond milk over medium heat. Stir in the maple crystals and salt and cook, stirring frequently, until the crystals dissolve, 1 to 2 minutes. Add the oil and stir to incorporate. Gradually add the powdered almonds, stirring as the mixture begins to come together into a dense mass and stick to the spoon. Continue cooking, while stirring vigorously, until the mixture is smooth and forms a ball, about 2 minutes; be sure to watch the flame—if the heat is too high, the fudge may become granular.

3. Transfer the fudge to the center of the prepared baking sheet and top with another piece of parchment paper. Working quickly and using a heavy-bottomed pan, flatten the mixture to a ½-inch thickness; use a small offset spatula or butter knife to straighten the edges to form a 6-inch square and flatten again, if needed. Let the fudge rest for a few minutes. Paint the fudge with a very light coat of edible gold powder, if using. While the fudge is still warm, dip a sharp knife in water and cut the fudge into 16 squares. Cool before serving.

4. Store the fudge in an airtight container (separating layers with a sheet of parchment paper) at room temperature for up to 5 days.

Chocolate Pudding

SERVES 10 TO 12

2 cups vegan, semisweet chocolate chips, melted

3 (13.5-ounce) cans full-fat coconut milk, refrigerated

½ cup agar flakes

Pinch of fine sea salt

1 cup maple crystals, coconut sugar, or raw turbinado sugar

1 tablespoon pure vanilla extract

1 tablespoon kuzu

Fresh or freeze-dried raspberries or strawberries and/or fresh mint, for serving (optional)

Whipped Coconut Cream (page 101), for serving (optional)

THIS MAKE-AHEAD, CROWD-PLEASING DESSERT is perfect for dinner parties and celebrations. Serve the pudding in small dessert bowls or tumblers for a pretty presentation. If you are unfamiliar with agar flakes, a plant-based alternative to gelatin, and kuzu, a gluten-free thickener, both used here, turn to page 32 to learn more.

1. Fill a large pot with about 2 inches of water and bring to a simmer over high heat. Wipe a large heat-proof bowl completely dry with a kitchen towel and put it on the pot over the simmering water, making sure the water is not touching the bowl. Reduce the heat to very low and put the chocolate in the bowl. Allow the chocolate to melt slowly, stirring as needed, until the chocolate is completely melted and smooth. Carefully remove the bowl from the pot and set aside.

2. Open the coconut milk cans and poke a spoon or butter knife through the thick layer of cream until you reach the coconut water. Pour off the coconut water from the cans of coconut milk into a medium pot. Stir in the agar flakes and let the mixture sit to bloom, 10 to 15 minutes.

3. To the coconut water–agar mixture, add the remaining coconut cream and salt. Bring to a simmer over medium heat, reduce the heat to low, and simmer until the agar is completely dissolved, about 10 minutes (to check if it has dissolved, tilt the pan forward—if you still see flecks of agar on the bottom, continue cooking).

4. Add the maple crystals and vanilla, and stir to dissolve. In a small bowl, dissolve the kuzu in 2 tablespoons of cold water, and add it to the coconut milk mixture. Whisk until the mixture thickens slightly. Add the chocolate and whisk to incorporate.

5. Transfer the mixture to a shallow pan. When the pudding has stopped steaming, place it in the fridge to firm up, at least 30 minutes and up to 60 minutes.

6. Before serving, purée the pudding in a food processor until smooth. Divide among serving dishes and top with raspberries, mint, and a dollop of Whipped Coconut Cream, if using. Leftover pudding may be refrigerated in an airtight container for up to 4 days.

Vanilla Bean Ice Cream

MAKES 1½ PINTS

2 cups raw cashews

2 vanilla beans, split, with seeds scraped and pods reserved

4 cups boiling water

¾ cup maple syrup

¾ cup brown rice syrup

Pinch of fine sea salt

SPECIAL EQUIPMENT

Ice cream machine

YOU WON'T BELIEVE HOW easy it is to make this rich and creamy vegan ice cream that counts on whole cashews for creaminess, rather than dairy cream. Feel free to use this as a template recipe for other ice cream flavors, too, as we have done with the Black Sesame (page 297) and Gingersnap (page 301) flavors.

1. In a large bowl, combine the cashews, vanilla seeds and pods, and boiling water and set aside for 30 minutes.

2. Discard the vanilla pods, transfer the cashew-water mixture to a blender, and blend until completely smooth, 1 to 2 minutes. (If the mixture doesn't blend silky-smooth, strain it through a nut milk bag or a fine-mesh strainer, lined with a double layer of wet cheesecloth, and then return it to the blender.) Add the maple syrup, rice syrup, and salt, and blend to incorporate. Pour the mixture into a large bowl and refrigerate until cold.

3. Transfer the cold mixture to an ice cream machine and churn according to the manufacturer's directions to a scoopable consistency, usually about 30 minutes. Transfer to a lidded container and store in the freezer for up to 3 months.

> **CHEF'S TIP:** We like to use a high-speed blender when making cashew ice cream because it completely pulverizes the nuts, eliminating the need to strain the mixture. Depending on the model, a standard blender can work just as well. If your blender doesn't pulverize the nuts all the way, simply strain the milk in step 2.

DESSERTS

Avocado-Lime Ice Cream

MAKES 1 QUART

4 small ripe avocados, halved, pitted, and peeled

1 cup agave syrup

¾ cup fresh lime juice (from 10 to 12 limes)

¾ cup canned full-fat coconut milk

¾ cup coconut cream

Pinch of fine sea salt

SPECIAL EQUIPMENT

Ice cream machine

CALLING ALL AVOCADO LOVERS! This distinctive vegan ice cream flavor, featuring everyone's favorite healthy fat, is equal parts rich and refreshing. The avocado gives this treat a velvety mouthfeel and stunning color, while the lime provides the tropical sour flavor we crave in the warmer months.

1. In a blender, combine the avocados, agave, lime juice, coconut milk, coconut cream, and salt until smooth and creamy.

2. Transfer the purée to an ice cream machine and churn according to manufacturer's directions to a scoopable consistency, usually about 30 minutes. Transfer to a lidded container and store in the freezer for up to 1 month.

Watermelon Granita

MAKES 1½ QUARTS

2 pounds seedless watermelon, cut into chunks (about 6 cups)

½ cup fresh lime juice (from about 8 limes)

⅓ cup agave syrup

Pinch of fine sea salt

Mint sprigs, for serving (optional)

SPECIAL EQUIPMENT

Nut milk bag or wet cheesecloth-lined fine-mesh sieve

GRANITA IS AN ITALIAN semi-frozen dessert similar to sorbet. Rather than being churned like sorbet or ice cream, though, *granita* is raked by hand using a fork, or shaved. It can be made from virtually any summer fruit and flavored with any citrus of your choice. You can also experiment with adding a little Italian liqueur to the mix—such as Campari or limoncello.

1. Purée the watermelon in a blender until smooth and strain through a nut milk bag, or a fine-mesh sieve lined with wet cheesecloth.

2. Rinse out the blender and pour the watermelon juice back in. Add the lime juice, agave, and salt, and blend to combine.

3. Pour the mixture into a large shallow dish (like a 9 × 13-inch glass baking dish); the mixture should be about ¼ inch up the side of the pan. Freeze until crystals have formed but the mixture is not yet frozen solid, about 1 hour.

4. Remove the pan from the freezer. Using a fork, scrape any ice crystals that have formed in the dish, being sure to get into the edges and corners of the pan. Return the pan to the freezer and continue scraping every 30 minutes until the mixture is thoroughly frozen, 3 to 4 hours. Serve with mint sprigs, if desired. Transfer to a lidded container and store in the freezer for up to 1 month.

Black Sesame Ice Cream

MAKES 1½ PINTS

2 cups raw cashews

2 vanilla beans, split, with seeds scraped and pods reserved

4 cups boiling water

¾ cup maple syrup

¾ cup brown rice syrup

3 tablespoons black sesame seeds, toasted, cooled, and finely ground (see Chef's Tips)

Pinch of fine sea salt

SPECIAL EQUIPMENT
Ice cream machine

WE JUST CAN'T GET enough of the delicate nutty flavor of this Black Sesame Ice Cream. And the pale-gray color? Gorgeous. Black sesame seeds are the same as white, except they have not been hulled. As a result, they are slightly more flavorful and retain more calcium than their more common hulled counterparts. If you can't find black sesame seeds, feel free to use white for a slightly less intense flavor.

1. In a large bowl, combine the cashews, vanilla seeds and pods, and boiling water. Allow to sit for 30 minutes.

2. Discard the vanilla pods, transfer the cashew mixture to a high-speed blender, and blend until completely smooth. (If the mixture doesn't blend silky-smooth, then strain it through a nut milk bag or a fine-mesh strainer lined with a double layer of wet cheesecloth, and return it to the blender.) Add the maple syrup, rice syrup, sesame seeds, and salt, and blend to incorporate. Pour the mixture into a large bowl and refrigerate until cold.

3. Transfer the mixture to an ice cream machine and churn according to the manufacturer's directions to a scoopable consistency, usually about 30 minutes. Transfer to a lidded container and store in the freezer for up to 3 months.

> **CHEF'S TIPS:** To toast the sesame seeds, place the seeds in a small skillet over medium-low heat. Toast, tossing frequently, until fragrant, about 3 minutes.
>
> To grind the seeds, use a coffee or spice grinder, a food processor, or a mortar and pestle.

BLACK SESAME
ICE CREAM
page 297

**AVOCADO-LIME
ICE CREAM**
page 296

STRAWBERRY-BASIL SORBET
page 300

Strawberry-Basil Sorbet

MAKES 1½ QUARTS

4 pints strawberries, hulled

1¼ cups maple syrup

¼ cup balsamic vinegar

¼ teaspoon fine sea salt

Pinch of freshly ground black pepper

¼ cup finely chopped basil leaves (½ ounce)

SPECIAL EQUIPMENT

Ice cream machine

THE INTENSELY SUMMERY AROMA of this dessert comes from the strawberries. Be sure to use the best-quality strawberries you can find, preferably local ones from a farmers' market. Taste the mixture at the end of step 1; since the sugar content of berries varies, you may need to add a bit more maple syrup. Remember, sweetness is tamed when something is frozen, so the base of the sorbet should taste a little too sweet before it goes into the ice cream machine.

1. In a blender, combine the strawberries, maple syrup, balsamic vinegar, salt, and pepper, and blend until smooth. Transfer to a bowl and whisk in the basil.

2. Transfer the mixture to an ice cream machine and churn according to the manufacturer's directions.

3. Scrape the sorbet into a shallow dish and freeze for an additional 40 to 60 minutes, until the sorbet firms to a scoopable consistency, before serving. Transfer to a lidded container and store in the freezer for 3 to 5 days.

Gingersnap
Ice Cream

MAKES 1½ PINTS

2 cups raw cashews

1 quart boiling water

¾ cup brown rice syrup

½ cup plus 3 tablespoons maple
syrup

1 tablespoon molasses

2 tablespoons fresh ginger
juice from about a 6-inch piece
(see page 74)

1 teaspoon ground ginger

⅛ teaspoon freshly grated nutmeg

Pinch of fine sea salt

SPECIAL EQUIPMENT

Ice cream machine

HERE WE USED OUR classic Vanilla Bean Ice Cream recipe (page 295) as a template to re-create a beloved childhood treat in ice cream format. Feel free to experiment with your own flavor creations. Matcha, hibiscus, and Earl Grey are just a few to try. If you want to use a flavoring that can be mixed right in (like matcha), incorporate it in step 2. And if you're going for flavors that need steeping (in this case, hibiscus and Earl Grey), combine them with the cashews and water and strain them out after step 1.

1. In a large bowl, combine the cashews and boiling water. Allow to sit for 30 minutes.

2. Transfer the mixture to a high-speed blender, along with the rice syrup, maple syrup, molasses, ginger juice, ground ginger, nutmeg, and salt. Blend on high speed for about 2 minutes, until the mixture is completely smooth. Pour into a large bowl and refrigerate until cold.

3. Transfer the mixture to an ice cream machine and churn according to the manufacturer's directions to a scoopable consistency, usually about 30 minutes. Transfer to a lidded container and store in the freezer for up to 3 months.

Chocolate Chip Cookie Ice Cream Sandwiches

MAKES 8 SANDWICHES

5 teaspoons flaxseed meal

3 tablespoons hot water

1¼ cups whole-wheat pastry flour

1 teaspoon baking powder

¼ teaspoon fine sea salt

¾ cup maple crystals

¼ cup unsweetened coconut cream (see page 34)

¼ cup coconut oil

1 teaspoon pure vanilla extract

¾ cup vegan chocolate chips

3 to 4 cups Vanilla Bean Ice Cream (page 295)

SPECIAL EQUIPMENT

Stand mixer

CHEF'S TIPS: If you don't own a stand mixer, use a hand mixer to cream the coconut cream, oil, and maple crystals together, and then use a wooden spoon to incorporate the flour mixture.

You may also cut the dough into 32 cookies, instead of 16, to make mini sandwiches.

THE TYPE OF FLOUR you choose is extremely important to the quality of your finished baked product—for example, you wouldn't use whole-wheat flour for a French macaron, nor would you use almond flour to make traditional pizza dough. These cookies call for whole-wheat pastry flour (WWPF). Since all three parts of the wheat kernel—bran, germ, and endosperm—are preserved when WWPF is milled, it has a milder taste than traditional whole wheat because of the type of wheat used (a soft red or white wheat, as opposed to the hard wheat used in whole-wheat flour). WWPF is an essential ingredient for many professional bakers because whole-grain nutrition can be added to baked items while maintaining a tender crumb. In this case, the resulting cookie is wonderfully delicate but chewy enough that it won't crumble when you bite into the ice cream sandwich. When sourcing vegan chocolate, it may not necessarily be labeled as such. Cacao itself has a very bitter flavor, which is why people traditionally add dairy and sugar to make it more creamy and sweet. Look at the ingredient lists and watch out for not only dairy, but dairy derivatives, such as whey and casein.

1. Preheat the oven to 350°F. Line a rimmed baking sheet with parchment paper and set aside.

2. In a small bowl, stir the flaxseeds with the hot water and set aside until the mixture thickens, about 5 minutes. In a medium bowl, whisk together the flour, baking powder, and salt. Set aside.

3. In a stand mixer fitted with the paddle attachment, combine the maple crystals, coconut cream, and oil, and beat on medium speed until smooth and creamy, about 1 minute. Add the flaxseed mixture and vanilla, and beat on medium-high speed until thoroughly combined, about 30 seconds. Reduce the speed to low and slowly add the flour mixture, combining just until the flour is incorporated. Use a rubber spatula to scrape down the sides of the bowl. Add the chocolate chips, and mix just until combined.

4. Spread the mixture onto the prepared baking sheet to create an 11-inch square. Bake until slightly golden around the edges, 10 to 12 minutes. Remove the pan from the oven and immediately cut the cookies into sixteen 3 × 3-inch squares. Set aside to cool completely on a wire rack. The cookies will be soft but will harden slightly as they cool.

5. To assemble the cookies, sandwich a scoop or 2 of ice cream between 2 cookies. Freeze the sandwiches to harden the ice cream before serving. To store leftover sandwiches, wrap them tightly in plastic wrap and freeze for up to 3 days.

Rolled Fig Cookies

MAKES ABOUT 24 COOKIES

OUR SLICE-AND-BAKE PINWHEEL COOKIES get their light-as-air shortbread texture from ground almonds and coconut oil. You can prep these a day ahead, and keep them refrigerated until you're ready to bake. Black mission figs give the spirals a dramatic contrasting color, but feel free to substitute dried Turkish figs or apricots if that's what you have on hand. These pair especially well with a steamy cup of chai.

FOR THE DOUGH

¼ cup plus 2 tablespoons blanched almonds (see Chef's Tip, page 173)

1½ cups unbleached all-purpose flour

¾ cup whole-wheat pastry flour

¼ teaspoon ground cinnamon

⅔ cup maple syrup

6 tablespoons melted coconut oil

Pinch of fine sea salt

FOR THE FILLING

2 cups dried black mission figs

1½ cups unsweetened apple juice

2 teaspoons pure vanilla extract

½ teaspoon ground cinnamon

Pinch of ground cloves

Pinch of fine sea salt

CHEF'S TIP: Be careful not to overprocess the almonds in the food processor because they quickly turn to butter.

1. Preheat the oven to 350°F. Line 2 baking sheets with parchment paper and set aside. Adjust the oven racks to the upper-third and lower-third positions.

2. Put the almonds in a food processor and grind to a fine meal. Transfer the ground almonds to a medium bowl and add the all-purpose flour, whole-wheat pastry flour, and cinnamon, and whisk to combine. In a separate bowl, whisk together the maple syrup, oil, and salt. Pour the maple syrup mixture into the almond mixture and stir to combine.

3. Divide the dough evenly in half. Flatten lightly to form 2 disks and wrap each one in plastic. Refrigerate for 15 minutes or up to 1 week.

4. While the dough chills, make the filling: In a medium pot, combine the figs, apple juice, vanilla, cinnamon, cloves, and salt. Simmer over medium-low heat until the figs are soft, 5 to 7 minutes. Drain the figs, reserving the liquid.

5. Put the softened figs into a food processor and purée to make a smooth, spreadable paste, adding 1 to 1½ cups of the simmering liquid as needed. Set the mixture aside to cool completely.

6. Working with 1 disk of dough at a time, roll out the dough between 2 pieces of parchment paper into a 10 × 6-inch rectangle that's about ⅛ inch thick. Trim off any excess dough to create even edges. Spread half of the cooled filling evenly over the dough and roll it jelly-roll style—starting from the left edge and rolling into a log toward the right—as tightly as possible. Wrap the log in the parchment paper and transfer to the freezer to chill until solid, at least 15 minutes or up to several months. Repeat with the remaining dough and filling.

7. Using a bread knife, slice the rolls crosswise into ¼-inch-thick rounds. Transfer to the prepared baking sheets, spacing the cookies 2 inches apart, and bake until lightly golden, 10 to 15 minutes, rotating the baking sheets between the top and bottom racks halfway through baking. Allow the cookies to cool for 5 minutes before transferring them, using an offset spatula, to a wire rack to cool completely. Store the cookies in an airtight container at room temperature for up to 5 days.

Easy Peanut Butter Cookies

MAKES ABOUT 20 COOKIES

1½ cups whole-wheat pastry flour

1½ teaspoons baking powder

½ teaspoon fine sea salt

¾ cup unsweetened creamy natural peanut butter, stirred well to emulsify

¾ cup maple syrup

⅓ cup canola oil

1 teaspoon pure vanilla extract

SPECIAL EQUIPMENT
Stand mixer

THESE COOKIES ARE CRISP, buttery, light, and very easy to make. Resist the urge to eat them straight out of the oven, as they will be crumbly when warm but will harden as they cool. If you don't own a stand mixer, blend the wet ingredients in a food processor, transfer the mixture to a bowl, and mix in the dry ingredients by hand.

1. Preheat the oven to 350°F. Line 2 baking sheets with parchment paper and set aside. Adjust the oven racks to the upper-third and lower-third positions.

2. Sift the flour, baking powder, and salt into a medium bowl. In a stand mixer fitted with a paddle attachment, blend the peanut butter, maple syrup, oil, and vanilla on medium speed until smooth. Reduce the speed to low, add the flour mixture, and mix just until combined.

3. Using a 1-ounce ice cream scoop (or using a tablespoon measure and scooping 2 tablespoons for each dough ball), scoop the dough onto the prepared baking sheets, spacing them about 2 inches apart. Press down on the cookies with the back of a fork to form ridges.

4. Bake until lightly golden, 10 to 15 minutes, rotating the baking sheets between the top and bottom racks halfway through baking. Cool before serving (on a wire rack, if you have one). Store the cookies in an airtight container at room temperature for up to 5 days.

Chewy Chocolate Crinkle Cookies

MAKES ABOUT 14 COOKIES

½ cup semisweet vegan chocolate chunks

¼ cup aquafaba (liquid from a can of chickpeas; see Chef's Tips)

Pinch of fine sea salt

½ cup plus 2 tablespoons maple crystals

3 tablespoons unsweetened cocoa powder, sifted

1 teaspoon pure vanilla extract

1 cup unsweetened shredded coconut

CHEF'S TIPS: While the liquid from both beans cooked at home and canned beans can be used for aquafaba, the latter is generally more fail-proof. The liquid from canned beans tends to be thicker and more viscous, and whips up more successfully, so it's definitely a better option for beginner aquafaba users.

Slowly integrating the sugar into the aquafaba helps to stabilize it. And if you can't find vegan chocolate chunks, you can chop vegan chocolate to make your own chunks, or replace chunks with chips.

THIS IS A GREAT recipe to have in your back pocket for potlucks, office parties, and bake sales where allergens may be of concern. While these vegan cookies are free of gluten, soy, and nuts, they are packed with rich, fudgy flavor. So what do we use to bind these divine bites of goodness if not eggs? The answer—aquafaba, which translates literally to "water-bean." And, yes, that's exactly what it is: chickpea water. Strange as it may seem, this liquid from beans can be coerced into a form that resembles an egg-white meringue by simply whipping it. Therefore, it's a credible, if not *in*-credible, egg replacement. Not only does the aquafaba act as a binder, but it contributes moisture to these cookies that are wonderfully chewy, almost brownie-like, with slightly crispy edges. For extra decadence, serve them alongside a scoop of Vanilla Bean Ice Cream (page 295) or, even better, sandwich a dollop of the frozen sweet between two of them.

1. Preheat the oven to 350°F. Line a baking sheet with parchment paper.

2. Fill a medium pot with about 2 inches of water and bring to a simmer. Wipe a medium heat-proof bowl completely dry with a kitchen towel and place it on the pot over the simmering water, making sure the water is not touching the bottom of the bowl. Reduce the heat to low and place the chocolate in the bowl. Allow the chocolate to melt slowly, stirring occasionally. Set aside to cool for about 5 minutes, or until it's barely warm to the touch.

3. Meanwhile, in a small bowl, combine the aquafaba and salt, and beat with a hand mixer or a whisk until foamy, about 3 minutes. Gradually sprinkle in the maple crystals while beating the aquafaba, until soft peaks form (which is when peaks just start to hold their form before flopping over). This can take anywhere from 10 to 15 minutes, depending on whether you're doing it by hand or using an electric mixer.

4. Using a rubber spatula, fold in the cocoa powder and melted chocolate until they are evenly incorporated, being careful not to deflate the meringue too much. Lastly, gently stir in the vanilla and coconut until everything is well combined. The mixture will become a very stiff dough.

5. Using a tablespoon measure, transfer the dough to the prepared baking sheet, spacing the cookies about 2 inches apart. Bake until slightly glossy and cracks appear on the top, about 15 minutes. Transfer the cookies to a wire rack to cool before eating (if you can wait). Store the cookies in an airtight container at room temperature for up to 5 days.

Coconut Lime Cream Tart

MAKES ONE 9-INCH TART

THE STEPS INVOLVED IN making this rich tart may be plentiful, but the results are absolutely worth it. The light and crumbly tart shell is made with a tropical-inspired mix of macadamia nuts and toasted coconut. The coconut milk base of the lime-flavored filling is set with agar, the sea vegetable–derived vegan gelatin substitute (see page 32). This dessert is perfect to make in advance for festive gatherings.

FOR THE CRUST

⅓ cup unsweetened shredded coconut

⅔ cup raw macadamia nuts

1 cup unbleached all-purpose flour

⅓ cup coconut oil, melted, plus more for greasing the pan

¼ cup maple crystals

¼ teaspoon fine sea salt

FOR THE FILLING

1 (13.5-ounce) can full-fat coconut milk

⅓ cup maple syrup

2 tablespoons brown rice syrup

1 tablespoon plus 1½ teaspoons agar flakes

¼ teaspoon fine sea salt

½ cup unbleached all-purpose flour

1½ teaspoons lime zest (from about 2 limes)

¼ cup fresh lime juice (from about 4 limes)

1 tablespoon toasted unsweetened shredded coconut, for serving (optional)

1 tablespoon lime zest, for serving (optional)

SPECIAL EQUIPMENT

9-inch tart pan with removable bottom

1. Make the crust: Put the coconut in a small skillet over medium-low heat and toast, tossing frequently, until lightly golden, 4 to 5 minutes. Transfer to a large bowl and set aside.

2. Put the macadamia nuts in a food processor and grind into small bits (be careful not to overprocess as the nuts may turn into butter). Transfer to the bowl with the coconut and add the flour, oil, maple crystals, and salt. Stir to combine and then use your fingers to rub the mixture together until it resembles a coarse meal. Transfer the dough to a greased tart pan and use your fingers to spread and press it evenly across the bottom and up the sides of the pan. Refrigerate the crust for 15 minutes or up to several days (in which case you should cover it with plastic wrap).

3. Preheat the oven to 325°F.

4. Place the tart pan on a baking sheet and bake until the crust is lightly golden, 15 to 20 minutes. Set aside to cool on a wire rack.

5. Meanwhile, make the filling: In a medium saucepan over medium heat, combine the coconut milk with the maple syrup, rice syrup, agar, and salt. Bring the mixture to a boil, then lower the heat to low and simmer, whisking frequently, until the agar is completely dissolved, 10 to 15 minutes (to check if it has dissolved, tilt the pan forward—if you still see flecks of agar on the bottom, continue cooking). Pour the mixture into a large bowl and set aside.

6. In the same saucepan over high heat, combine the flour with ¾ cup cold water, whisking constantly until the mixture thickens, about 2 minutes. Turn off the heat and, while whisking, slowly pour in the coconut milk mixture. Whisk in the lime zest and juice. Return the filling back to the large bowl to cool slightly, stirring frequently to prevent the mixture from setting, about 10 minutes. Pour the filling into the cooled tart shell and refrigerate until the filling is cool and completely set, about 1 hour. Sprinkle with the toasted coconut and lime zest, if using, and serve chilled. Refrigerate for up to 2 days.

Zesty Lemon Cake

with Whipped Lemon Coconut Cream

MAKES ONE 8-INCH, 2-LAYER CAKE

FOR THE CAKE

⅓ cup melted coconut oil, plus more for greasing the pans

1 cup whole-wheat pastry flour

1 cup unbleached all-purpose flour

1 teaspoon baking powder

1 teaspoon baking soda

1 tablespoon lemon zest (from about 1 lemon)

1 teaspoon fine sea salt

1 cup maple syrup, at room temperature

⅔ cup unsweetened almond milk, at room temperature

¼ cup fresh lemon juice (from about 2 lemons)

2 teaspoons lemon extract

1 teaspoon pure vanilla extract

1 teaspoon apple cider vinegar

THESE LEMONY LAYERS HAVE a nice moist crumb that are frosted with a decadent coconut cream, which is neither too sweet nor heavy. Like our Coconut Lime Cream Tart (page 310), we use agar flakes (see page 32) to thicken the dairy-free frosting. Feel free to double this recipe and make a four-layer cake for extra-special celebrations.

1. Position a rack in the center of the oven and preheat the oven to 350°F. Grease and flour two 8-inch cake pans and line the bottoms with parchment paper.

2. In a large bowl whisk together the flours, baking powder, baking soda, lemon zest, and salt. In separate bowl, whisk together the oil, maple syrup, milk, lemon juice, lemon and vanilla extracts, and vinegar until smooth. Pour the wet ingredients into the dry and whisk until well combined. Divide the batter evenly between the 2 prepared pans.

3. Bake the cakes until they spring back to light pressure and pull away from the sides of the pans, about 18 minutes. Remove the cakes from the oven and set aside in the pans on a wire rack to cool for about 15 minutes, then turn them out from the pans and cool completely on the rack.

4. Meanwhile, make the frosting: Prepare a large ice bath. In a small saucepan, whisk the coconut milk and agar flakes (or powder) together and set aside for 5 minutes, then bring the coconut milk–agar mixture to a boil over medium-high heat and simmer until all the agar has dissolved, whisking constantly to avoid scorching, about 7 to 10 minutes.

5. In a blender, combine the coconut cream, agave, lemon zest and juice, and salt, and blend until smooth. Add the coconut butter and blend to combine. Slowly add the hot coconut milk–agar mixture to the blender and blend to combine.

6. Using a rubber spatula, transfer the frosting to a medium bowl and place it in the ice bath until completely chilled, about 20 minutes (you can also refrigerate it, which will take at least 40 minutes). The frosting should be thickened and able to hold its shape, like a traditional buttercream.

ingredients and recipe continue

FOR THE FROSTING

1 (13.5-ounce) can full-fat coconut milk

3 tablespoons agar flakes, or 1 tablespoon agar powder

1¼ cups (12 ounces) coconut cream

¾ cup agave syrup

2 teaspoons lemon zest (from about 1 lemon)

¼ cup lemon juice (from about 2 lemons)

Pinch of fine sea salt

1 (14-ounce) jar coconut butter (1½ cups), softened to room temperature (see Chef's Tips)

7. After the frosting has become firm, you can either pulse it in the food processor a few times until smooth, or stir it by hand until smooth. (Don't overprocess it in hopes of making this frosting fluffy, as it's quite thick; it separates easily and will break into greasy clumps. See Chef's Tips, if this happens.) Use immediately to frost the cooled cake layers. To do this, position one layer on a plate or cake stand. Spread a generous ½ cup frosting evenly on top of the base layer, then carefully set the second layer on top of the base, positioning it evenly on all sides. With a rubber spatula, scrape the rest of the frosting onto the top of the cake. Using an offset spatula, spread the frosting across the top of the cake and down the sides. Serve at room temperature, but store refrigerated and bring back to room temperature before serving, which may take up to an hour or so.

CHEF'S TIPS: If your coconut butter does not soften at room temperature, you may warm it on the stovetop by placing the glass jar in a pan of simmering water that reaches about three-fourths of the way up the sides of the jar and warm it until the butter softens. If your coconut butter is in a plastic container, scoop it out into a heat-proof container first. While you want the butter softened, you do not want it melted. If this happens, put the melted butter in the fridge to stiffen up. If the edges harden, scrape the hard pieces into the cooled butter, and stir vigorously until you get a consistency that is smooth and spreadable, like nut butter.

If the frosting separates when whisking (or using a food processor), heat it in a double boiler over the stovetop and stir well to bring it back together. Chill before attempting to whip it again.

French Walnut Tart

MAKES ONE 9-INCH TART

2 batches Basic Pastry Crust
(page 98)

½ cup maple syrup

⅓ cup brown rice syrup

2 tablespoons barley malt syrup

1 cup store-bought or homemade
Almond Milk (page 61)

2 tablespoons creamy unsalted
cashew butter or other nut butter

½ teaspoon fresh lemon juice

Pinch of fine sea salt

1 tablespoon arrowroot starch

1 teaspoon pure vanilla extract

¼ teaspoon orange extract
(optional)

1 tablespoon brandy (optional)

3½ cups toasted walnut halves,
coarsely chopped (see page 56)

Whipped Coconut Cream
(page 101), for serving (optional)

SPECIAL EQUIPMENT

9-inch tart pan with removable
bottom

DECADENT AND IMPRESSIVE, THIS tart is composed of crunchy walnuts in a sweet gooey filling enveloped in a flaky, light crust. Think of it as a European equivalent to pecan pie (speaking of which, feel free to use pecans instead of walnuts). As compared to most of our desserts, this treat is quite rich, so you only need a small sliver to satisfy your sweet tooth. Don't be put off by the lengthy ingredient list—the procedure for making the tart is actually quite simple.

1. Preheat the oven to 350°F.

2. Remove the dough from the refrigerator and allow it sit at room temperature for 5 to 10 minutes. On a lightly floured surface, roll out one disk to a 12-inch round that is about ⅛ inch thick. Carefully lift the dough and slide it into a tart pan with a removable bottom, gently pressing it into the sides and bottom. Trim the overhang and refrigerate the dough in the tart pan while you prepare the filling. Roll out the second crust to a ⅛-inch-thick round and slide it onto a piece of parchment; place this dough in the refrigerator as well.

3. In a medium pot, combine the maple, rice, and barley malt syrups. Bring them to gentle boil over medium-high heat and then whisk in the almond milk, nut butter, lemon juice, and salt; set aside.

4. In a small bowl, stir together the arrowroot and 2 tablespoons cold water until dissolved. Add the arrowroot slurry, vanilla and orange extracts, and brandy (if using) to the pot and whisk again until smooth. Stir in the walnuts, reduce the heat to low, and stir until the mixture thickens slightly. Remove from heat and cool slightly.

5. Remove the crusts from the refrigerator and pour the walnut mixture into the tart shell. Place the top dough over the filling and press the edges down onto the rim to seal, then press and trim any overhang. Use a paring knife to make a few steam vents in the top crust. Place the tart pan on a rimmed baking sheet and bake until the crust is firm and golden, 30 to 40 minutes. Cool for at least 25 minutes before slicing. Serve with Whipped Coconut Cream, if desired. The tart can be served slightly warm or at room temperature. Store covered at room temperature.

Rich Flourless Chocolate Cake

MAKES ONE 8-INCH CAKE

3 tablespoons flaxseed meal

7 ounces (2 standard-size bars) vegan dark chocolate (72% cacao or higher), roughly broken into chunks

1 cup unsweetened applesauce

½ cup maple crystals, coconut sugar, or turbinado sugar

½ cup unsweetened cocoa powder

1 tablespoon ground coffee

½ teaspoon sea salt

IF YOU'RE LOOKING FOR a moist and fudgy chocolate dessert that doesn't require any fancy techniques or equipment to put together, this is it. Instead of eggs—which give most flourless chocolate cakes their structure—this recipe utilizes flaxseed meal as a binder, along with applesauce, which adds moisture. This cake is so rich, you need only a little bit to satisfy that after-dinner sweet craving, so we recommend slicing it into 16 pieces. Serve it with Vanilla Bean Ice Cream (page 295) or Whipped Coconut Cream (page 101) to balance out the intense chocolate flavor.

1. Preheat the oven to 350°F. Grease the bottom and sides of a round 8-inch baking dish with coconut oil and line the bottom with a parchment paper round.

2. In a medium bowl, combine the flaxseed meal with 9 tablespoons of water. Let stand while you prepare the rest of the ingredients.

3. Fill a large pot with about 2 inches of water and bring to a simmer over high heat. Wipe a large heat-proof bowl completely dry with a kitchen towel and put it on the pot over the simmering water, making sure the water is not touching the bowl. Reduce the heat to very low and put the chocolate in the bowl. Allow the chocolate to melt slowly, stirring as needed, until the chocolate is completely melted and smooth. Carefully remove the bowl from the pot and set aside.

4. In a large bowl, combine the applesauce, maple crystals, cocoa powder, coffee, salt, and flaxseed mixture, and stir to thoroughly combine. Stir in the melted chocolate. Pour the mixture into the prepared baking dish and bake until the cake pulls away from the sides of the pan, about 1 hour and 10 minutes. Cool to room temperature then cover the baking dish with foil or plastic wrap and refrigerate to cool completely, preferably overnight.

Coffee Flan

SERVES 6

3½ cups unsweetened almond milk

2 tablespoons agar flakes

½ cup maple syrup

¼ cup good-quality instant coffee

1 tablespoon kuzu

Neutral oil (such as canola), for greasing the ramekins

¼ cup maple crystals, coconut sugar, or raw organic sugar

½ cup toasted pecans, coarsely chopped (see page 56)

USUALLY A FLAN COUNTS on eggs, milk, and sugar for its trademark creamy texture, but in ours we use our two favorite plant-based thickeners instead: kuzu and agar. The alchemy of the two creates a rich, custardy vegan flan (kuzu adds shine and agar sets the mixture, akin to gelatin; see pages 32 and 33). The almond milk, coffee, and maple add a rich, sweet flavor to the velvety texture of this dessert. Other than pecans, you can top it with a little shaved chocolate or a few chocolate-covered espresso beans for a stylish touch.

1. In a medium pot, combine the milk and agar and set aside for 5 minutes. Bring the mixture to a boil over medium-high heat, reduce the heat to low, and simmer, uncovered, until the agar is completely dissolved, about 5 minutes. Stir in the maple syrup.

2. Dissolve the coffee and kuzu in ½ cup water, whisking until no lumps remain. Stir into the milk-agar mixture and simmer over medium-low heat until slightly thickened, about 5 minutes. Remove from heat.

3. Lightly oil 6 ramekins (or small tumblers) and sprinkle 2 teaspoons of maple crystals in the bottom of each ramekin.

4. Divide the custard among the ramekins and refrigerate until completely set, about 45 minutes.

5. To serve, run a paring knife around the sides of each ramekin to separate the flan from the dish, invert each onto a plate, and top with the pecans. (Alternatively, serve the flan directly out of the ramekins.)

Apple Galette

MAKES ONE 6-INCH GALETTE

Ⓢ Ⓝ

All-purpose flour, for dusting

1 batch Basic Pastry Crust
(page 98)

1 tablespoon coconut oil

2 Granny Smith apples
(approximately 1 pound), peeled,
cored, and thinly sliced (see
Chef's Tip)

3 tablespoons maple crystals,
coconut sugar, or turbinado sugar

¼ teaspoon ground cinnamon, plus
more for the bread-crumb mixture

1 teaspoon pure vanilla extract

1 tablespoon plain bread crumbs

1 to 2 tablespoons maple syrup,
for glazing

CHEF'S TIP: While slicing
apples, soak them in bowl
of water with lemon juice to
prevent browning. For every
2 cups of water you use, add
the juice of half a lemon.

ONE OF THE MOST important elements of making tender and flaky pastry is the temperature of your ingredients. The fat should be very cold when you're looking to make a flaky crust; the bits of fat (in this case, coconut oil) melt during baking, creating air pockets that result in flaky layers. Once the dough has chilled and rested (a critical step to relax the gluten and prevent your crust from being tough), it should be slightly softened before you roll it out to prevent it from breaking (you should be able to feel a tiny bit of softness when you press your finger into it). Alternatively, if the dough sets too soft and warm when you roll it out, pop it back in the fridge for a few minutes. Serve this flaky, fragrant galette with a scoop of Gingersnap Ice Cream (page 301) for a spicy contrast to the apples.

1. Lightly dust a sheet of parchment paper with flour and put the dough in the center. Put a second piece of parchment paper on top of the dough and, using a rolling pin, roll out the dough until it's about a ¼-inch-thick, 6-inch circle. Remove the top piece of parchment, dust the dough and rolling pin lightly with flour, and continue rolling the dough until it is a ⅛-inch-thick, 9-inch circle.

2. Place an 8-inch round cake pan in the center of the circle and, using a sharp knife, cut a circle around the pan to create even edges. Transfer the parchment with the dough to a baking sheet and chill in the refrigerator.

3. Meanwhile, heat a medium skillet over medium heat and add the oil. Add the apples and cook, stirring occasionally, until they are slightly tender but not mushy, 4 to 6 minutes.

4. Transfer the apples to a bowl and gently fold in 2 tablespoons of the maple crystals, cinnamon, and vanilla. Refrigerate until cool.

5. In a small bowl, combine the bread crumbs, the remaining 1 tablespoon of maple crystals, and a pinch of cinnamon. Sprinkle the bread-crumb mixture into the center of the prepared dough round, leaving a 1½-inch border around the edges. Fan the apples in 2 layers of concentric circles over the area covered with the bread-crumb mixture. Gently fold the edges of the dough up about 1 inch over the apples, creating an overlap. Place the baking sheet in the refrigerator to chill the galette until firm, about 30 minutes.

6. Preheat the oven to 375°F.

7. Bake the galette for 15 minutes, then remove it from the oven and use a pastry brush to glaze it with the maple syrup. Bake until the crust is golden bowl, 15 to 20 minutes more. Cool, slice, and serve.

Enzymatic Fruit Salad Parfaits

SERVES 4

MORE THAN JUST A sweet ending to a big meal, the fresh fruits in this light dessert actually promote good digestion. Pineapple contains bromelain, an enzyme known to help break down hard-to-digest protein, and ginger has been used throughout history in many cultures to help maintain digestive health and soothe tummy troubles. The blueberries and mangoes are both excellent sources of antioxidants and fiber, which are also essential to proper digestion. Fun fact about the mango: Often referred to as "the king of fruits," it is one of the most consumed fruits in the world.

1 ripe mango, peeled, pitted, and cut into medium dice

½ medium ripe pineapple, skin removed and cut into small dice

1 cup blueberries

1 tablespoon fresh ginger juice from a 2-inch piece (see page 74)

1 teaspoon lime zest

¼ cup fresh lime juice (from 3 or 4 limes)

1 tablespoon agave syrup

Pinch of fine sea salt

½ bunch mint leaves, cut into thin ribbons (chiffonade), plus 6 small mint leaves for serving

1 cup Whipped Cashew Cream (page 101)

1. In a large bowl, gently toss together the mango, pineapple, and blueberries.

2. In a small bowl, stir together the ginger juice, lime zest, lime juice, agave, and salt. Drizzle over the fruit and and let sit for 15 minutes.

3. Toss the fruit with the sliced mint and divide the salad among 4 parfait glasses or dessert bowls. Top with the Whipped Cashew Cream and mint leaves, and serve.

Dark Chocolate Bark

with Pistachio, Orange, and Sea Salt

MAKES ABOUT TEN 3-INCH PIECES

1 thin-skinned orange, very thinly sliced

¾ cup shelled pistachios, toasted and coarsely chopped (see page 56)

¼ cup hazelnuts, toasted, skinned, and coarsely chopped (see page 56)

¼ cup hulled pumpkin seeds, toasted (see page 56)

1 tablespoon sesame seeds, toasted (see page 56)

1 tablespoon chia seeds

1 teaspoon orange zest

¼ teaspoon ground cardamom

12 ounces vegan dark chocolate (65% cacao), coarsely chopped

2 teaspoons flaky sea salt

SPECIAL EQUIPMENT
Candy thermometer

CHEF'S TIPS: Orange chips can be made up to several days in advance and stored in an airtight container at room temperature.

If you have a dehydrator, you may use it to make the chips. You can also buy them in specialty stores— just make sure they have no added sugar.

THE TRICK TO BEAUTIFUL and professional-looking glossy chocolate bark is to temper the chocolate while you melt it. This is a simple process, in which you melt a portion of the chocolate and then slowly add the remaining chocolate a bit at a time. When you temper the chocolate, you avoid "fat bloom"—white splotches on the surface of the chocolate—the result of cocoa fat separating and rising to the surface. Other tips for successfully working with chocolate include making sure your bowls and mixing tools are completely dry (as even a drop of water can cause chocolate to become gritty) and to avoid over-heating the chocolate, as this causes it to become dull and clumpy. If you have a candy thermometer, you may use it for a more precise measurement of temperature. You can find them online or in specialty kitchen stores for around $15.

1. Preheat the oven to 150°F. Lay the orange slices in a single layer on a parchment paper–lined baking sheet and bake until the slices are dry but still slightly sticky, about 3 hours. Remove from the oven and set aside to cool. Once the oranges are cool enough to handle, break them into shards and set aside. Reserve the parchment-lined baking sheet.

2. In a large bowl, combine the pistachios, hazelnuts, pumpkin seeds, sesame seeds, and chia seeds. Sprinkle with the orange zest and cardamom and toss again. Spread the mixture in a single layer on the reserved baking sheet and set aside.

3. Fill a large pot with about 2 inches of water and bring to a simmer. Wipe a large heat-safe bowl completely dry and place it over the simmering water, making sure the water doesn't touch the bottom of the bowl. Reduce the heat to low and place about three-fourths of the chocolate in the bowl. Allow the chocolate to melt slowly, stirring as needed, until it reaches 88°F to 90°F (if you dab the chocolate on the inside of your wrist it should be hot, but not burning). Remove the bowl from the pot and gradually stir in the remaining chocolate, waiting until the pieces fully melt before you add the next. Continue until all the chocolate is added and keep stirring until the chocolate cools slightly (if it cools too much, it will become thick and dull, in which case, set the bowl back over the boiling water and stir until the chocolate reaches 88°F to 90°F again).

4. Pour the chocolate over the nuts and seeds to cover the mixture and set aside at room temperature for a few minutes to set. When the chocolate is semicool but still tacky, sprinkle with the flaky salt and orange shards. Refrigerate until the bark cools completely and is firm, about 1 hour.

5. To serve, break into bite-size pieces. Store leftover bark between pieces of parchment paper in an airtight container in a cool, dry place.

Fudgy Carob, Banana, and Tiger Nut Flour Brownies

MAKES SIXTEEN 2-INCH SQUARES

½ cup coconut oil, melted, plus more for greasing the pan

4 ripe bananas

1 vanilla bean, seeds scraped out

¾ cup tiger nut flour

⅓ cup carob powder

1 teaspoon ground cinnamon

1 teaspoon baking soda

¼ teaspoon fine sea salt

THESE MOIST, FUDGY BROWNIES are gluten- and, despite their name, nut-free. Tiger nut flour does not come from nuts, but from a small root vegetable native to Africa. When ground into a flour it is almost sweet in taste and does not leave an aftertaste or gritty texture (as some other gluten-free flours do). You can find tiger nut flour in most large supermarkets or health food stores today. The most noteworthy fact about this baked good: There is no added sugar. The only sweetness comes from the bananas, flour, and carob, which is naturally sweeter than cocoa.

1. Preheat the oven to 350°F. Brush an 8 × 8-inch baking pan with oil and line it with parchment paper, with 2 sides overhanging.

2. In a food processor, purée the bananas, vanilla seeds, and melted oil.

3. In a medium bowl, sift together the tiger nut flour and carob powder. Whisk in the cinnamon, baking soda, and salt. Stir until well combined. Add the flour-carob mixture to the food processor and pulse until just combined, 4 or 5 times. Using a rubber spatula, scrape the batter into the prepared pan.

4. Bake until lightly firm to the touch and the batter pulls lightly away from the edges, about 30 minutes. Cool the brownies for 20 minutes before removing from the pan. Lift the parchment to remove the brownies when cool and cut them into 16 squares. Store in an airtight container in the refrigerator for up to 5 days or in the freezer for up to 3 months.

CHAPTER 10

Juices & Brews

Carrot, Celery, and Ginger Juice

SERVES 4

THIS ENERGIZING ELIXIR MAKES a great afternoon pick-me-up. If you prefer juices on the sweeter side, feel free to add an apple to the mix.

1 bunch flat-leaf parsley, stemmed

2 bunches celery (about 15 stalks), trimmed

1½ lemons, peeled

2-inch piece of ginger

10 large carrots, ends trimmed

Cut the produce to fit the juicer feed tube. Juice all the produce in the order in which it is listed. Skim off and discard the foam, and serve immediately.

Mango Lassi

SERVES 2

LASSI IS A TRADITIONAL yogurt-based Indian drink that can be either sweet or savory. Mangoes are a great source of vitamins C and A, as well as powerful enzymes that aid in digestion. Enjoy this as a light breakfast, midday snack, or soothing treat after a spicy meal.

1 ripe mango, peeled, pitted, and coarsely chopped

1 cup dairy-free yogurt

½ cup ice, plus more for serving (optional)

Pinch of sea salt

1 or 2 mint leaves, for serving

In a blender, combine the mango, yogurt, ice, and salt, and purée until smooth. Pour into glasses and add more ice, if desired. Garnish with the mint leaves.

Green Juice

SERVES 4

1½ large cucumbers, peeled if not organic, ends discarded

¾ lemon, peeled

1 cup fresh pineapple chunks (about ¼ pineapple)

1-inch piece of ginger

1½ large zucchini, trimmed

6 large kale or collard leaves, washed and trimmed, stems intact

½ cup stemmed fresh flat-leaf parsley (about ¼ bunch)

3 large celery stalks, trimmed

WE LIKE TO THINK of juice as a supplement, not as a meal replacement, as the ongoing fad would have you believe. Fresh juice is a fantastic way to enjoy the micronutrients and phytochemicals of a large quantity of fresh produce—after all, it is not easy to eat several pounds of vegetables in one sitting. However, if you have been an attentive student thus far, you already know that since it is stripped of its fiber-rich pulp, juice is not a whole food and relying on juice alone as the source of your nutrition may leave you less than satiated.

Cut the produce to fit the juicer feed tube. Juice all the produce in the order in which it is listed. Serve immediately.

CHEF'S TIPS: When purchasing produce specifically for juice, it's best to use organic, if possible. Since you're mostly using whole fruits and vegetables with their skins intact, you could be exposing yourself to a large dose of residual pesticides if you opt for nonorganic produce.

It's a good idea to follow not-so-juicy greens and herbs with a watery piece of produce, like celery, to help get as much of that concentrated green goodness out of the machine as possible.

Ginger, Turmeric, and Lemon Tea

SERVES 1 (MAKES 1 CUP)

HERE IS ONE OF our favorite home remedies for a variety of common ailments like a sore throat, cough, and nausea. The ginger is warming, soothing, and contains natural antibacterial properties; the lemon lends antioxidant powers; while fresh turmeric is touted for its anti-inflammatory benefits. If you can't find fresh turmeric root at your market, substitute with ½ teaspoon ground turmeric.

1 cup boiling water

½-inch piece ginger, finely grated (about 1 teaspoon)

1 teaspoon freshly grated turmeric root

Juice of ¼ lemon

½ teaspoon maple syrup (optional)

In a mug, combine the water, ginger, turmeric, lemon, and maple syrup, if desired. Let stand for 10 minutes. Strain before serving, if desired.

Sweet Brew

with Citrus Fruit

SERVES 6

KUKICHA, A JAPANESE TEA made from twigs and stems, is a longtime favorite around here, and although seen in Japan as a peasant tea, it has been popularized by its central use in the macrobiotic diet. It lends an earthy, woody flavor to this blend, which is warming and nourishing.

3 kukicha tea bags (see page 338 for resources)

2 mint tea bags

4 thin lemon slices

4 thin orange slices

4 cups unsweetened apple juice

1. Bring 4 cups of water to a boil in a large pot over high heat.

2. Turn off the heat and add the kukicha and mint tea bags, and the lemon and orange slices. Cover the pot and steep for 5 minutes.

3. Discard the tea bags and add the apple juice to the pot. Stir and serve warm in mugs.

Pomegranate, Blueberry, and Ginger Elixir

SERVES 4

BRIGHT AND REFRESHING, THIS luscious drink made from antioxidant-rich fruits like pomegranate and blueberries, is deeply satisfying. It's perfect for a hot summer day.

4 cups unsweetened pomegranate juice

1 pint blueberries

¼ cup fresh ginger juice from about a 6-inch piece (see page 74)

2 tablespoons agave syrup

Combine the pomegranate juice, blueberries, ginger juice, 1 cup of water, and agave in a blender and purée. Serve over ice.

Chilled Carrot Hazelnut Chai

SERVES 4

1 cup hazelnuts, soaked overnight and drained

2 pitted dates, soaked in hot water until soft and drained

1 teaspoon ground cinnamon

½ teaspoon pure vanilla extract

¼ teaspoon freshly grated nutmeg

⅛ teaspoon fine sea salt

3 cups fresh carrot juice (see Chef's Tip)

SPECIAL EQUIPMENT
Nut milk bag or a fine-mesh strainer lined with cheesecloth

THE EARTHY SWEETNESS OF the carrots, balanced by the distinctive taste of the hazelnuts and the spice of the cinnamon and nutmeg, makes for a refreshing combination. This chai is a sophisticated alternative to iced tea or lemonade during the warmer months. Use the leftover hazelnut pulp in smoothies or homemade granola.

1. Purée the hazelnuts with 2 cups of water until the mixture is creamy and the pulp is fairly homogenous, 2 to 3 minutes. Pour the hazelnut milk through a nut milk bag or fine-mesh strainer lined with wet cheesecloth, and into a bowl, pressing on the pulp to extract as much liquid as possible. Set aside.

2. Return the hazelnut pulp to the blender and process again with 2 more cups of water. Blend thoroughly and strain again, combining the second batch of milk with the reserved milk. Reserve the pulp for another use and rinse the blender.

3. Pour the milk back into the blender and add the dates, cinnamon, vanilla, nutmeg, and salt, and purée until smooth. Add the carrot juice to the nut milk mixture and blend again. (If your blender is too small, you may blend the chai in 2 batches.) Pour into glasses and serve chilled.

CHEF'S TIP: Note that 2 pounds of carrots, scrubbed, trimmed, and juiced, yield about 3 cups of juice. If you don't have a juicer, you can make carrot juice in a high-speed blender by puréeing 2 cups of chopped carrots with enough water to help blend and straining the liquid through a nut milk bag.

Coconut Oil
omeganutrition.com

Maple Syrup
petessweets.com

Maple Crystals
Butternut Mountain Farm
37 Industrial Park Drive
Morrisville, VT 05661
butternutmountainfarm.com

Barley Malt
Suzanne's Specialties
suzannes-specialties.com

Tempeh
Barry's Tempeh
growninbrooklyn.com

**Spices, Specialty Legumes,
and Indian Cookware**
Kalustyan's
123 Lexington Avenue
New York, NY 10016
foodsofnations.com

**Fermenting, Canning,
and Sprouting Equipment**
culturesforhealth.com

Cold Press/Low-Speed Juicers
omegajuicers.com

High-Speed Blenders
vitamix.com

**Specialty Baking and
Cake Decorating Supplies**
N.Y. Cake
56 W. 22nd Street
New York, NY 10010
nycake.com

Knives
Mercer
mercerculinary.com

Cookware
All-Clad
all-clad.com

Chef's Uniforms
OK Uniform
253 Church Street
New York, NY 10013
okuniform.com

**Japanese Products
and Cookware**
(kuzu, umeboshi, suribachi,
sea vegetables, kukicha tea, etc.)
Natural Import Company
naturalimport.com

Brown Rice Syrup
Lundberg Family Farms
lundberg.com

RECIPE CREDITS

Chef Elliott Prag: Miso Soup (page 136)

Chef Olivia Roszkowski: Almond Mozzarella (page 62); Shiitake Crumble (page 72); Yuca Focaccia with Zucchini, Tomatoes, and Red Onion (page 194); Fudgy Carob, Banana, and Tiger Nut Flour Brownies (page 324); Sweet Potato-Cassava Tortillas (page 94); Kimchi Fried Rice (page 198)

Chef Jay Weinstein: Curried Couscous Salad with Almonds and Raisins (page 189)

Friday Night Dinner menu by **Chef's Training Program class 252B:** Pulled Barbecue Mushroom Sandwiches with Kale Slaw (page 240)

Friday Night Dinner menu by **Chef's Training Program class 233B:** Roasted Summer Vegetables with Mint Pesto, Almonds, and Currants (page 181)

Friday Night Dinner menu by **Chef's Training Program class 261B** Butternut Squash and Pepita Blue Cheese Cannelloni with White Bean Broth (page 248).

TEXT BOX CREDITS

Chef Elliott Prag: "Eating in Harmony with Tradition" (page 25) and "Finding Balance with Intuitive Eating" (page 256)

Chef Celine Beitchman: "Why Soy Is Steeped in Controversy" (page 31)

Chef Ann Nunziata: "Using Alternative Sweeteners" (page 29); "Eating the Rainbow" (page 161); and "Breakfast as Self-Care" (page 261)

Chef Olivia Roszkowski: "A Friday Night Dinner Like No Other" (page 234)

Chef Jill Burns: "Why We Eat Sea Vegetables" (page 116) and "Finding Balance with Intuitive Eating" (page 256)

ACKNOWLEDGMENTS

This book reflects over forty years of plant-based cooking knowledge developed in a culinary school founded by Annemarie Colbin, PhD, a leader in the field of holistic health and culinary wellness. This book would not have been possible without the collective efforts of the individuals who make culinary education come to life and is a testament to the commitment and dedication necessary to be culinary authorities. Thank you to the chef instructors—Susan Baldassano, Celine Beitchman, Alexandra Borgia, Jill Burns, Richard LaMarita, Ann Nunziata, Elliott Prag, Barbara Rich, Olivia Roszkowski, Jay Weinstein, and Hideyo Yamada, who work tirelessly to deliver educational excellence to aspiring chefs and engaged home cooks. We'd also like to extend heartfelt gratitude to Myriam Fieulleteau and her team for their incredible support, and, of course, a big thank-you to Coadi Robertson and Judith Shapiro for making logistics magic happen.

Thank you to everyone at the Clarkson Potter team for helping make this cookbook dream a reality: Angelin Borsics, Amanda Englander, Raquel Pelzel, Andrea Portanova, and Mia Johnson. A big thank-you to the amazing photographer, Christina Holmes, and food stylist, Jason Schreiber, for bringing our recipes to life. Finally, thank you to literary agent extraordinaire, Sharon Bowers, for guiding us through this exciting journey.

Thank you, devoted recipe testers, for your time and diligence: Susan Ball, Nancy Sobel Butcher, Teresa Catanas, Nathalie Montoya Curraba, Jacqui Errigo, Abbie Gellman, Alexis Brooke Hall, Elaina Kaufman, Emily Knapp, Chandley Logsdon, Keesha O'Galdez, Abigail Orzolek, Nicole Papantoniou, Martha Rakowicz, Michelle Siriani, Christina Spano, Leah Vanderveldt, Alisa Wadell, Amy Weisinger, and Gretchen Worsley.

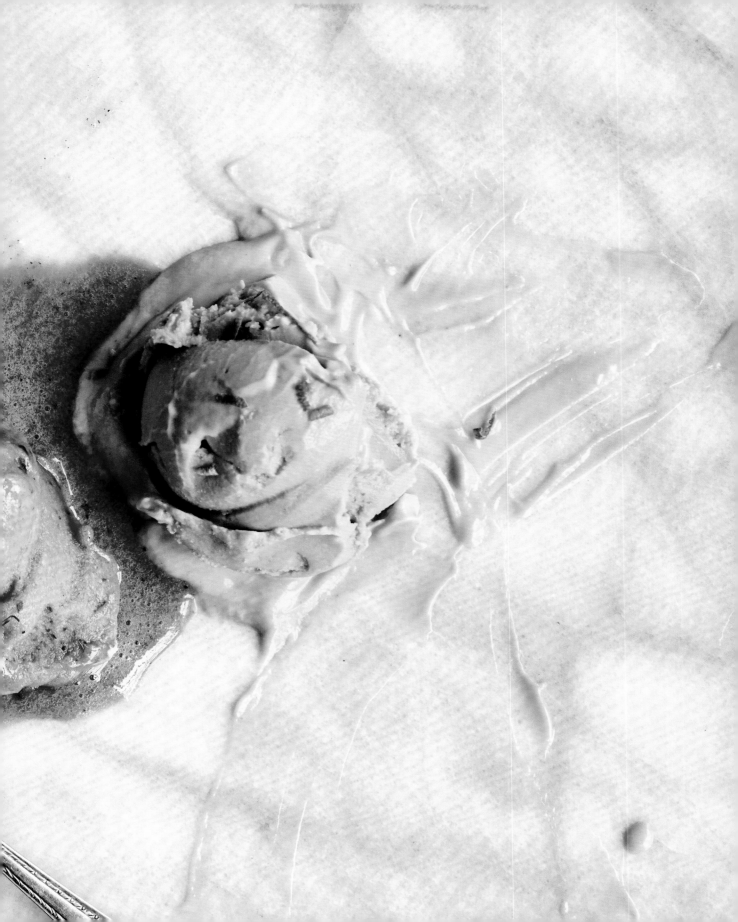

Copyright © 2019 by Natural
Gourmet Cookery Corporation
Photographs copyright
© 2019 by Christina Holmes

Published in the United States by Clarkson Potter/
Publishers, an imprint of the Crown Publishing Group,
a division of Penguin Random House LLC, New York.
crownpublishing.com
clarksonpotter.com

CLARKSON POTTER is a trademark and POTTER
with colophon is a registered trademark of
Penguin Random House LLC.

Library of Congress Cataloging-in-Publication Data
Names: Holmes, Christina, photographer. I Natural
    Gourmet (New York, N.Y.), author.
Title: The Complete Vegan Cookbook : Over 150
    Whole-Foods, Plant-based Recipes and Techniques;
    photographs by Christina Holmes.
Description: First edition. I New York : Clarkson Potter/
    Publishers, [2019]
Identifiers: LCCN 2018020623 I ISBN 9781524759810 I
    ISBN 9781524759827 (ebook)
Subjects: LCSH: Vegetarian cooking. I Cooking (Natural
    foods) I Natural Gourmet Center (New York, N.Y.) I
    LCGFT: Cookbooks.
Classification: LCC TX837 .N43 2019 I DDC
    641.5/636—dc23 LC record available at
    https://lccn.loc.gov/2018020623

ISBN 978-1-5247-5981-0
Ebook ISBN 978-1-5247-5982-7

Printed in China

Book and cover design by Mia Johnson
Cover photography by Christina Holmes

10 9 8 7 6 5 4 3 2 1

First Edition